PLAYING WITH FIRE

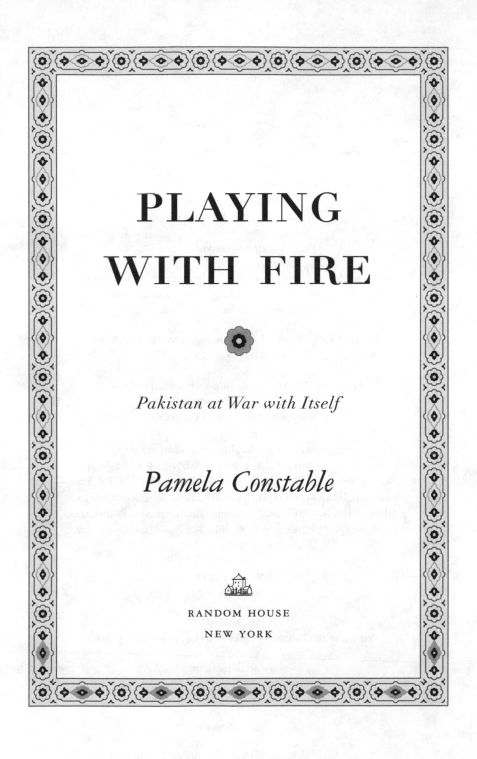

PLAYING WITH FIRE

Pakistan at War with Itself

Pamela Constable

RANDOM HOUSE

NEW YORK

Published in the United States by Random House, an imprint of
The Random House Publishing Group, a division of
Random House, Inc., New York.

RANDOM HOUSE and colophon are registered trademarks of
Random House, Inc.

Library of Congress Cataloging-in-Publication Data
Constable, Pamela.
Playing with fire / Pamela Constable.
p.   cm.
Includes bibliographical references and index.
ISBN 978-1-4000-6911-8 (alk. paper) — ISBN 978-0-679-60345-0
(ebook)   1. Pakistan—Politics and government—1988–   2. Pakistan—
Social conditions—21st century.   3. Islam and politics—Pakistan.
4. Islam and state—Pakistan.   5. Islamic fundamentalism—Pakistan.
6. Democracy—Pakistan.   7. Constable, Pamela—Travel—Pakistan.
I. Title.

DS389.C65 2011
954.9105'3—dc22
2011012621

Printed in the United States of America on acid-free paper

www.atrandom.com

2   4   6   8   9   7   5   3   1

First Edition

Book design by Christopher M. Zucker

God's purpose for man is to acquire a seeing eye and an understanding heart.

—JALAL AL-DIN RUMI, A.D. 1207–1273

CONTENTS

Introduction   *xi*

CHAPTER 1
The Flood   3

CHAPTER 2
Sahibs   25

CHAPTER 3
Honor   50

CHAPTER 4
Hate   73

CHAPTER 5
Khaki   92

CHAPTER 6
Talibanization   130

CHAPTER 7
The Siege   159

CHAPTER 8
The Girl from Swat   *182*

CHAPTER 9
Justice   *210*

CHAPTER 10
Drones   *237*

CHAPTER 11
The Murder of Democracy   *266*

Epilogue   *289*
Acknowledgments   *295*
Notes   *297*
Index   *313*

introduction

PAKISTAN IS A VAST and diverse society of some 175 million people who inhabit scattered pockets of clan and class, religion and ethnicity, poverty and power. It has a thousand separate worlds that may coexist at close quarters but never intersect.

It is a tribal chief sleeping with an arsenal under his bed; a fashion model strutting across a stage; a beggar gulping soup in a Sufi shrine; a fiery cleric exhorting acolytes to martyr themselves for Islam; a tiny girl making bricks all day in the sun; a society bride in glittering crimson; a colonel watching his son receive a medal for bravery; a family of flood victims waiting in an empty tent.

Pakistan is a country of existential as well as cultural contradictions, some of which have not been resolved since it was founded six decades ago. It is a constitutional democracy in which many people feel they have no access to political power or justice. It is an Islamic republic in which many Muslims feel passionate about their faith but are confused and conflicted over what role Islam should play in their society.

It is a proud nuclear power that yearns for global respectability but mistrusts its neighbors and resents its allies. It is a teeming hive of activity in which many people feel too trapped to move. It is a national security state under siege from terrorists that selectively coddles violent extremist groups.

This book is an attempt to explain to Western readers what Pakistani society is like today: what matters to Pakistanis, how they live and work, what frustrations and hopes they harbor, whom they fear and admire, and what forces shape their lives and opinions.

It is not an investigative work aimed at ferreting out the secrets of powerful institutions or radical movements. It does not try to keep up with every incremental news development or to predict what lies ahead for the war on terror and the ambivalent relationship between Pakistan and the United States.

Rather, it is an attempt to create a backdrop for a dangerous and fluid moment in the history of a troubled but important country, and to explain what is enduring and changing in its life as a nation. It is an attempt to explain such puzzles as why Pakistanis have a love-hate relationship with the West, why the coup-prone army remains the nation's most respected institution, and why the feudal mind-set still dominates politics. It explores why a country with such enormous economic potential has failed to educate and employ a majority of its people, and why a nation founded with such high hopes as a modern Muslim democracy has struggled so painfully to live up to them.

In all of these issues lurks the same, central question: why is Pakistan, with its huge military establishment, democratic form of government, and tradition of moderate Muslim culture, failing to curb both the growing violent threat and the popular appeal of radical Islam?

OVER THE PAST DECADE, I have traveled widely in Pakistan and explored many of its worlds, from Sufi shrines to Deobandi seminaries, from fashion shows to flooded villages, from brick quarries to bombed bazaars.

The most important thing I have learned is that many Pakistanis feel they have no power. They see the trappings of representative democracy around them but little tangible evidence of it working in their lives. They feel dependent on, and often at the mercy of, forces more powerful than they: landlords, police, tribal *jergas*, intelligence services, politicized courts, corrupt bureaucrats, and legislators tied to local power elites. People do not trust the system, so they feel they need a patron to get around it. This in turn makes everyone complicit in corruption, especially its victims.

The feeling of powerlessness and injustice, which people expressed everywhere I went in Pakistan, is perhaps the most significant factor in explaining the appeal of the Taliban and other religious extremists. They appear to offer justice in a society where that is hard to come by, even if people may not understand what the extremists' brand of justice would look like. They also offer an opportunity for those who feel excluded, especially the young and poor, to join a movement that has elements of a moral crusade or revolution, even if it seems like thuggery from the outside.

The second important thing I learned is that in Pakistan, truth is an elusive and malleable commodity. In Afghanistan, another country where I have spent a lot of time, things are often spelled out in black and white: fight or die, eat or starve, guest or enemy. Afghans survive by making hard choices, but they make them with defiant pride. In Pakistan many things are gray and murky, and people survive by playing the angles, ducking their heads, and reinventing themselves. Truth is elastic, fleeting, and subject to endless political manipulation.

Major assassinations are rarely solved, and there is often a feeling that it is convenient for them not to be solved. Court cases are chaotic affairs with myriad versions of events, suspects pressured to confess or recant, and innocent people charged or released through bribes. Political promises are easily made and rarely kept. People are considered foolish if they pay taxes, creating a permanent culture of tax evasion. The current president has been accused and jailed in numerous corruption cases but never convicted, and the truth will probably never be known.

In foreign affairs, central aspects of Pakistan's behavior toward other nations are either covert, duplicitous, or routinely denied, such as the longtime official fiction that Pakistan extended only moral and political support to the insurgency in Kashmir, or the recent official fiction that Pakistan has not maintained links to selected Islamic militant groups as a source of potential pressure on India and strategic depth in Afghanistan. After the terrorist siege in Mumbai in 2008, Islamabad denied for weeks that the surviving commando belonged to a Pakistani militant group that had been officially banned but secretly supported by the state for years.

When those at the top of a society routinely prevaricate and obfuscate, hypocrisy becomes a way of life and the state cannot expect or demand that ordinary citizens will behave honestly. When political pressure and corruption filter down to the pettiest legal case or the smallest bureaucratic transaction, a government cannot ask its citizens to rise above them. When Pakistanis today quote Mohammed Ali Jinnah's speech in 1948, in which the new country's founding father called on its young civil servants to resist political pressure and serve the people honestly, they do so with chagrin.

THE THIRD THING I began to understand was the deeply—sometimes frighteningly—emotional nature of many Pakistanis' attachment to their religion. Pakistan is not a theocracy, but it was founded as a Muslim nation, its laws are written in conformity with Islam, and the vast majority of its inhabitants are Muslims. Yet its citizens receive a barrage of confused messages about what it means to be a Muslim, what is the correct meaning of sharia or jihad, and what is the proper relationship between the state and religion.

When there is violence against religious minorities, be they Shiites or Christians or Ahmedis, it is sometimes tacitly condoned by influential people who should know better. When terrorist attacks take place and innocent people are killed, these same influential people—officials, politicians, talk show hosts, religious leaders—often cast blame on vague foreign enemies, rather than acknowledging the menace of violent homegrown extremists who harm the society, the state, and the religion of Islam. When a militant group is banned but its leaders are freed time after time, it sends a confusing signal to the public about what the state views as right and wrong.

Many Pakistanis are extremely passionate about Islam and easily roused to anger in its defense. To an extent this fervor correlates with class and education. In a society where millions are barely literate, raised to revere rather than question, and exposed to limited sources of information, they can be easily swept up in mob hysteria against anyone accused of insulting their religion. Police, courts, and political leaders are often reluctant to intervene, either from sympathy or from fear of backlash by powerful Islamic groups and their followers.

There are also influential people in Pakistan, including highly educated opinion makers, who deliberately equate national pride and patriotism with unquestioned support for Islam, no matter what form it takes. Some seem to be promoting a dangerous clash of civilizations with the West for purely domestic political or religious purposes.

This deliberate conflation of religion and state, famously rejected by Jinnah in 1947, was revived and promoted heavily during the Cold War era of the 1980s, when military ruler Mohammed Zia ul-Haq launched a campaign to "Islamize" the nation. It has continued to filter through society ever since, accompanied by the proliferation of Islamic seminaries, of which there are now more than twenty thousand across the country, teaching an estimated two million students. Many of these establishments are moderate and mainstream, but others are unregulated, unregistered nurseries of hate.

Since the attacks of 9/11 and the wars in Iraq and Afghanistan, there has been a growing tendency toward a more muscular or conservative religious attitude among Pakistanis as well as Muslims elsewhere, from pop singers and politicians to cricket players and TV hosts. Many Pakistanis today abhor the punitive extremism of the Taliban, yet they deeply resent the West and feel stridently defensive about Islam.

That is how someone such as Faisal Shahzad, a middle-class

college graduate and air force official's son living in Connecticut, could be persuaded to plant a bomb in Times Square—just as easily as someone such as Ajmal Kasab, an urban lower-class dropout with no prospects or heroes, could be persuaded to launch a jihad against the city of Mumbai.

IN THE FIRST FOUR months of 2011, a series of events brought Pakistan's internal contradictions into sharply dramatic relief. They highlighted the violent divergence of religious convictions among ordinary Muslims, the cultural divide between rural and urban notions of justice, the abysmal level of mistrust between allied military and intelligence establishments in Islamabad and Washington, and the official incompetence or perfidy that allowed al Qaeda's fugitive leader, Osama bin Laden, to live for years just a few blocks from Pakistan's equivalent of West Point, where he was killed in a secret raid by U.S. Navy Seals.

The first issue exploded just after the New Year, with the successive, hate-driven assassinations of two liberal Pakistani officials, Punjab Province governor Salman Taseer and Federal Minister for Minority Religious Affairs Shabbaz Bhatti. The two men had little in common: Taseer was a brash, wealthy, and secular Muslim politico; Bhatti a devout Christian advocate from a Punjabi village. What they shared was an outspoken commitment to religious tolerance, a cornerstone of Jinnah's founding vision for Pakistan.

Taseer was gunned down by one of his own police guards, who proudly confessed he had acted out of righteous anger against someone he considered an infidel and a blasphemer. Instead of revulsion, the crime generated a perverse groundswell of popular support for the jailed killer. Religious groups hailed him as a hero of Islam and passed out his posters at exuberant rallies. The civilian government, stunned by the backlash, hastily distanced itself from proposals to reform the draconian blasphemy law and promised the newly empowered forces of intolerance that not a word of it would be touched.

Six weeks after Taseer's murder, unknown assailants shot Bhatti to death in what appeared to be a Taliban hit. His slaying silenced the leading voice of Pakistan's 20-million-strong Christian minority, which had come under increasingly frequent harassment, ostracism, and violent attacks as the growing ranks of Islamic extremists spread poison between Muslim and Christian neighbors in working-class communities. This time there was more public indignation, but it was soon overshadowed by outrage over Koran-burning incidents in the United States, which stoked Muslim fears of a Western assault on Islam.

Another growing source of suspicion and tension between the United States and Pakistan—despite their official partnership in the war on Islamic terrorism—was the role of covert American military and intelligence operations inside Pakistan. This included a campaign of missile strikes by CIA drone planes on militant targets near the Afghan border and rumored ground operations to spy on extremist groups. American officials had long suspected Pakistan of secretly shielding some militants, despite its adamant denials, thus necessitating covert action.

These tensions erupted in a nationwide furor in January, when Raymond Davis, a burly CIA contractor, shot dead two young men who were following his vehicle on motorbikes in Lahore; a third was struck and killed by a U.S. embassy vehicle. The incident confirmed Pakistanis' worst suspicions about U.S. spy activities and created an awkward dilemma for Washington, which needed to placate its allies in Islamabad but prevent Davis from being publicly tried in Pakistan.

After weeks of wrangling over his diplomatic status, the problem was solved in a way that protected U.S. spycraft but exposed both governments as uncomfortable coconspirators. Under Islamic laws that allow blood money to forgive crimes, the families of the three victims were paid off just as Davis's trial was due to start, and he was whisked out of the country. This humiliating denouement was immediately followed by a major CIA drone strike that killed dozens of villagers, provoking a rare public protest by Pakistan's army chief and a derisive retort from U.S. intelligence agents, who suggested the army was posturing to protect its ties with Islamic militant groups.

The depth of U.S. suspicions became much clearer on the night of May 2, when President Obama suddenly called a news conference and announced that Osama bin Laden had just been killed in a secret raid by U.S. Special Forces on his guarded mansion in Abbotabad, Pakistan, a garrison city near the capital.

For the United States, the death of the iconic al Qaeda leader was a triumphant and cathartic ending to a multiyear manhunt for the figure behind the 9/11 terror attacks. For Pakistan, it was a huge embarrassment. The location of bin Laden's hideout suggested that the country's military-intelligence establishment, which had received many millions of dollars in U.S. aid to fight terrorism, was either grossly incompetent or complicit in hiding the world's most wanted terrorist. The elaborate secrecy of the American raid suggested the latter, and no amount of defensive spluttering seemed likely to repair the damage to relations between the United States and its nuclear-armed ally.

The third setback for Pakistan's pretensions as a moderate, modernizing society came in an equally sensitive domestic arena. It pitted the stubborn power of traditional rural mores—with their primitive forms of justice, stratified social hierarchy, and routine abuse of women—against the hopes for change embodied in an increasingly independent justice system headed by an iconoclastic crusader and champion of popular rights.

The case of Mukhtar Mai, a peasant woman from southern Punjab, had outraged the world nearly a decade earlier. Mai, then thirty-three, told police she had been gang-raped by a group of men, on the orders of a village council, in crude retaliation for an alleged tryst in a sugarcane field between her thirteen-year-old brother and a girl from a higher landowning caste. Fourteen men were initially charged in the crime, and the case wound its way through Pakistan's notoriously slow court system while Mai was internationally acclaimed as a heroine for women's rights.

Over the years, lower courts and appeals panels acquitted most of the defendants, leaving the Supreme Court as Mai's last hope for vindication. But on April 21, nearly nine years after the incident, a high court panel acquitted all but one man of rape. The two justices in the majority showed a keen understanding of male-dominated village mores and power politics—yet they expressed little empathy for Mai, suggesting her story was "flimsy" or had been concocted by others.

Only the lone dissenting judge seemed to understand what was at stake, and what it had taken Mai to report the crime in the first place. "An illiterate woman of rural humble background mustered tremendous courage to stand up against powerful influential culprits to bring them to justice," he wrote. But in the end the justice system failed her, and all rural women facing abuse at the hands of powerful local forces. The justices sent a strong, if perhaps unintentional, signal that the ancient customs of rural and tribal justice in Pakistan, as cruel and unfair as they might be, would not be easily dislodged.

YET FOR EVERY ENDURING problem in Pakistan—feudalism or corruption, militancy or injustice—there are signs of change and pockets of hope. Unfortunately forces for change can also become compromised or work against themselves. The independent judiciary, destroyed by military rule and then restored by the extraordinary lawyers' movement, has set an inspiring example in some cases, but it has proven hidebound in others or provoked political and institutional confrontations that Pakistan can ill afford.

The remarkable rise of the independent media, especially private TV news channels, has exposed scandals and abuses, and it has made officials more accountable than ever before. Yet often news and commentary stray into sensationalism and ad hominem attacks, and influential talk show hosts frequently pander to public fears and prejudices rather than calling for fairness and facts.

Civil society movements, once confined to the small urban elite, are beginning to spread. In towns all over Pakistan, lawyers and journalists and educators are working, often alone and in danger, to bring social justice and progress to people who have been neglected by the state, trapped by debt peonage, or imprisoned by tribal tradition. The devastating floods of 2010 exposed the extremes of rural poverty and provoked a crise de conscience among wealthy elites.

The influence of Sufi shrines and culture has also provided oases of compassion and serenity, and a crucial antidote to the forces of hate, exclusivity, and aggression that increasingly thrive in a defensive and emotionally charged religious environment. Access to technology and higher education is beginning to trickle down the social scale, offering the fast-growing younger generation an alternative to the rote learning of madrassas. The new phenomenon of grassroots leaders and women becoming involved in politics is beginning to shake the complacency of a top-down political party system.

But change is not coming fast enough. The majority of poor Pakistanis still feel excluded from politics, educational opportunities, jobs, and justice. They have become accustomed to paying bribes instead of taxes, and to seeking favor from corrupt politicians instead of demanding service from the state. They look for someone to blame for their plight, and it is easy for them to be persuaded that foreign enemies of Pakistan and Islam are the cause, when often the problem starts at home.

Pakistan has more potential than many other developing nations to thrive and progress, to become stable and prosperous and democratic. It is not a failed state, as some have asserted. But unless its military leaders retrain their sights from rivalry with India to the far greater threat of Islamic extremism, and unless its civilian leaders work harder to educate, employ, and engage a frustrated young populace that soon will be the largest in the Muslim world, they may be condemning a new generation of Pakistanis to make bricks, mop floors, or put on suicide vests.

—ARLINGTON, VIRGINIA, MAY 2011

PLAYING WITH FIRE

CHAPTER I

THE FLOOD

EACH SUMMER, WHEN THE monsoon rains arrive, millions of villagers across Pakistan celebrate the drenching downpour that brings welcome refreshment from long sweltering days in the fields and long restless nights in rooms with no fan to stir the heat. But when the monsoon came in June 2010, relief quickly turned to panic.

This time the rain was heavier than anyone could remember, and it did not stop. The Indus and Sindh rivers, usually half parched and harmless, rose and spilled over their banks. Water broke through earthen dikes and spread across fields where rice, wheat, cotton, and sugarcane were ripening for harvest.

The rains and flooding continued for weeks, transforming fertile fields into vast stagnant lakes and reducing mud-walled farm compounds to tiny islands. Families perched on trees and rooftops, waiting for rescue by army boats and helicopters, and watched helplessly as their terrified goats and buffaloes were swept away by the surging waters.

"There was a woman clinging to a tree trunk with water all around her. She was holding a baby in her arms," said Ashraf Jatoi, a local official in southern Punjab. "We told her to reach out and grab our hands, but the water was very deep and fast. The baby slipped and was carried away," he said, still shaken weeks after the experience. "She kept crying, 'My boy, save my boy.' There was nothing we could do but put her in the boat and take her to safety."

More than eighteen hundred people lost their lives in the floods. More than a million and a half lost their homes. Several million more fled to higher ground, hastily piling bed frames and cooking pots and infants onto bullock and donkey carts. They trudged across the sodden land in a ponderous human exodus that looked very much like Partition, the vast and chaotic spasm of migratory flight that had accompanied Pakistan's abrupt separation from India and its violent birth as a nation sixty-three years before.

Between June and September, more than five million acres—about 20 percent of Pakistan's arable land—was inundated and rendered temporarily barren. International lending institutions estimated that almost $10 billion worth of damage was done to roads, buildings, bridges, and irrigation systems. Pakistan officials said $40 billion in long-term agricultural production had been lost.

As the rain swelled riverine systems to bursting and the cataclysmic tide swept across the agricultural landscape, it disrupted communities, livelihoods, and systems that had governed rural life for generations. And as television crews sent back dramatic footage of rooftop rescues, flooded farms, and desperate flight, the coverage exposed the depth and breadth of Pakistan's rural poverty—a phenomenon that to the world, and to many Pakistanis as well, had been largely invisible.

The floods reinforced some stereotypes about Pakistan and shattered others. They provoked an outpouring of compassion from a society often accused of selfishness and indifference to the poor, but they also highlighted the inadequacy of civilian authorities to deal with a major crisis, giving the army an opportunity to demonstrate its superior capabilities and burnish its historic self-image as a national savior.

Islamic groups, some of them violent extremists, rushed in to provide relief and support for flood victims, improving their public credibility and associating their names with compassion, while the country's elected president left an indelible image of remote disengagement at the top of Pakistani democracy, helicoptering to a vacation in his luxurious villa in the north of France while the floods rose at home.

International donors were wary and grudging. Foreign governments were concerned about Pakistan's reputation for rampant corruption and feared much of the aid would never reach the victims. Sympathy was also dampened by the growing number of terrorist attacks abroad traced back to Pakistani sources.

In a country of enormous unmet potential, founded as an experiment in Muslim democracy but increasingly identified with suicide bombings, honor killings, military coups, and nuclear rivalry, the floods added a new catastrophe to the list—and became a metaphor for everything that had failed in Pakistan during half a century.

IN AUGUST I SPENT two weeks wandering through the flood zones of Punjab and Sindh. In many places the water had receded and the danger had passed, but a more profound and far-reaching despair had set in.

In Punjab, a riverside town resembled Pompeii, with streets of knee-deep mud where fishing boats were stranded at odd angles. Cornfields had been churned into sandbars and canals overflowed with useless, contaminated water. Farmers lost a lifetime of toil and investment, the animals they had tended for years swept away forever and the fields they had plowed a hundred times covered with stagnant black water.

A leathery, sunburned man in Kot Adoo, wearing a stained tunic and waiting in line for a relief ration card, wept as he recounted how he had watched from a roof while his two goats and only buffalo were carried off by the current, struggling and bleating, until they vanished in the storm. "It was very hard. They were my savings and my income, but I also felt a kind of love for them," he admitted shyly.

The other men in line looked haggard and dirty, as if they had neither slept nor washed since the floods had driven them from home a month before. When asked what their greatest problem was, they said they were desperate to find fodder for the animals they had managed to save. "My buffaloes are groaning from hunger. We go out and scavenge in the fields, but the land has been ruined and there is not enough," said one.

In Sindh I walked through a vast, historic cemetery in the town of Thatta where hundreds of displaced families had camped among the tombstones. Volunteer doctors from a religious charity were dispensing cough syrup and antibiotics in a tent, and snake charmers were trying to coax life into a pair of exhausted cobras in a basket, hoping to make a few rupees from the refugees.

An hour away was a fishing village on the edge of the Sindh River, where not a single hut had been left standing. A small girl was washing dishes among the reeds. Half a dozen young men were diving for fish in a stretch of water that had once been a road. An old man was darning a torn net he was not sure he would ever use again. "I spent my entire life on the water, and I have never been afraid of it until now," he said.

On the outskirts of Karachi, where a dozen makeshift camps had been set up in vacant fields, I met displaced families from northern Sindh, where flooding had wiped out dozens of villages. They huddled in a daze, with little to do but calm their fretting children and wait. As they told their stories of escape and loss, what struck me were the harsh conditions of their lives *before* the floods—lives of permanent debt, primitive routine, customary constraint, political powerlessness, and economic immobility.

Many had come from some of the poorest and most neglected districts in the country. One of them, Jacobabad, was found in a 2010 survey to have the lowest literacy rate in Sindh, followed closely by the surrounding districts. Some of the worst-inundated areas had no drinking water systems, and victims stranded by floodwaters also suffered from thirst.

These Pakistanis had few skills, no plans, and no communities left. The floods left huge swaths of cropland unusable for years, widening the gulf between feudal owners, who could easily survive their losses, and peasants and small farmers, who were wiped out.

One older couple, Pura and Bannu Jawan, had lived in a mud hut in Shikarpur District. They and their sons tended 10 acres of wheat for a landlord who owned 300. They earned no wages but received 900 kilograms of wheat at harvest time. Water was always in short supply, and they had to spend 1,500 rupees each week on fuel to operate an irrigation pump.

Their only valuable possessions were a few thousand rupees in savings and Bannu's wedding jewelry, which they kept in a metal trunk. When the flood warnings came, an army truck whisked them to a nearby town for safety. Their son and daughter-in-law went back to look for the money and ornaments but never returned. Now their home was a sweltering tent with a sleeping, orphaned grandson.

In the next tent was a younger couple with eight children. No one in the family had ever been to school. The husband, Azeem, said he wanted to go home and see if his land was still there. The wife, Hani, was silent at first, but suddenly she spoke up.

"I want my children to be civilized," she said. "In our tribe children only memorize the Koran, but there is a school in this camp. My husband says he is too old to learn, but people who read can shop better and learn the news, and the landlord's men can't cheat them on the grain shares. If this flood has brought us to a school, then maybe it is God's plan."

MOST MAJOR NEWS IN Pakistan comes from its volatile, densely packed cities—suicide bombings in Karachi, protest marches in Lahore, teeming refugee camps in Peshawar. But almost two-thirds of Pakistan's inhabitants, more than 120 million people, still live in rural areas, and 87 million make their living straight from the land.

Agriculture dominates the national economy, with crop production and livestock contributing 31 percent of the total gross domestic product (GDP). Of the four provinces, Punjab and Sindh are the big breadbaskets and export producers, with hundreds of thousands of acres planted in cotton and food crops. In 2008–9, Pakistan produced 50 million tons of sugarcane, 24 million tons of wheat, 11.7 million bales of cotton, and 6 million tons of rice.

Much of Pakistan is extremely arid, and its crops are heavily dependent on man-made irrigation, including an elaborate system of canals built by the British a century ago. It also faces a chronic water shortage that is becoming more acute each year and that could seriously jeopardize its ability to feed a population that continues to grow at more than 3 percent a year. Some analysts call water scarcity the single greatest threat to Pakistan's stability and survival.

The water crisis has been aggravated by official corruption and indifference, global warming, interprovincial rivalries, resistance to dam construction, and poor canal maintenance. One of Pakistan's major water sources is the Indus River, which originates in India. Its flow is apportioned according to a bilateral treaty, but Pakistan often accuses India of diverting water, and Islamic extremist groups have begun capitalizing on the emotional issue.

The Indus first reaches Punjab, the richest agricultural province, then flows on down to the poorer and drier lands of Sindh. In 2009, one economic report said the mighty Indus had "shrunk to a canal, and in some areas shriveled to little more than a puddle." The terrible irony of the next monsoon was that it turned the useless puddle into a destructive sea.

At the time of Partition, land ownership in Pakistan was highly concentrated among a few families, with about 7 percent of farms occupying more than half the arable land and a handful of vast feudal estates accounting for one-third. In the 1950s and 1970s, two modest land reform programs broke up many large holdings, and today 93 percent of Pakistani farms are less than 10 acres in size.

Yet many wealthy landowning families were able to skirt these limitations by parceling out property among dozens of relatives. Today large plantations still occupy 40 percent of the total cultivated area, and the power of the landlord clans is reinforced by their continued dominance in regional and national politics.

Pakistan has made impressive strides in reducing the level of absolute poverty, measured by individual calorie consumption, from more than two-thirds of the populace in the 1980s to less than 30 percent today. It is not a nation of starving people, though many Pakistanis rarely eat eggs or meat and subsist mainly on sugared tea and chappatis (wheat pancakes fried in oil), which they use to mop up dal, a lentil gruel with onions and chili peppers for spice.

But most Pakistani poverty is rural, and most rural Pakistanis are poor—field hands who receive abysmally low wages, tenant farmers paid in crop shares, migrant laborers permanently in debt to their bosses, and millions of small independent farmers who survive at the mercy of weather, pests, world food price fluctuations, and natural disasters such as the monsoon floods of 2010.

Despite the formal breakup of feudal lands, the feudal mind-set persists—especially in southern Punjab and northern Sindh—perpetuating the wide social gulf between peon and patron, and reinforcing the bonds of paternalism and loyalty that keep many illiterate villagers trapped on the land rather than seeking education and opportunities elsewhere.

Most rural Pakistanis live and die in small, circumscribed worlds that have barely changed for generations. Often their children do not attend school, or drop out after a few years. Families need them to work in the fields and may see little benefit in sending them to class. Girls are married off early to keep them chaste and safe within the clan. Teachers are hard to recruit and keep in remote areas, and thousands of rural "ghost" schools sit empty, while bureaucrats collect their operating fees.

The result is abysmal rural literacy rates and a burgeoning population of unskilled young people who will probably never rise above their parents' learning or earning levels. The national literacy rate is officially 57 percent, but it is only 36 percent for women. In some rural areas of Sindh and Balochistan, less than 20 percent of women are able to read, add and subtract, or even write their name.

The situation is even worse in the northwest tribal areas, where militant groups often recruit unoccupied young men from poor villages. In a 2010 poll conducted for the New America Foundation in the tribal areas, only 20 percent of adult respondents said they worked full-time, less than half said they had finished sixth grade, and fully 29 percent said they had never attended school at all.

Rural life has other priorities. It is ruled by the changing seasons and by unquestioned traditions of honor, duty, and vengeance. Villagers are subject to the decisions of the *waderas,* hereditary rural chiefs, and *sardars,* hereditary tribal leaders. In the rural areas, people are bound together by the traditions and kinship of their *baraderi,* a word whose definition lies somewhere between "caste" and "brotherhood."

Daily activities are divided by gender. Men gather at mosques or elders' homes to discuss marriage alliances and disputes with neighboring clans. Women rarely leave their homes and never mingle with unrelated men. Families are happy if a son is born healthy or a daughter is engaged; they are unhappy if a new calf dies of colic or the landlord's bookkeeper cheats on their share of the crop.

The old nomenclature persists too, although it represents a dying way of life. Landless peasants are still known as *haris* and landowners as *zamindars,* although some *zamindars* are also *waderas,* which makes them responsible for handling the problems of *haris* in their area: property disputes, illness, debts, crimes, and family crises.

Even today, many *haris* have never been to school, never owned a plot of land, and never earned more than a few hundred dollars or a few sacks of grain for a year's hard toil. They may own a cow or a buffalo, which they have borrowed heavily to purchase, but their only luxuries are likely to be an electric fan or a bicycle.

They turn to their *baraderi* elders for advice and to the landlord for loans. At election time, they usually vote for the candidates their elders support, and in return they are guaranteed a patron to intervene on their behalf with the police and unblock bureaucratic hurdles. They do not make news, hold protests, travel farther than the nearest city, or dare imagine any other life.

———————————

"THIS IS HOW IT works. All the land here belongs to one family, and everyone in this village works on their land. It has been that way for generations," explained Mohammed Rafi. "The women do the field labor and they get paid 120 rupees cash [$1.40] a day. They sow and cut corn, wheat, rice, potatoes. The men work in the fields too, but they also go to the cotton factory or the potato warehouse because they can earn more there, about 240 rupees a day."

Rafi, fifty-eight, was a sugar mill worker and the most educated man in a village of forty homes. The village lay off a road in southern Punjab lined with shimmering fields where families hacked at walls of wheat with sharp scythes. It was the autumn of 2009, the end of a long growing season. Tractor carts chugged along, loaded with mounds of sugarcane. Little boys splashed in brimming canals; little girls cut fresh fodder for buffaloes that snoozed beside mud huts adorned with drying dung cakes.

Rafi stood in the doorway of his house, greeting neighbors as they walked to the backyard mill next door that ground flour for chappatis. A cluster of children headed for the tiny shop that sold candy and soap. One girl of ten, wearing a uniform and carrying a vocabulary book, pointed to several pictures and read the words "butterfly" and "helicopter."

Another girl, about two years older, said she worked in a house in Lahore, cooking and cleaning for a rich family who paid her 1,800 rupees a month. She had never been to school and did not know how old she was. "They let me come home to visit sometimes, and then my sister goes instead," she said.

Rafi said more village children were going to primary school now than a decade ago, but that it was hard for them to rise further. His nephew had finished high school and his diploma hung in the front room, but the young man seemed bored and bitter. "I want to work with computers, but you have to know someone in the city to get that kind of job," he said.

When I asked Rafi about the landowners, he said they were old-fashioned but not cruel. The village was generally peaceful because everyone was from the same *baraderi,* but if there was serious trouble—a dispute over stray cattle, a robbery, an accident—families always went to the landlord, never the police.

"The landlord takes care of everything, even the smallest problems, but we cannot go against him. At voting time he says whom people should vote for, and everyone does," Rafi explained. Politics, he observed, "is a game for the elites. The people are helpless. We cannot afford to have a different opinion. He can throw us off the land immediately, even if we have been here for fifty years."

One day, Rafi said, the landlord will die, and his son will inherit the land. "He will be from a younger generation, with more education and a less feudal way of thinking," he said. "Then maybe things will begin to change."

THERE WERE PREDICTIONS THAT the floods of 2010 would bring a revolution to rural Pakistan; that cowed and complacent villagers would be roused to demand compensation for their ruined fields; that the government's glaringly inadequate response would discredit political leaders and the protracted economic damage would shake up the traditional rural power system.

The chaotic and inadequate response by a hodgepodge of civilian agencies reinforced the impression of a bloated and dysfunctional state. Thousands of people waited for hours, pressed together in long lines, to obtain ration cards, food, or medical checkups.

Federal and provincial officials made repeated visits to the flood zones, but most were little more than VIP tours in guarded convoys that reinforced the gulf between the rulers and the ruled. Dignitaries made brief speeches, gave news conferences, and met with local officials, but they had little interaction with flood victims.

People squatted patiently on lawns outside government buildings where visiting officials were scheduled to speak, but they were cordoned at a safe distance by police with bamboo poles, who occasionally barked or prodded stragglers back into place. When the visitors emerged from their meetings, they were whisked away in convoys of

SUVs, and the police made sure no one came near enough to bother them.

President Asif Ali Zardari's ill-timed trip to Europe made matters worse. Instead of canceling his meetings and cutting short his vacation as news of the flooding worsened, he seemed to personify regal indifference as TV newscasts showed him landing in a helicopter at his French villa and then hopping to his luxurious home in London. Although Zardari later spent several weeks in relief camps in Sindh, the jet-setting getaway indelibly reinforced his reputation as a remote, self-indulgent leader.

Everywhere I went in rural Pakistan, both before and after the floods, people expressed enormous frustration and anger at the corruption and injustice around them.

In many flooded areas, people complained of officials or interest groups taking advantage of the crisis. In Punjab, people said local officials were steering relief aid to their supporters and that rich landlords were diverting floodwaters away from their property, even hiring workers or guards to break through embankments. In Sindh, there were reports of business mafias sending fake victims to squat on land designated for displaced families, and of rural politicians promising victims land and jobs in Karachi in order to foment competition with their urban rivals.

There was a time when such a natural and economic disaster might well have provoked a popular rebellion. In the 1970s, millions of workers and peasants were inspired by the ringing socialist rhetoric of Zulfiqar Ali Bhutto, a feudal landlord by birth but a charismatic populist whose election slogan was *"Roti, kapra aur makan"*—bread, clothing, and shelter for all.

Bhutto founded the Pakistan People's Party (PPP) in 1967, which championed the idea of Islamic socialism, and as prime minister, he proposed a variety of reforms aimed at reducing the power of the wealthy elite. But the antagonisms of class and ideology he aroused were seen as a dangerous threat by the permanent military and civilian establishment.

He was eventually convicted of conspiring to murder a rival and hanged in prison by the army. This humiliating demise also ended a tumultuous time of social fervent and replaced it with an era of iron-fisted military rule in which fledgling labor unions, left-leaning parties, and liberal media outlets were simply shut down.

In the years after, politics reverted to a game between rival elites that gave democracy a bad name, leading to ugly institutional clashes and another military intervention in 1999. Labor organizations remained weak and human rights activities were largely confined to the urban elites. Parliament was opened up to women and minorities but remained dominated by wealthy landlords and industrialists.

In the short run, though, the floods stirred a dramatic awakening of conscience among affluent Pakistanis at home and abroad. Unlike previous natural disasters, such as the 2005 earthquake in remote and mountainous Kashmir, this one was on full public display. Enterprising crews from Pakistan's new private TV channels filmed families forging through torrents and stranded on rooftops. In the process, they ripped the protective cover off a hidden pastoral existence of quiet suffering and submission.

Appalled by the dramatic scenes unfolding on their screens, private individuals and charities rolled up their shirtsleeves and stepped into the breach. Doctors volunteered at displacement camps; restaurant owners delivered vats of food. Hundreds of thousands of people donated to relief appeals advertised on Pakistani TV stations or the Internet.

Suddenly, in a society known for corruption, tax evasion, and class snobbery, compassion became fashionable and entrepreneurs recognized the opportunity to do well by doing good. Banks and cell phone companies established appeals for drinking water and literacy programs. A real estate tycoon named Malik Riaz Hussain offered to donate 75 percent of his fortune to rebuild flooded communities—and challenged other business owners to do the same.

The charitable impulse was also in part a patriotic reaction to the wary, tepid response from the international aid community. Many Westerners associated Pakistan with terrorism and corruption and were reluctant to donate large quantities of aid that might be stolen or misused. The presumption of official corruption was so strong that some foreign donors and governments bluntly insisted on channeling flood aid through private charities.

Several Pakistani religious groups seized on the moment to denounce Western callousness as well as Pakistani government incompetence, at the same time polishing their own charitable credentials and increasing their name recognition among a rural peasant population that was normally far removed from their urban lower-class bases.

Jamaat-e-Islami, a large Sunni political party with a strong middle-class membership and a strategic agenda of theocracy, sent volunteer doctors and social workers into refugee camps. Jamaat-ud-Dawa, the educational and charitable wing of a banned anti-India militia group, Lashkar-e-Taiba, rushed to set up roadside relief stations in areas the slower official apparatus had not yet reached. In the process, thousands of grateful victims came to associate their black-and-white banners with beneficence instead of bombs.

Some clerics also spread the message that the floods were a punishment from God because Pakistanis had sinned against Islamic values, a message intended to resonate among poorly educated Muslims searching desperately for meaning in the disaster.

In the Punjabi village of Marripura, where the angry Indus had filled fancy riverside homes with mud, I asked people what they thought of that explanation. A young man spoke up eagerly. "It's a wake-up call from God," he said firmly, identifying himself as a seminary teacher home for a visit. "God says those with nice houses should care for those with none, or it is a sin." An older villager shook his head and mumbled, "It's just the rain. Don't turn it into a sin." The others said nothing.

WHILE PAKISTAN'S RURAL SOCIETY remains largely trapped in the past, its urban world is careering toward a dynamic but perilous future. The population of its cities—especially the large metropolitan magnets such as Karachi and Lahore, and the gritty industrial zones such as Faisalabad and Sialkot—has expanded seven-fold since 1950. Karachi, a sprawling port city on the Arabian Sea, is home to 18 million.

Ethnic migrants, conflict refugees, and ambitious young villagers with a few years of schooling are packed into slums and working-class districts. Shabby three-tiered apartments, strung with laundry and smelling of reheated cooking oil, line narrow twisting alleys with gutters of green stagnant sewage. Boys in dirty tunics throw rocks at yelping puppies and lug frayed sacks full of scavenged tin and glass to scrap sellers with scales, who usually cheat them and chase them away.

For those without skills or connections, there are a thousand occupations in the cities—errands to run, offices to guard, and streets to sweep. Wizened drivers ferry passengers in ancient wooden-wheeled tonga carts, pulled by tired horses with jutting hip bones and open sores beneath their harnesses. Younger, more daring drivers whiz among traffic in zippy three-wheeled taxis called motor rickshaws.

If a newcomer has some education and a local relative to help him navigate and grease the city job market, he can land a full-time position for minimum wage—about 6,000 rupees a month—as a city bus driver, a waiter in a fast-food restaurant, or a textile machine operator.

But there are far too few formal jobs available for the fast-growing populace, so most poor city dwellers find niches in the informal or "black" economy. This encompasses a vast array of activities, from selling mangoes on the sidewalk to exchanging foreign currency in the illegal *hawala* trade, which funnels billions of rupees from overseas workers into the untaxed, informal economy each year. Women sell homemade pastries wrapped in newspapers; men squat beside stacks of tools or paintbrushes all day, hoping for a few hours' cash work.

The most volatile problem facing the cities is the population explosion. More than half of Pakistanis today are under age fifteen. The number of inhabitants has doubled since the 1960s and increased by 50 million in the last twelve years alone, to an estimated 176 million. Even though families are larger in the countryside, competition for space, jobs, and basic amenities is much greater in the cities.

With the formal employment market expanding much more slowly than the population, Pakistan faces an imminent youth explosion that will trap many young people in dead-end urban jobs and may push others into the arms of criminal gangs or Islamic guerrillas.

The recent exodus of flood victims toward cities such as Thatta, Karachi, and Multan is likely to exacerbate the contest for cheap quarters and unskilled jobs and to put more pressure on overburdened city infrastructures, including water and sewers. As cities become more crowded, street crime, noise, and pollution take a toll on people's nerves and health.

Public education is widely available in the cities, but the quality of urban schools is often poor. Parents complain that classes are crowded, textbooks are scarce, and teachers are unqualified, absent, or cruel. Some families end up sending their children to religious seminaries, where tuition is free and pupils receive more attention—but may be vulnerable to extremist indoctrination. Others send them to private academic courses by borrowing money or working extra jobs, but poor children in old clothes sometimes feel like unwelcome misfits.

Hundreds of thousands of teenagers work in cities instead of going to school, despite labor laws passed in the 1990s that prohibit children under fifteen from performing heavy work such as mining and those under fourteen from working at all.

Boys often work with their fathers in fruit markets, repair dented cars in greasy workshops, or deliver smuggled TV sets on the backs of bicycles. Older girls often work as live-in domestic servants for wealthy families, earning pennies a day and sleeping in tiny back rooms. Younger ones thread fragrant flowers into tiny garlands, then stand on traffic islands during rush hour, selling them to drivers to hang on their rearview mirrors.

At a crowded bus stand on the highway to Peshawar, I spotted a boy of about twelve wandering among the crush of commuters, selling herbal twigs used as toothbrushes. He said his parents were refugees from Afghanistan and that he had nine brothers and sisters. I asked him if he could read, and he grabbed my notebook eagerly. In neat English script he wrote: "My name is Ismail Khan. My father name is Noor Ahmed. I want to school, but my family need, my work is better to feed them."

As he hoisted his bag of twigs and turned away, the boy murmured something in Afghan Pashto, and my translator caught it. "This is now my fate," he said.

KURIANWALA ROAD, A WIDE industrial artery that shoots straight through the city of Faisalabad, is lined with drab, high-walled compounds that look like prisons. Each has a small sign out front: Haseeb Spinning Mills, Jamal Textile Industries, Faisal Fabrics, Habib Calico Weaving.

Inside are huge noisy hangars, filled with rows of men and machines that spin white Pakistani cotton into yarn and thread, which other men and machines weave into bolts of cloth, which still others dye and stitch to make baby-blue bedsheets or terra-cotta bath towels for the latest bulk order from Walmart or Fieldcrest.

These modern, shift-work factories are the lifeblood of Pakistan's urban economy, light-years from the village huts where nimble-fingered girls spin cotton on tiny wooden spools and weave carpets on hand-and-foot looms. Even though more than half of the nation's workers still toil in agriculture or other rural occupations, migration to the cities has created a vast pool of semiskilled and semieducated young men desperate for any work they can find.

In this fast, gritty, highly competitive world, textiles are king. Pakistan is the world's fourth-largest producer of cotton and its third-largest consumer. The spinning, weaving, and apparel industries have been the main drivers of Pakistan's export economy for half a century, creating the most jobs and bringing in the most foreign exchange.

In 2008, despite several consecutive years of reduced investment and other difficulties, Pakistan produced 26 million tons of textiles and clothing, far more than any other products, including food, steel, medicines, fertilizers, cars, leather goods, and electronics. The textile industry employed 13 percent of all workers and accounted for 18 percent of the GDP.

For any single young man from a working-class family in Punjab with a basic education but no connections that will open the doors to an entry-level government post, the best hope of finding a formal job with standard hours and wages and some chance of promotion is at a textile mill in a big manufacturing town such as Faisalabad or Sialkot.

Inside the mills, the noise can be deafening and the air is filled with fibers that irritate the lungs. But there are cheap bunks in nearby hostels, and if a mill worker saves carefully and avoids temptation, he can send a few thousand rupees home each month.

"The work is not too difficult, and after a few days the noise doesn't bother you. I earn 6,000 rupees [about $90] a month and send half to my mother," said Sabar Iqbal, nineteen, a power loom operator who was eating a lunch of chappatis and lentil soup with his shift-mates outside a factory that spins yarn.

Iqbal said he shared a bunkroom with eight other workers for 350 rupees each a month, and his only complaint was that the electricity often went off at night. "Then it's hard to sleep, and the mosquitoes bite you," he said with a resigned shrug.

Unlike villagers in rural Pakistan, where the socioeconomic structure is stratified and fixed in stone, poor city dwellers face a dilemma of rising but frustrated expectations. They watch more news and debate; they learn more about rights and justice; they feel the bustle of commerce and the lure of technology while remaining trapped in dead-end sweeper and porter jobs; they see more clearly the gulf between themselves and the rich.

Lower-class urbanites stand in line for hours to buy rationed flour and sugar while hearing about mill owners hoarding food to drive up prices. They swelter through summer nights without electricity during power cuts, while the wealthy enjoy generator-powered air-conditioning. They cram into stifling buses while cabinet ministers are caught driving untaxed SUVs. They wear the same greasy tunics every day while elegant models swirl and pout for cameras during Fashion Week.

In the past several years, the combustible combination of rising food costs and power shortages has turned Pakistan's cities into flashpoints for discontent. Throughout 2008 and 2009, inflation climbed steadily. Thousands of people lost factory jobs and slipped into poverty. Homes were left without light or fans, and commuter bus fares tripled.

The new Zardari government, trying to shore up the most vulnerable families and buy time for economic recovery, boosted spending on social programs and emergency aid. But belated infusions of cash could not compensate for years of inadequate social spending and months of runaway inflation that slashed the value of bare-bones salaries; by the time the government pledged to raise the minimum wage to 7,000 rupees, the bonus was already moot.

In Barakaho, a gritty suburb of Islamabad, an unusually violent protest broke out at a market one afternoon in the spring of 2010, resulting in dozens of arrests. A day or two later, I drove there with my translator and sat down at an outdoor tea stall. Within minutes, a dozen men in stained and frayed tunics, some of them too old to be digging ditches, crowded around me and begged for a day's work.

When I took out my notebook, they all pressed forward and began talking at once. Bus fares had doubled and their children had to walk to school. Flour and sugar had tripled. Construction projects had stopped and no one had been paid. The rioters, they said, had been speaking for all of them.

"Every common man knows they were right," said one man named Bashir. He had seven children, and at age sixty he was still working as a day laborer. "Flour used to be 260 rupees a bag and now it's 600.

The bus from Aabpara used to cost 12, and now it's 25. The drivers cheat you and the buses are owned by high society people who are tied to the government. The whole system is corrupt."

I asked Bashir if there was any Pakistani leader he admired, and he thought for a moment. "Ayub was an honest man, but we haven't had one since," he said, referring to President Ayub Khan, a reformist dictator of the 1950s and 1960s.

"This bunch are all liars and thieves, and they don't care about the poor," he said bitterly, and the men around him nodded in agreement. "The police can beat us, but someday the people will come out on the streets, like they did in France, and nobody will be able to stop them."

THE OTHER OUTLET FOR public anger and frustration is Islam. For decades, Pakistanis seeking solace in hard times have flocked to the shrines of Sufi saints, benign mystical figures from Muslim history. There they prayed and lit candles, received free meals, and made offerings to the saints they hoped would find them a job, cure their arthritis, help them conceive a child, or send their creditors away.

But in recent years, harsher schools of Islamic thinking have also been on the rise in Pakistan. These are groups with ambitious and aggressive agendas to defeat India and its foreign allies, counter Western vulgarity and secular influence in society, or build a theocratic state through violent means if needed.

They recruit members in lower-class urban working districts, operate thousands of seminaries in cities and towns, send student activists onto campuses, preach Friday sermons against the evils of political corruption and Western immorality, and call on disaffected, disenfranchised Muslims to join their crusades.

Some of the groups are mainstream political parties; others are underground militant organizations such as the Taliban. They tap directly into the frustrations of poor Pakistanis and adapt their messages to widen their appeal.

In addition to providing charitable relief to flood victims during the 2010 monsoon, groups such as Jamaat-ud-Dawa and Jamaat-e-Islami have begun holding rallies and protests on popular issues including water and power shortages. They also appeal to class resentments, calling for a religious and moral revolution against the corrupt Pakistani state and the self-indulgent, "un-Islamic" ways of the wealthy.

Faisalabad, the headquarters of Pakistan's textile industry, where thousands of migrant mill workers were thrown out of work by power shutdowns, is also known as a center for radical seminaries and mosques. Several suspected terrorists have been captured there over the years, including the alleged al Qaeda military commander Abu Zubayda, and several Pakistanis linked to bombings in Lahore and Rawalpindi.

In the summer of 2010, Abid Qaiyum Suleri, director of the Sustainable Development Policy Institute in Islamabad, wrote an essay warning of a new "mullah-Marxist nexus" in which Islamic extremists were using "Robin Hood–style strategies" to capitalize on popular despair and anger against distant, selfish elites.

The growing "Talibanization" of Pakistan, Suleri wrote, was not just a product of Islamic hard-line ideology but of common outrage against "chronic hunger, endemic corruption, unfair courts," and government neglect. He warned that it was easy for extremists to create "parallel states" when the formal state failed its citizens, and to brainwash lost and hungry people by offering them security, justice, and a "confirmed place in heaven."

Not everyone is open to the militant message. In fact, a majority of Pakistanis from all social classes say they disapprove of Islamic extremist groups, but attendance at radical mosques is concentrated in poor urban areas, and directionless young men—conditioned to authoritarian culture, with few role models or outlets for their energies—can become easy prey for recruitment into radical suicide missions.

Ajmal Kasab, the lone surviving member of a terrorist squad that assaulted the Indian city of Mumbai in 2008, was a young, jobless dropout from a poor urban family in Punjab. In court testimony and a detailed confession, he said he and a friend had been in a market in Rawalpindi, plotting to buy a gun and rob shops, when they were approached by a man who offered them a chance to join an important religious mission. After just a few months of intense physical and mental conditioning, they were transformed into robotic mass killers.

While a strong majority of Pakistanis reject terrorism and could not imagine bombing a hotel or a market as a form of protest, they also identify Islam as a religion of positive moral values, which often seems to clash with the behavior of the nation's leaders.

Ordinary people everywhere express the same sense of personal impotence, of grudging collusion in a corrupt system much bigger than they, and of anguished yearning for a chance to matter, to belong, or to change the way things are. When asked to name the most important quality in an ideal leader, they tend to say the same thing: "First, he should be a good Muslim."

FOR MANY PAKISTANIS TRAPPED at the bottom of a stratified and hierarchical society, the patterns of submission are too ingrained and the hole too deep to escape. Men are driven to desperate and violent acts—which often are directed at themselves and those they love.

During 2009, when inflation, unemployment, and power shortages were taking an especially heavy toll, I noticed that the papers were carrying more police briefs about fathers strangling their children in bed, or husbands shooting their wives and themselves. The brief reports almost always mentioned that the man had lost his job, been evicted, or gone deeply into debt.

But it was not until I spent several days in Pakistan's brick kilns that I came to understand how an entire way of life, dependent on a simple system of production, could become a trap from which families and generations had almost no escape.

The kilns are remote, self-contained worlds, carpeted in thick red dust, where clay-colored figures squat all day in the sun, shaping balls of mud into bricks and setting them out in rows to dry. More than 200,000 migrant laborers work in kilns across Pakistan, earning a few hundred rupees a day.

Small children squatted beside their fathers, rolling mud bricks on the quarry floor. Older boys loaded bricks on the little quarry donkeys, which trudged to the kilns and then trotted back on their own. Soot-streaked men shoveled coal into underground ovens, while chimneys overhead billowed trails of black smoke across the pale dawn sky.

The kiln families live in encampments of brick huts beside the quarries, cut off from schools and shops. Most eventually borrow money from the owners and became permanently indebted. Legally they are free to quit, but many never earn enough to leave. If they move to a new kiln, their debt moves with them. "It can stay with you for life, like a pair of invisible handcuffs," one worker told me.

Kiln work is hot and dangerous, and many workers have old burn marks on their arms and legs. But there is another, horrifying hazard that some willingly risk in their desperation to get out of debt: selling their kidneys in the clandestine organ trade. I had read about this practice, in which brokers reportedly took poor men for operations in secret clinics and paid them cash, but I had never quite believed it.

One day when I was visiting a quarry in Punjab, I asked some brick workers if they knew anyone who had gone through this ordeal. They nodded and pointed me toward a thin, grizzled man who was sitting in the shade. His name was Imam Baksh; he said he was forty-five, but he looked sixty.

Baksh said yes, it was true. He had sold his left kidney to a clinic for 80,000 rupees several years ago, and he had felt tired ever since. When I looked skeptical, he sighed and pulled aside his earth-stained tunic to reveal a long diagonal scar. "The worst part," he said, "is that I still haven't paid off my debt."

CHAPTER 2

SAHIBS

THE HOMES OF PAKISTAN'S affluent classes, in manicured urban neighborhoods such as Gulberg in Lahore and Clifton in Karachi, have an atmosphere of hushed, museum-like stillness, discreetly expensive taste, and familiar privilege. The floors are polished stone or old wood, the sofa pillows are fluffed, the tea tables are arrayed with silver and alabaster objects. There are no children's toys or tennis sneakers strewn about, no forgotten coffee cups or piles of half-read books.

The inhabitants are cordial, cultured, and well-read. The men are lawyers and legislators and industrialists; their wives are artists and educators and human rights activists. The professional men wear Western business suits to work; the politicians favor traditional, starched white *kameez* tunics over billowing *salwar* pajamas. The women wear soft, flowing tunic-and-trouser ensembles in fashionable rainbow hues and loose diaphanous head scarves, called *dupattas,* as a gesture to modesty.

Many affluent families own ancestral plots of farmland, where tenant farmers have sharecropped for generations, and yet they bristle at the suggestion that they might be considered feudal landlords. Some are eccentric and ostentatious, building ornate mansions with vast marble foyers, pillars, and balustrades, and far too many rooms.

Former prime minister Nawaz Sharif, who comes from a family of wealthy Punjabi industrialists, built a fantasy estate near Lahore with his own private zoo and peacocks roaming the grounds. When he was overthrown in 1999 and sent into exile, the army gave guided tours of the estate as an example of self-indulgent excess among the civilian elite.

But most of Pakistan's wealthy families are discreet, insular, and highly protective of their privacy. They move seamlessly between worlds, often traveling to second homes in London or New York or Dubai. They send their sons and daughters to Oxford or Stanford— but then summon them home to marry within their circle and enter the family sugar or cement business. On weekends, they retire to private clubs or farmhouses and attend endless rounds of engagement parties and hotel weddings among interlocking circles of extended, intermarried families.

Despite their genteel pretensions and tasteful salons, though, the world of Pakistan's elite is one that depends on the cowed subservience of others—a silent and invisible class of servants whose function is to clean, cook, launder, tend the roses, guard the gate, walk the dog, wash the car, bring the tea.

It is a world made possible by the enormous gulf between rich and poor—a gulf that is less gaping than in the poorest pockets of Africa and Asia, but remains more pronounced than in most other developing countries in South and Central Asia, such as India or Bangladesh.

It is a world made possible by the lack of social mobility and meaningful democratic representation, by hour and wage laws that are never enforced, by taxes that are rarely collected, by a police and intelligence apparatus that represses the poor. It is made possible by desperate need and self-censoring submissiveness on one end and by a sense of immutable hierarchy and privilege on the other.

A foreign visitor who enters this world is treated to articulate and reasonable-sounding opinions in good English, along with sweet milky tea and freshly baked snacks on silver trays. Yet the visitor soon discovers that it is impossible to carry on a polite conversation for more than several minutes, because the host or hostess is constantly interrupting to tell a servant to *do* something: bring more tea, remove a plate, turn on a light, switch off a fan.

Most of these duties the speaker is perfectly capable of performing with little effort or inconvenience, but that is not the point of this ritual. The point is that each request, no matter how politely framed, no matter how genteel the patron, reinforces the gulf of class and place that has long kept Pakistani society stagnant and stratified instead of allowing it to become dynamic, creative, and diversified. The servant enters noiselessly, complies with the order and retreats, sometimes literally moving backward on bare feet.

Members of the upper classes tend to have moderate religious views and to regard radical Muslim clerics as shrill and lower-class. They attend funerals and Friday prayers, but they are not obsessively pious. Many men, especially older or retired bureaucrats and military officers, enjoy drinking whisky and singing along to sentimental South Asian ballads known as *ghazals* at private stag gatherings, growing happier and more off-key as the lubricated evening wears on. Not infrequently, crude jokes or patronizing stories about mullahs will be shared.

Affluent Pakistanis have been among the major targets of extremist Islamic violence in the past several years, and they have had to adjust their lifestyles accordingly. Two of the country's main luxury hotels, the Islamabad Marriott and the Peshawar Pearl Continental, were decimated by suicide bombers within nine months of each other; the Marriott was rebuilt as an elegant fortress, but the whirl of weddings and retirement dinners slowed to almost nothing.

As the pace of urban terror attacks picked up after mid-2007, schools and shopping centers were also targeted, requiring extra guards and security measures. Most foreigners left the capital, and enrollment in exclusive private schools dropped. By 2009, the leafy VIP enclaves and government districts of Islamabad were completely surrounded by concentric circles of police checkposts, barbed wire, and barricades. The newest luxury hotel there, the Serena, was designed as a nearly impenetrable hilltop fortress.

Yet there was always a sense of unreality about the threat that loomed out there in the dark. The elite tended to dismiss Islamic militancy as a Pashtun tribal problem that could be handled by the army, as the ideology of a tiny lunatic fringe that could never obtain political power, or as a by-product of the wars in Afghanistan and Kashmir that would eventually fade away. Few upper-class people seemed to make the connection between Pakistan's persistent poverty and the growing menace of radical Islam—in part because they too were Muslims, and in part because they were insulated from both.

SINCE THE 1950S, PAKISTAN has been said to be ruled by twenty-two families of old landowners and industrialists, who enjoyed wealth and political connections from the time of Partition and passed them on to succeeding generations. This exclusive club has gradually expanded (though not always willingly) as the economy has diversified from the traditional mainstays of food, leather, and textiles into lucrative new areas such as electronic media, real estate, computers, and cell phones.

Rapid urbanization and rising education levels have also begun to pry open the political sanctums once reserved for the upper classes, allowing nouveau riche upstarts and even a few working-class leaders to win seats in the national legislature. Yet even a cursory glance through the rosters of Pakistan's wealthiest clans includes numerous references to marital alliances that reinforce the patterns and power of concentrated wealth.

Members of the Pakistani establishment deeply resent criticism by outsiders and are keenly sensitive to foreign moral judgments on their way of life, and they adamantly reject Pakistan's international image as a nation of feudals and fanatics. Rural landowners immediately deny being feudal; industry barons reject accusations that they are part of a cartel; and tribal leaders insist they are committed to the new, post-tribal way of doing things.

Pakistanis love their country, and they yearn for the international stature they consider their due as a nuclear power that helped the West defeat communism in Afghanistan. Yet they also know there are seeds of truth in the criticism; that their nation was cursed almost from birth by oligarchism, militarism, and poor leadership; and that even today many aspects of Pakistani life are cruelly unfair.

"Pakistan is the best place on earth to be rich," a successful business executive acknowledged to me in a moment of candor. He expressed compassion for the struggling poor and disapproval of the spoiled elite, yet he also confided that he rarely ventured from his hectic but insular world of professional meetings, private clubs, and weddings or other social obligations.

"Here you can get away with anything, have all the luxuries of life, pay no taxes, and have many servants," he said, expressing both general disapproval and personal chagrin. "Too many people have no collective vision. They don't think about the society. Everyone only thinks of himself."

Many wealthy Pakistanis give generously to medical and educational charities, especially during emergencies such as the monsoon floods of 2010. They also pay lip service to the egalitarian and compassionate mores of Islam. Yet they are terrible snobs and spiteful gossips. Their history of repeated military interventions makes them especially sensitive to rank, while their reliance on servants reinforces a classist mentality. When a prominent lawyer in Lahore was accused of beating his servant girl to death in 2010, the legal fraternity immediately closed ranks around him.

"From the beginning, our problem has been the lack of a national bourgeoisie," said Aitzaz Ahsan, one of Pakistan's best-known attorneys and democratic activists, as well as a published historian of South Asia. "India had a vigorous trading and manufacturing class, and a tradition of liberal intellectualism; we did not. Their social structures were conducive to democracy; ours were not." During the

Cold War, he added, power became a "marriage between the feudals and the mullahs and the military"—a relationship that remains largely unchanged.

I asked Ahsan, a leader of the lawyers' protest movement to restore the independent judiciary in 2007, why more people in his profession had not condemned the death of the servant girl in Lahore. He sighed and shrugged. "Everyone has servants in Pakistan. There is always someone below you to sweep the floor. Some masters are better than others, but the mind-set doesn't change."

THERE ARE A THOUSAND reasons why Pakistan has failed to develop its economic potential and why the wealth at the top has not sufficently translated into growth and inclusion for the masses. Many problems, from foreign tariffs to domestic terrorism, cannot be attributed to upper-class attitudes and business practices.

Pakistani manufacturers have long faced high barriers in the West to exports such as textiles and shoes, and officials have begged American administrations for years to open up markets, with little result. Foreign investors have been scared away by vertiginous shifts in government economic policies, from mass nationalizations to mass privatizations, as well as by recurring military interventions in power. The state has shortsightedly failed to invest in higher education and technology, while countries such as India, Chile, and Turkey were busy producing engineers and programmers.

Since the mid-2000s, an escalating wave of terrorist attacks has created a cloud of insecurity that sent investors fleeing, diverted extra resources to defense, and robbed the economy of more than $43 billion between 2004 and 2009, according to the Pakistan Economic Survey. Many terrorist attacks are aimed at high-profile symbols of elitism and sites frequented by foreign visitors, notably the Marriott Hotel in Islamabad, which was decimated by a truck bomb in September 2008, and the Pearl Continental in Peshawar, which collapsed in a similar attack several months later.

Historically, Pakistan has hardly lacked for gung-ho entrepre-

neurial spirit. Its first business leaders were Indian Muslims such as
Yousuf Saigol and members of the Memon and Chinioti trader clans,
who fled from Mumbai or Calcutta to cities such as Karachi and
Faisalabad and Lahore in the newly created Muslim homeland. They
came with great hopes and ambitions, bringing their jute or cotton
milling machines with them. The phenomenon was known as the
Pakistani gold rush.

But the indigenous environment that awaited them was essentially that of landed feudalism, a sedentary and paternalistic system
frozen in the past. Throughout Punjab and Sindh, a few families in
each district controlled thousands of acres, from which peasants and
tenant farmers extracted crops while their owners did little but collect the profits. There was neither economic incentive nor legal compulsion to spread the wealth around, so it began to accumulate in the
hands of millers, manufacturers, and bankers too.

According to critical analysts such as Ayesha Siddiqa and histori-
ans of Pakistan's private sector such as Shahid-ur Rehman, the business model that developed in Pakistan was a closed system based on
cozy relationships with banks, officials, and regulatory agencies,
which produced quick profits for the owning class but stymied competition, innovation, and improvements that have allowed more successful developing countries, such as Bangladesh and Indonesia, to
expand their middle-class professional sectors and forge ahead in the
global economy.

The high concentration of private wealth was evident as early as
1959, when Pakistani officials announced that twenty-two families,
topped by the Saigol, Dawood, Adamjee, and Amin business groups,
controlled more than two-thirds of all industry, 70 percent of insurance, and 80 percent of banking. Laws were passed to curb monopo-
lies and create more competition, but they were ineffective and
poorly enforced. In 1970, one expert calculated, forty-three groups
or families owned half of all nonbanking businesses listed on the
Karachi stock exchange.

The tumultuous events of the next four years turned this cozy
world upside down. First, an independence movement in East Paki-

stan was brutally suppressed and the region seceded, creating Bangladesh, and many Bengali businessmen went with it. Then Zulfiqar Ali Bhutto became prime minister, winning on a populist platform of social and economic justice, and announced a massive nationalization program of the private sector aimed at ending the monopoly of the twenty-two families and other "robber barons."

Between 1972 and 1975, Bhutto nationalized more than thirty companies in heavy industries such as steel and chemicals, then extended the takeover to private banks, insurance, shipping, schools, cooking oil and cotton processors, and other areas of the economy. His aim was to halt the concentration of wealth in the hands of a few and to make Pakistan self-sufficient in key industries.

But critics said Bhutto's radical scheme had permanently damaged the "psyche" of the entire sector, while nationalization tended to benefit the growing Punjabi business community over the older Karachi firms. Some entrepreneurs left Pakistan for good. Others scaled back plans to modernize or expand industries at home, leaving Pakistan reliant on imported machines to process its cement, sugar, and cotton while other developing nations moved into electronics and services.

The military coup by General Zia ul-Haq in 1977, followed by the imprisonment and hanging of Bhutto, snuffed out the fires of social upheaval and swung economic policies 180 degrees. Zia and his finance minister Nawaz Sharif, a politician from a wealthy Punjabi industrialist family who would later become prime minister twice, set out to reprivatize as many nationalized businesses as possible.

But instead of restoring health to Pakistan's ailing private sector, privatization made it sicker. Throughout the 1990s, during two periods of rule by Sharif and two by his archrival Benazir Bhutto, the privatization process became a game of grab and run. Instead of investing in solid projects, many business groups colluded with corrupt officials to make quick profits. They borrowed huge sums without collateral, created and dissolved ghost factories, purchased state assets at token prices, avoided paying taxes, defaulted on shaky loans, or deferred repaying them indefinitely.

The losers in this scheme were the Pakistani treasury and public. By 1995, the state was owed more than 108 billion rupees in bad business credit. Dozens of companies were found to have created phantom businesses to launder loans that were actually used to purchase luxuries such as lavish homes in Dubai. Major defaulters and beneficiaries of loan write-offs, granted by both the Bhutto and Sharif governments, included some of Pakistan's wealthiest business families—the Manshas, Saigols, Hashwanis, Habibs, Bhuttos, and Sharifs.

Business in Pakistan has always been linked to political and regional loyalties, but the war between the Bhuttos of Sindh and the Sharifs of Punjab was an unusually blatant case of rival leaders wielding political power to sabotage their opponents' business interests. While in office, both Benazir and Nawaz selectively used tax laws, import licenses, and business permits to reward loyalists and punish opponents. While out of power, both levied impassioned charges of corruption against each other's families. Sharif accused Bhutto's husband, Asif Ali Zardari, of using front men to buy sugar mills and hotel land; Bhutto accused Sharif of taking kickbacks on a new highway, manipulating customs duties, and milking banks.

Neither leader was ever prosecuted or convicted for any crime, but both paid a high price for their behavior. Bhutto's two governments were dismissed in 1990 and 1996, and Sharif's first was dismissed in 1993. The presidential order removing Bhutto the second time said that "corruption, nepotism," and rule breaking had become so widespread that the government could not function and public faith had "disappeared." It also accused Bhutto and Zardari of purchasing a luxury home in England and two villas in France, presumably with ill-gotten gains.

The order firing Sharif in 1993 was almost identical, saying that "mal-administration, corruption and nepotism have reached such proportions" that they violated his oath of office and undermined the constitution. His second removal from office in 1999 was far more dramatic; accused of trying to stage a coup against the army chief, General Pervez Musharraf, Sharif was arrested, sent to prison, and forcibly exiled to Saudi Arabia.

By the time Musharraf seized power, the public was fed up with the shenanigans of its two main civilian leaders, whose decade in power had given the very concept of democracy a bad odor. The general, who detested both politicians, was able to consign them to exile with little protest. He then turned to the economic elite, vowing to end corrupt crony practices and prosecute the worst defaulters, who by then had cost the state some 130 billion rupees in bad loans. Using an agency called the National Accountability Bureau (NAB), the regime began investigating major loan defaulters and demanding they pay up.

To prove he meant business, Musharraf actually sent army soldiers to arrest several chronic defaulters. One of them was Nasim Saigol, an officer of numerous Saigol family operations, including its flagship, Kohinoor Textile Mills. His elegant ivy-covered home in Lahore was surrounded by uniformed troops, and one of the most prominent men in Pakistan was detained at his doorstep and taken away in a military truck. It was a deliberate slap in the face of the entire business elite, which only weeks before had strongly endorsed the bloodless military coup against Sharif.

The NAB went on to prosecute some eighteen hundred cases of corruption and recover nearly $3.4 billion in assets, but Musharraf squandered his credibility and cost the NAB much of its clout in 2007 when he issued his infamous National Reconciliation Order. A clumsy and desperate attempt to secure Musharraf's reelection, the order granted amnesty to hundreds of bureaucrats, politicians, and businessmen accused of corruption and other crimes, including Zardari and Benazir Bhutto.

Today, Zardari is president and Pakistan's leading business moguls, including the Saigol clan and others pursued by the NAB, still sit atop a pyramid of wealth and economic opportunity that has widened considerably in the last decade but is still far too narrow. The country is no longer run by twenty-two families; a few hundred business groups, plus a handful of military-run enterprises, now control most of the wealth. Lists of the richest businessmen include most of the iconic names from half a century ago—some of whom have since lost fortunes and rebuilt them—along with a handful of new entries in cutting-edge fields such as cellular communications, electronic media, and real estate.

At the very top is textile and cement magnate Mian Muhammad Mansha whose Nishat Group owns some thirty diversified companies including a major bank, and who is reported to be worth $2.5 billion. He is closely allied with the Saigols, who remain the dominant power in Pakistani textiles and the country's wealthiest business clan. As the family fortune has been divided among various relatives, its investments have flourished and diversified into cars, chemicals and appliances. Nasim Saigol and his brother Asif are each reported to be worth about $850 million.

An extraordinary number of Pakistan's business and banking families are interrelated by marriage, which has helped protect their wealth against outside rivals and multiplied their links to various seats of power. One of the main early alliances was the marriage of Yousuf Saigol's daughter in about 1970 to Mian Mansha, whose family established further marital bonds with the Elahi and United groups.

The practice has continued to the current generation, such as the 1994 wedding between a Dawood and a Dewan. But while most marriages in Pakistan are still arranged, such unions these days are usually the result of affluent young people moving in the same elite social circles, rather than their elders' business strategies. Glossy society magazines feature swank parties in Karachi and Lahore with stylish young men and women flirting and posing, something unheard of in their parents' time.

Both the Bhutto and Sharif clans still rank high on the list of the very wealthiest Pakistanis. The Sharifs control dozens of sugar and cement mills, steel foundries, and other production plants, and they spend weekends at their park-like Raivind estate outside Lahore.

Shabbaz Sharif wields enormous power as the chief minister of Punjab, and Nawaz bides his time as president-in-waiting. He has been so adroit at sheltering wealth that in 1999, he was reported to pay only 3,000 rupees in income taxes. The foyer of his country house is guarded by twin statues of leopards, a reminder of his personal and party ballot symbol, the tiger.

But Zardari, the current president, is both far more publicly identified with corruption and far better positioned to benefit from public office. He is said to be worth about $1.8 billion, much of it associated with alleged kickbacks and other shady business dealings from his two-time tenure as the prime minister's spouse.

Zardari spent more than eight years in prison on charges of money laundering and kickbacks, which earned him the indelible nickname "Mr. Ten Percent." He has never been convicted of a crime and enjoys legal immunity as long as he remains in office, but his presidency has been overshadowed by pending legal cases.

While efforts to punish and curb corruption have come and gone, monitoring groups have consistently rated Pakistan's business environment and reputation among the most corrupt in the world. They use the term "corrupt" in a broad sense, to include patronage and privileges as well as the cruder business of bribery and kickbacks. They also point out that such practices are publicly accepted and weakly prosecuted despite the existence of numerous anticorruption laws and agencies.

"There is probably no multinational or national company which does not support the 'need and greed' of the public sector official," the private group National Integrity Systems said in its 2003 study of Pakistan. The single largest casualty of this systemic rot, it added, has been in lost development opportunities. With both the bureaucracy and its local clients clinging to the status quo and throwing up obstacles to innovation, many foreign agencies and private investors simply give up.

More than just a crime, such groups warn, corruption is a mindset that spreads throughout society, and its major casualty is a warped

public notion of right and wrong. "Hardly any aspect of life is untouched" by financial corruption, nepotism or "misuse of privileges,"
the National Integrity Systems study warned, describing these habits as "socially accepted" and "deemed inevitable." Children are
brought up knowing that their "fathers, relatives and neighbors are
corrupt," and that it is a normal part of the society around them, the
study said. Palms are greased for the smallest transaction, and "none
are ashamed of being the giver or the taker of bribes."

Even after a decade in which four elected governments were
thrown out amid charges of corruption or power abuse, Transparency
International said in its 2008 report, there is an "unchanging" public perception in Pakistan that corruption is "widespread, systemic
and deeply entrenched at all levels of society and government."

One result of this perception is that young professionals entering
the business world are drawn to new fields such as communications
technology (rather than more traditional sectors such as textiles) and
to multinational corporations (which are seen as more efficient and
merit-based than domestic ones). Even older professional workers,
who might well benefit from corrupt practices, express the same
preferences.

A few Pakistani officials openly acknowledge the problem—and
their limited ability to do anything about it. In 2009, Sohail Ahmad,
then chairman of the Federal Board of Revenue—the equivalent of
the American Internal Revenue Service—described to me a national
culture of acquisitiveness, ostentation, and tax avoidance. So deep is
the aversion among Pakistanis to paying taxes, especially among
business owners, that Sohail estimated the government collects less
than one-third of the revenues it should. His crusade to implement
a value-added tax met with adamant opposition from business leaders and failed to pass Parliament.

"We have become a high-spending consumer society without the
means to support it," Sohail said in an interview in his wood-paneled
office, which he confided was too lavish for his taste. "Everyone wants
to get and spend money, so they are willing to sacrifice other values

and principles," he said. "It bothers me that people have all these private parties and weddings that don't reflect the real situation in Pakistan."

A MAMMOTH STEEL STRUCTURE rises beside a highway in rural Punjab. This multistory factory, a labyrinth of steel catwalks and conveyor belts and machines that grind and clatter and hum, can crush up to 7,000 tons of sugarcane a day. The noise is deafening, and it never stops. The scent is strangely cloying, and there are fine bits of sweet dust in the air.

The machines devour stalks of sugarcane and crush it into pulp, then send it to other machines that extract the juice and convey it to rows of enormous steel vats, where it is boiled and reduced to syrup. At the end of the maze, a stream of white crystalline sugar pours out of a funnel and into a row of white 40-kilo bags, each weighed and stamped with the name Tandlianwala Sugar Mills, Ltd. When the factory is running all shifts, it can produce 14,000 bags in twenty-four hours.

The owner of this state-of-the-art mill is Humayun Akhtar Khan, a trim, athletic man with a graduate degree in chartered accountancy. He speaks perfect English, wears Oxford shirts, collects abstract art, and presides over an efficient corporate headquarters in Lahore. His family has invested many millions of dollars to build a chain of profitable sugar mills on once-idle land, and he views himself as a progressive, cutting-edge entrepreneur whose operations have brought jobs, development, and higher living standards to the surrounding communities.

More than just a factory, Tandlianwala is a self-contained community with lanes of neat brick rowhouses for the full-time staff of 1,200, an elementary school and clinic, landscaped rose gardens, and orange groves. "More than 80 percent of them stay with us, because we treat them like human beings, with dignity," the mill manager told me. "If we were feudal, nobody would stay."

Yet Khan is also a member of the traditional, interlinked elite that dominates the Pakistani economy, a man equally at home in all spheres of influence and well positioned to navigate the ways of doing business in Pakistan. He is an elected member of the national senate and the son of a late prominent army general, which gives him lifetime access to the self-contained military world. His connections with banks and officials help him negotiate loans on favorable terms, while his legislative seat gives him a voice in national finance and industrial policies.

Sugar is a critical commodity in a country where people consume vast amounts of sweet tea, soft drinks, and cakes, using about 4 million metric tons of sugar a year. For the poor it is a major source of energy that sustains them during long days in fields or factories. For the affluent, it is a staple ingredient in the endless weddings, birthdays, and family gatherings that dominate social life. So important is satisfying the national sweet tooth—and so sensitive is the public to sugar scarcity and price hikes—that a shortage in the 1960s contributed to the fall of the country's military ruler, Ayub Khan.

Sugar is also very profitable. Pakistan is among the top five producers of sugarcane in the world, employing more than two million seasonal laborers at harvest time, and sugar refining is its second-largest agrobusiness after flour milling. According to the National Accountability Bureau, a majority of the country's eighty-plus sugar mills are owned by political families from both major parties, including the Sharifs and the Bhuttos, as well as by members of Parliament and several military-controlled enterprises.

To critics in the Pakistani press, labor movement and liberal intelligentsia, Khan and his fellow mill owners are greedy "sugar barons" and cartel conspirators whose sole aim is to keep the price of their product high—by hoarding warehouse stocks, taking advantage of crop shortfalls, or colluding on agreed prices—while paying as little as possible to those who grow and cut the cane.

"In Pakistan, the sugar industry is actually a political industry in which powerful politicians on all sides are involved," said a 2009 statement from the Pakistan Sugar Mills Workers Federation that described how the big millers cheat small growers through fake middlemen, then manipulate sugar prices by pressuring the government to stimulate or discourage exports depending on how much cane has been harvested.

In the summer of 2009, Pakistan confronted another major sugar crisis. In April, retail prices were running at about 36 rupees per kilo, but by August, they were reaching 60 rupees, market shelves were empty, and people were waiting for hours in long, hot lines outside state utility stores that sold small, rationed amounts of sugar at subsidized prices. In a few lines, scuffles turned into riots.

Private TV channels covered the crisis aggressively, interviewing angry consumers and accusing the politically connected mill owners of hoarding and colluding to drive up the prices. The judiciary also waded into the crisis when the Lahore High Court unexpectedly fixed the sugar price at 40 rupees and the Supreme Court upheld the order.

When I interviewed Khan, the senator and mill owner, he offered a detailed, reasonable-sounding defense of how his business functioned. He blamed the government for failing to import extra raw sugar when Pakistani cane production fell, and for setting fixed prices to win points with consumers instead of letting the market adjust. He also accused the authorities of unfairly protecting large sugarcane growers—who happened to include two government ministers—with whom the millers were locked in a permanent war over price and quality.

"People love to hate the rich and the industrialists; they love to call us a cartel and a sugar mafia," Khan said with a disarming laugh. "They want to believe certain things about us, that the mills are all owned by feudals and politicians, but it's only about 20 percent. Most of the owners are regular businesspeople. They say we are highly protected, but we are not. I cannot hoard or manipulate or collude, but I am not breaking the law if I sell my stock at the right time to maximize my profits," he asserted. "This crisis is all because of government intervention, and because people are always playing politics. The press loves it too. When there are no suicide bombs, sugar is a good issue."

I NEVER ACTUALLY MET a feudal landlord in Pakistan, or rather I never met anyone who admitted to being one. I did, however, meet a number of people who fit the description and were willing to talk about their world. Most of them were also politicians, which meant they were articulate, educated, self-aware, and careful not to sound like medieval barons.

All of them agreed that the system needed to change, and that Pakistan could not survive much longer in the global, increasingly knowledge-based economy as long the majority of its inhabitants remained illiterate peasants. Yet sooner or later, all of them ended up defending the old rural ways and expressing nostalgia for them in paternalistic terms. They spoke of local inhabitants as "my villagers" or "my voters," which could just as easily have been "my children."

Despite the gradual breakup of most large plantations over the past half century, some families in Sindh and southern Punjab still control huge farms with thousands of tenants and workers. One study of Pakistan's wealthy families by journalist Shahid-ur Rehman found that as recently as the mid-1990s, two of the largest and wealthiest landlord clans in Sindh, the Jatois and the Mahers, still owned 100,000 acres and 80,000 acres respectively, even at a time when land reform laws limited individual land holdings to 150 acres.

Both families were also political dynasties, long associated with the Pakistan People's Party but later split between party factions. The patriarch of the Jatois served in India's parliament before Partition, and his son Ghulam Mustafa Jatoi was elected to Pakistan's General Assembly seven times and named acting prime minister in 1990 after Benazir Bhutto was fired. When he died in 2009, all four of his sons were serving as provincial or national legislators.

The Mahers, whose territory includes some of the poorest, most illiterate, and most hidebound villages in Pakistan, were once said to own everything in Sindh from the Grand Trunk Road to the Indian border, which meant they effectively owned all the people who lived there too. Many of their leading members have also served in the national and provincial legislatures, as federal and provincial ministers, and as district officials.

Despite their prominent role in Pakistani democracy, however, the two clans have been at each other's throats for decades. Since the 1980s they have fought a bloody feud that led to more than two hundred deaths and required repeated government mediation as recently as 2008. The clashes were sparked by multiple grievances, including the kidnapping and forced marriage of women, but at bottom they were violent contests over land and power. Both sides have been accused of hiring criminals and using local police to kill, kidnap, and victimize villagers as a form of political retaliation.

Yet even as they denounce the violence, these agricultural patriarchs cling to an image of rural life as a pastoral idyll and assert that the collapse of law and order is largely due to the gradual breakdown of the feudal system itself.

"I still get up at four in the morning to walk my lands. I check on the [rice] paddy. I meet people in my *hijra,*" said Ghaus Bux Maher, a soft-spoken, gray-haired member of Parliament, referring to the traditional, open-air verandah where rural leaders welcome visitors and receive petitions from the public. "But now things are different. Eighty percent of my villagers have their own lands now. State law gives it to them," he said. "We are still landlords, but we are not feudals."

Maher made it clear he regretted the changes, especially the reduced powers of the *waderas,* landlords who held inherited positions as judges and peacekeepers among local peasants. "The old system was better; you handled a few people and everything was under control," he said. "Now the *haris* are better off. They have solid houses and more crops to sell, but there is no law and order anymore. The old system and the old values are gone, but nothing has replaced it."

Even if the size of their realms is no longer what it used to be, the habit of power survives among the rural elite, and the vulnerable are often abused. When flooding threatened to inundate large areas of Sindh and Punjab in the summer of 2010, many small farmers complained that big landlords deliberately had rising water diverted from their property so that it flooded the lands of poorer and less powerful neighbors.

Even the younger generation of landowners, who usually have studied abroad and acquired democratic affectations, can revert to cruder, droit du seigneur attitudes back on the farm. One professional friend in Lahore told me his old school classmate, a Punjabi landlord's son, had invited him for a visit to their estate. "He said he could get me a peasant girl if I were interested," the friend reported in disapproval.

The landlord I knew best in Pakistan was someone I had always associated with Islamabad, where her home was one of the capital's leading political salons. Abida Hussain is a formidable woman and career politician with iron-gray hair, a deep sonorous voice, and strong opinions about everything.

She is also an outspoken liberal activist and a Shiite Muslim, which along with her gender makes her a rarity among Pakistan's landlord class. Her family made a fortune in the cardboard packaging business, which makes milk and juice cartons sold in grocery shops across Pakistan every day. It has also been involved in politics for years: one uncle was Pakistan's first ambassador to England, and another became finance minister.

A longtime People's Party member, Hussain served as ambassador to Washington in the early 1990s, as well as holding numerous cabinet posts. For most of the past twenty-four years, she has held a seat in the National Assembly from Jhang, deep in southern Punjab. I had often heard her speak of her "constituency" when we met at her home in Islamabad, but I had not realized she was also talking about a number of villages connected to a large area of agricultural land that had been in her family for several generations.

When I asked her about land ownership in Jhang, Hussain gave a throaty laugh. "They call me a big bad feudal," she said, shrugging off the epithet. Then she dropped the smile and began patiently explaining that her family's original tract of several thousand acres had been reduced twice under land reform programs in the 1950s and

1970s. After that, she said, she had sold off even more chunks and invested the proceeds in private schools and media publications.

Hussain still owns a large farm in Jhang, with a prize herd of horses and a variety of crops. Although there are hundreds of peasant farmers in her district, she describes her role as a mix of neighborly agricultural consultant and political problem solver, giving one person advice on seed improvement and another a reference for a son or daughter applying to college in the capital.

"My drawing room is always full of humble folk, and they get the same tea and savories as everyone else," she said. "You don't find that in the home of a general or an industrialist. In the countryside, things are different."

WHEN PEOPLE SPEAK OF Pakistan's potential, they often point to Karachi, a fast-paced, traffic-clogged metropolis of 18 million that is much more like São Paulo or Mexico City or Mumbai than any other city in Pakistan. It has a stock exchange, a huge commercial seaport, highways with overpasses, dozens of banks, and hundreds of factories. It has elegant art galleries, dazzling fashion shows, and a 20-mile beach everyone is too busy to visit.

Geographically, Karachi is located in Sindh Province, but few people there speak Sindhi. The metropolitan area is self-governed by a middle-class Urdu-speaking immigrant party, the Muttahida Qaumi Movement (MQM), and its hectic, vertical life seems utterly removed from the slow, surrounding plains of rural poverty and feudal tradition—a Chicago ringed by El Salvador.

Karachi is also one of the most violent cities in Asia. It is home to a volatile mix of criminal and business mafias, political shock troops, Islamic sects and militant factions, and warring ethnic enclaves. Every time I have visited Karachi as a journalist, it was invariably to cover a spate of political assassinations, an outbreak of ethnic warfare between the Pashtuns and the Mohajirs, or a terrorist bombing such as the one that exploded during a peaceful Shiite Muslim procession in January 2010.

Many natives of Punjab tend to look down on Karachi as a social and demographic disaster, and successive national political and economic upheavals have gradually elevated the economic status of Punjab Province, a center of cultured history and genteel affectations, above this rough-and-tumble port city. But Karachi remains the nation's Wall Street, while its cosmopolitan spirit, resilience, and mobility continue to attract ambitious people of every class, religion, and ethnic group.

Above all, Karachi is a city of immigrants. It was founded by wealthy Urdu-speaking "sailor businessmen" who migrated from India at the time of Partition, and it was built largely on the sweat of Afghan migrants who fled to northwest Pakistan from Soviet occupation, civil war, and other calamities, then gradually filtered south. Diversity is welcome, and everyone has a chance to claw his way up. Old-timers attribute this to the longtime dominance of the private sector, in contrast to the sluggish state bureaucracy and landed political cronyism that dominate power in the rest of the country.

"The reason Karachi succeeds is because everything here is based on competition. We are the engine of Pakistan and we keep the economy going. Here you have to keep moving to survive, but everyone is welcome to come and try," said Siraj Telli, a longtime business association leader in Karachi who runs a Pepsi bottling and distribution operation. Corruption, sycophancy, and moral laxity are the bane of Pakistan, he declared.

"You have to have standards. It may be normal some places to steal 10 percent, but in Pakistan people steal 90 percent and they don't care what happens to anyone else," Telli said, exaggerating for effect. "Political leaders get too much power and it goes to their heads. The army is more disciplined and professional. Now they have become corrupt too, and I pray they don't step in and take over again, but they are still a better institution."

The Karachi entrepreneurial model has many levels and niches, from the wood-paneled clubs where English- and Urdu-speaking captains of industry dine to the gritty lairs of the trucking and construction cartels dominated by ethnic Pashtun refugees.

The well-heeled residents who attend art openings and dinners in Clifton, the seaside enclave made famous as the site of Benazir Bhutto's family home, have no more in common with factory workers who inhabit the gritty industrial wastes of Orangi than, say, senior bureaucrats living in Islamabad's policed residential suburbs have with the ragged garbage pickers of the capital's hidden Christian slums.

What's different about Karachi is the critical mass of people in the middle: the secretaries and bookkeepers, restaurant managers and printers, taxi owners and factory foremen, Internet technicians and bank clerks who represent Pakistan's impatient urban middle class. People with such ambitions exist in cities and towns all over Pakistan, and their numbers are growing fast. The problem is that in most places, there is not enough modern economic activity and job market growth to absorb them. Too much wealth is sent abroad rather than being reinvested at home; too little has been spent to build competitive colleges and graduate schools; too few taxes are collected and too many bribes are paid; too many bureaucratic hurdles are placed in the path of start-up businesses; and too many educated young people are turned away from professional government positions because they don't have the right political connections.

Middle-class frustrations are more subtle, but no less real, than the desperate rage of jobless people demonstrating against high sugar prices and bus fares. Members of this group are less likely to become suicide bombers than teenagers recruited from poor villages and slums. Yet they are far from impervious to the moralistic message of Islamic extremist groups, who have worked hard to stoke popular perceptions of U.S. and European aggression against Muslims everywhere, and to capitalize on public anger and disappointment with the current elected government.

Shahid Javed Burki, a former Pakistani finance minister and longtime World Bank economist, described present-day Pakistan as a wobbly, three-tiered nation that could easily collapse. At the top, he wrote in a 2009 essay, a tiny elite of a few million have "sealed themselves off from the rest of society," with their own security, education, health, and power systems. At the bottom are some 75 million poor, struggling to survive and marginalized from public life, who view the state as "an indifferent and increasingly irrelevant presence."

While the government urgently needs to find ways to engage the desperate poor as productive wage earners, Burki argued, the key to Pakistan's future is the emerging but confused urban middle class of about 85 million. This is the class, he pointed out, that has generally voted for mainstream political parties, believed in upward mobility, and produced the lawyers and civic leaders who campaigned to restore the independent judiciary.

These are people of modest means and practical ambitions: the elementary school teacher who saves up to buy a cheap domestic car to drive to work, the office clerk attending storefront computer classes at six in the morning, the evening-shift security guard finishing a two-year degree in bookkeeping. These are the people, economists such as Burki say, who should be moving up, saving money, and expanding the economy.

Instead, this class is uncertain and unhappy, "waiting for leadership to emerge" that will mobilize its energies, employ its skills, and reinforce its democratic instincts. Some, who are drifting toward the religious right, must be lured "back to the fold" of mainstream Islam. "The battle for Pakistan," Burki concludes, will be "to keep the middle class convinced that their best option is to put their faith in the Pakistani state."

I met many people in Pakistan who fit this class description. One was a young bank officer I used to see every few weeks in Islamabad, wearing a coat and tie, smiling pleasantly behind a desk. One day I spotted him outside, smoking a cigarette and pacing back and forth. I said hello, and he gave me a sharp, beseeching look. "I have to get out of here," he blurted. "This environment is so stifling. It's all about relationships. I want to show someone what I can do, what I can learn. Can you find me a job with a foreign company?"

Another was a textile factory manager in Faisalabad, a man in his fifties named Mohammed Khan. His desk was pin-neat and his office had no windows. He was clearly a practical person, dedicated to his work and proud of his mill. He began by listing the myriad problems ailing Pakistan's textile industry—devastating power shortages, rising costs, government mismanagement, tariff barriers in the West, and cutthroat competition between the spinning industry, which makes thread, and the weaving industry, which produces cloth for sheets, towels, and shirts.

Then, somehow, the conversation grew more anguished and more universal. Suddenly the manager was leaning forward in his chair, confiding to a stranger his frustration with the way things are done in Pakistan, and his deep concern for the future of his country.

"There are more than 1,000 people working at this mill. We have talent, modern machines, and excellent materials. But I am the manager and it is my responsibility to set a good example, or I can't pressure the workers to do what's right," he began, and I realized he was speaking metaphorically.

"What we lack is good leadership. The government is too busy surviving to do its job and make consistent policies and plan ahead. Nothing is done on merit or criteria. The mind-set is only about money and interests. We have laws on conflict of interest, but look at all the federal ministers and MPs who own units in the garment industry, or in sugar. Nobody votes for people with education and ability, only for those they think will do them favors."

Khan took a breath, surprised at his own frankness. I asked him if things had been better during Musharraf's tenure, when the economy boomed for a few years and the military government promised to prosecute corruption and run a tight ship.

"My father was an officer and I respect the military, but that's not the solution either," he answered. "Every time a dictator comes in, things shut down and we have to start over. Nobody lets democracy or the market flow free. The only reason we survive as a nation is because we are hardworking people. Otherwise the politicians would throw Pakistan into the sea."

A few months after this encounter, I met a young man from Peshawar who had just graduated from one of Pakistan's best engineering schools but had been unable to find a job in his field. His résumé was tucked in a slender portfolio, and his English was perfect.

"The problem with Pakistan is that there isn't enough room in the economy for people like me," he said. "The multinationals skim off the cream of every graduating class, and all the rest of us end up working as office clerks. All those years, all that study. Who do I blame? How do I go back home? What do I tell my father?" He gave a bitter laugh. "Sometimes I think this is what makes people become terrorists."

CHAPTER 3

HONOR

A POISED YOUNG WOMAN named Rukshana sat on a neatly made cot in a small white room, next to her husband, Amir. She seemed sad but determined. Tears came to her eyes several times as she recounted the events that had brought them to this hiding place, a government-run shelter near the capital, but she firmly brushed them away.

It seemed hard to believe, sitting in that quiet room in the spring of 2010, but Rukshana was under a death sentence. At age twenty-five, she had set off a public firestorm that threatened an entire way of life—simply by refusing to submit to tribal custom in her village and marry another, much older man in compensation for a legal dispute.

In the past, Rukshana's story would never have become public knowledge. She and Amir most likely would have been hunted down, dragged back to their village in rural Sindh, and stoned to death by their own relatives and neighbors, on orders from the council of local elders, known as a *jerga*. There would have been no police investigation, no attempt to stop the punishment, no call for cooler heads to prevail. What mattered, in Pakistani tribal society, was keeping the peace, obeying the judgments of the elders, and avenging the injured "honor" of families whose wives or daughters had attempted to escape the iron boundaries of tradition.

But this time, several transformative elements came into play that cast an uncomfortable spotlight on the case and lent an unprecedented measure of protection to the victims. One was the national media, which leaped on the story and kept it in the public eye. The other was the justice system, which was beginning to emerge from years as a handmaiden of the elite under the newly restored chief justice of the Supreme Court, Mohammed Iftikhar Chaudhry, an iconoclastic reformer who took a personal interest in this case.

Rukshana also benefitted from the fact that she had managed to attend high school and college, even though she came from a deeply conservative rural background. This enabled her to imagine life beyond village culture and gave her the courage to defy authority in circumstances where most other young women would have meekly submitted.

On a broader level, though, hers is a tale of the struggle between two sets of powerful institutions. One is a traditional system that has provided peace and order in rural Pakistan for generations, but in the process has held back social development and the emancipation of women—the only cure for a population explosion that is dragging Pakistan into debt and poverty. The other is a set of modern institutions—the press, civil society, the legal establishment, and the courts—which are beginning to find their independent strength and to free their society from such traditional constraints.

Across Pakistan today, the tribal system is under assault. Its hereditary leaders are facing pressure to adapt with the times, abandon the decision-making tradition of male-only community *jergas* and cede their authority to the state. In some places things are changing, as the level of public education and awareness rises. But in others, such as Rukshana's region of northern Sindh, the elders—often in concert with local politicians and landowners—still forcefully cling to their power and way of life.

"Back home, the entire establishment is against me," Rukshana said with a faint smile, looking suddenly small and vulnerable beneath her head scarf. "If we go back, our lives will be in danger. Our families are under enormous pressure. The imam has issued a fatwa against us and the police chief will arrest us and take us to the elders. My mother supports me, but my brothers are looking everywhere for me. They say even if it takes them twenty years to find me, they will kill me. Nobody will forgive me, because I have violated the norms of our society. My life is worth nothing now."

EVEN TODAY, AFTER YEARS of negative publicity about honor crimes and efforts to promote women's rights in Pakistan, Rukshana's story is shockingly commonplace. According to two women's rights groups, the Aurat Foundation and the Violence Against Women Watch Group, there were 475 confirmed cases of honor killings across Pakistan in 2008 and 604 in 2009. Overall, the groups reported more than 16,000 confirmed cases of violence against women during those two years. In 2009 alone, 1,384 women were murdered, 1,987 abducted, 928 raped, and 608 assaulted by relatives, and 683 committed suicide. Another 274 were sexually assaulted, 50 were burned by stoves, and 53 had acid thrown on them. The majority of incidents took place in Punjab, followed by Sindh. Activists said they believe the number of unreported occurrences of killings and abuse is much higher.

Many of the reported incidents took place in rural villages with strong tribal influence, but others occurred in cities within working-class and occasionally more affluent families. Most often, the cases involved *zina,* the crime of committing illicit sex, and especially *karo-kari,* the act of forbidden elopement, in which the offending couple were usually caught, judged, and ritually murdered by their own relatives or by members of a *jerga.* There were numerous other cases in which women were burned, mutilated, or disfigured, usually at the hands of jealous husbands or of fathers and brothers whose marriage arrangements or authority they had resisted.

In 2003, Pakistan's Supreme Court upheld the right of any sane adult Muslim woman to marry the man of her choice. But the crushing power of custom and community often rendered law irrelevant, and a spate of new cases highlighted the cruel and grotesque punishments meted out to young women who dared insist on that right, not only in tribal villages.

The case that drew the most international attention was that of Mukhtar Mai, an illiterate villager from southern Punjab. In the summer of 2002, Mai, then thirty-three, told police she was gang-raped on the orders of an impromptu tribal council to avenge accusations that her adolescent brother had engaged in illicit sex with a girl from the higher-caste Mastoi clan. The boy had allegedly been kidnapped and sodomized by the Mastois, an equally cruel and criminal act, but the clan demanded further recompense for its lost honor.

The elders of Mai's family proposed marrying her to the girl's brother, a time-honored custom for settling disputes, and according to one version of the story, she was in fact married to him for several days and concocted the rape story. But Mai said the men of the accusing clan had summarily "sentenced" her to be raped, dragged her to a house where several took part in the punishment, and then pushed her out naked in front of the village. Satisfied, the aggrieved clan then withdrew its accusation against Mai's younger brother.

Instead of committing suicide, as another tribal woman might have done under such humiliating circumstances, Mai went with her family to the police and filed charges. Soon her story was all over the Pakistani media. Six of her attackers were quickly tried and sentenced to death, though five were later acquitted on appeal. After a series of legal battles, the Supreme Court intervened and ordered the retrial of all fourteen men originally accused. In April 2011, however, the court acquitted all but one remaining defendant, basically saying it did not believe Mai's story.

Mai's outspoken courage brought her international acclaim, including being honored by the United Nations and named *Glamour* magazine's woman of the year in 2005, but it subjected her to a second victimization by powerful forces at home. President Musharraf initially blocked her from traveling abroad, claiming she would "tarnish" Pakistan's international image. Senior officials pressured her to drop the charges against her rapists, and she told interviewers she was afraid of being harmed by landlords. When she founded a village project to encourage girls to stay in school and learn about their rights, the compound was raided.

Finally, in 2009, this world-famous icon of women's rights was forced once more to submit to tribal custom back home. Pressured to become the second wife of a man she did not want to marry, she finally consented because to refuse would have ruined the lives of two other women. It is a common custom in rural Pakistan to marry several girls from one family to several boys from another to reinforce tribal bonds. In the case of a feud, the reverse can happen. Two of Mai's sisters, married to men from her suitor's family, would have been forcibly divorced.

THE EXTRAORDINARY DIVERSITY OF Pakistan—and the extremes of class and culture that have made it so difficult to unify and move ahead—is nowhere more starkly evident than in the lives of its 80 to 90 million women. The contrasts in their daily routines and occupations, marital relations and family responsibilities, freedoms and constraints are so stark that the women of Pakistan truly might as well be living in several different nations and centuries.

These differences are rooted in a complex, often overlapping mixture of social, economic, ethnic, religious, and cultural causes—from illiteracy to gossip to ancient tribal codes. They illustrate how difficult it is to define, unite, and change a society where people have a wide array of beliefs and convictions about the proper role of women in a Muslim society.

In sophisticated urban settings such as Lahore and Karachi, thousands of middle- and upper-class girls study to become doctors and lawyers, psychologists and teachers. Some are sent abroad to study, and many are encouraged to pursue modern careers and callings. Young "Westernized" women of means also frequent stylish clubs, art exhibits, concerts, and fashion benefits, where they pose for society magazines such as *Goodtimes,* a glossy Lahore publication. They wear expensively tasteful *salwar kameez* in soft silks or cottons, and they rarely cover their heads except with loose *dupattas* that constantly slip out of place.

Pakistan's burgeoning fashion industry is a daring demimonde that flouts social convention and flaunts sexuality, although safely within the confines of big-city society. It is also one of the few fields in which women can become economically successful as models or designers. Annual fashion weeks in Lahore and Karachi have become exotic extravaganzas that feature provocatively clad models, androgynous male designers, and all the haute gossip of Paris or Milan. Fashion insiders relish the brash and bewildering contradiction they represent in a country most outsiders view as caught in the grip of Islamic terrorists and feudal barons.

Celebrity marriages in Pakistan are also hot topics of gossip, speculation, and scandal, much the way soap operas distract people everywhere from humdrum routines and pressures. In the spring of 2010, the conflict-weary nation breathlessly followed the intrigue-filled engagement between Shoaib Malik, a former national cricket team captain, and Sania Mirza, an Indian tennis star. The story had everything: spicy rumors that Malik had broken off a previous engagement to marry Mirza, special appeal for sports fans, and an obvious diplomatic angle because of the perennial hostility between India and Pakistan.

Yet even in the upper classes, there are strictly observed cultural limits. Single girls in Pakistan do not drink alcohol in public or date in the Western sense. They do not live alone and rarely even share apartments with friends. What happens while they are studying in London or in Los Angeles touring is one thing, but at home, most young women live with their parents until they marry, and almost all marriages are still arranged by their families. Usually the fiancé is someone within an extended social circle of family friends, and fairly often he is a cousin or other blood relative.

Increasingly, engaged couples from professional families know each other socially and are able to test their chemistry, especially since cell phones and the Internet have made flirtation, private chats, and even clandestine trysts much easier to manage. But often the groom is a virtual stranger, called home from work or study abroad for the formal engagement and later the marriage ceremony.

Weddings remain the social glue of Pakistan, whether they take place in a remote village square or a five-star hotel. Families are expected to invite even the most distant relatives to multiday festivities or else face ruinous gossip. The bride's parents are also expected to spend lavishly on a dowry for the groom's family, with the quantity of money and gifts, such as a motorcycle or refrigerator, depending on his stature.

At their crudest, marriage negotiations can become pecuniary haggling sessions in which the choice of bride or groom may change at the last minute if a better deal is struck or a more elaborate dowry is offered. Several governments have tried to set legal limits on dowries, but social convention has proven stronger. Only the Taliban, whose methods are harder to resist, have managed to impose such spending caps in the tribal regions under their control.

Separations are increasingly common as social life becomes more complex and mobile, but divorce is frowned on by all classes and rare in rural or tribal communities. Men from poorer and more traditional families occasionally insist on invoking the Islamic right to instantly divorce a disobedient or childless wife by simply declaring "I divorce you" three times, but often the multiple bonds between rural families—where several sisters may be married to several brothers—discourage this.

Although "honor" crimes are generally associated with lower-class and rural Pakistan, the urban upper classes are not immune to the same cultural pressures that produce them, especially in cases of divorce, elopement, and illicit romances. In a notorious incident in 1999, Samia Sarwar, a twenty-nine-year-old middle-class woman seeking a divorce from an abusive husband, was shot dead in her lawyer's office in Lahore. Her killer, though never caught, reportedly had been hired by her own mother and father—a medical doctor and businessman—out of shame over her affair with an army officer.

Violent domestic abuse is also common in upper-class homes, Pakistani activists say, but more easily hidden behind the walls of exclusive residential compounds than in close-knit villages and crowded urban slums where neighbors hear everything and gossip constantly. In a rare exception, an elegant society woman named Tehmina Durrani, divorced from a prominent politician and long-time confidant of Zulfiqar Ali Bhutto, published a shocking memoir in the 1990s called *My Feudal Lord,* which described years of vicious abuse at his hands. The book scandalized Pakistani society, but critics discredited Durrani as mentally unstable and motivated by revenge.

Domestic abuse is even more common by male employers and household heads against female servants, where both class and age differences exacerbate the man's sense of impunity and the woman's sense of helplessness. Many affluent urban families, including educated professionals, employ young girls from poor villages as cheap and docile house servants, paying their families a few dollars a month. Under 1991 child labor laws, the minimum age for legal labor is fourteen years for light work and fifteen for heavy work, but the law is widely ignored, and girls are especially vulnerable to abuse—both by their own families, who essentially sell them, and by those who hire them.

One young professional woman I knew started a program to provide free elementary school classes for young children who work, often as housemaids, garage mechanics, or garbage scavengers. She said some families who employed girls as servants were very reluctant to let them attend school, and that many of her own friends, all affluent college-educated women in their twenties, showed little interest in her project or made fun of her and made her feel like a misfit.

"My girlfriends spend a fortune on their clothes—they buy one outfit for the same amount we pay a teacher for one month—but I can't get them to donate, and they think I am eccentric for doing this," said the young woman. "Their families all have child servants, girls of ten who wash their clothes, and they think they are doing them a favor. Here everything is about how you look and what you have, not who you are. Everything is for show. People are complacent and apathetic. They are afraid that if they help poor people, they will just keep asking for more. When I say I want to help poor children, they say, 'Oh, you must not be from here. You must have just come from America.'"

Occasionally, a news story sheds light on a common practice that is usually hidden behind guard booths and garden walls in affluent residential areas. One such case was the death of Shazia Masih, a twelve-year-old housemaid, who died of unexplained injuries in a Lahore hospital in January 2010.

Masih was from a Christian family, a minority that is predominantly poor and generally relegated to certain low-level unsanitary jobs such as cleaning and collecting garbage. She earned $12 per month. What made her death so sensational was that her employer, Chaudhry Mohammed Naeem, was a prominent attorney and a former president of the Lahore High Court Bar Association, which had played a leading role during the Musharraf era in the peaceful movement to restore democracy and the independent judiciary.

According to press reports, the girl had been beaten and abused frequently in the lawyer's home, and a hospital autopsy found she had suffered numerous wounds from sharp and rusty instruments. The report listed possible contributing causes of death as physical torture, mental torture, and malnutrition. Naeem, his wife, and several other relatives were arrested but immediately released on bail. They claimed she had not been abused but was suffering from an infectious disease.

The federal government paid Masih's parents 500,000 rupees in compensation, and her case became a cause celebre among the Christian advocacy groups; thousands of people attended her funeral at a Catholic cathedral. But Lahore's legal fraternity closed ranks around their colleague Naeem, gathering outside the court when he was arraigned and angrily protesting against sensationalistic TV coverage of the case. The Pakistani Christian Association claimed no lawyer was willing to represent Masih's family because of threats, but an uncle of hers was arrested on charges of providing minor workers to employers, further muddying the moral waters.

Some weeks later, I was interviewing a group of lawyers in Rawalpindi about the problems of justice in Pakistan. They were all member of the city bar association, which had been at the forefront of the legal movement for democracy and judicial independence. When I asked them about the Masih case, one lawyer shook his head in chagrin.

"Every one of us knew it was wrong, but when it comes to your own kind, morality is wishful thinking," he said. "You Americans have your ideals, but we don't even have proper institutions yet. Our own movement is new and it is still evolving. We wanted to come out with a resolution on this case from our bar association, but we were not up to it. There were so many factors involved. I am sorry to say, we never did come out."

The plot grew even murkier when police officials said their investigation showed Masih had not been killed at all but suffered from both a skin disease and mental illness. Some lawyers sympathetic to Naeem also said she had fallen down the stairs. The *Nation,* a progovernment newspaper, quoted an unnamed police official as saying the abuse charges were "totally baseless and concocted." Masih's parents were playing into the hands of the nonprofit "mafia," he said, and the entire case was a "planned game to mint money."

IN THE PUBLIC AND political life of major urban centers, Pakistani women are active and visible in increasing numbers. Many were inspired by the example of Benazir Bhutto, an elegant but tough leader who was elected prime minister twice during the 1990s. Her socially progressive views emboldened a generation of young women from the working and middle classes, as well as the affluent elite, to become politically engaged and speak up for their rights.

Today, with a boost from government quotas, there are more than 100 women in the upper and lower houses of the national legislature and another 137 in provincial assembly seats. A few high-profile women, such as legislator Sherry Rehman and activist Asma Jehangir, are eloquent and outspoken advocates for human rights and democracy, while others represent conservative rural regions and religious parties, including the daughter of Jamaat-e-Islami founder Qazi Hussain Ahmed.

Hundreds of thousands of women work as teachers all over the country, and a small but growing number enter professions such as law and medicine. Educated women have long formed the backbone of Pakistan's still-small but vociferous civil society movement, holding up banners at protest rallies and pressing for democratic causes. A large number of women work in journalism, and they include some of the country's most influential writers and columnists, from nationalist Shireen Mazari to liberal Kamila Hyat.

In the middle and working classes, however, there are still strong social pressures against women being seen in public or coming into contact with strange men. Very few shopkeepers, restaurant servers, factory workers, and office clerks are women, and the only acceptable outside occupation for poor urban women is as domestic servants. Public transportation is viewed as a source of potential harassment or importuning by strange men, and many husbands or fathers do not want women in their families to take buses or vans to work or school.

Middle-class women often attend college, and increasing numbers of them take office or professional jobs, especially with multinational companies or international agencies. The majority, though, settle quickly after marriage into child raising and social activities within their extended joint family; their education level serves chiefly as a factor in compatible matchmaking.

In rural areas, the taboos are even stronger. Although many peasant women work in the fields alongside their husbands and sons, it is extremely rare for them to participate in public meetings or leave their villages unescorted by a *mahram,* or close male relative. Within a few miles of Lahore or Karachi, female literacy rates fall below 20 percent, the average age of marriage drops into the teens, and the number of births per mother rises. The deeper one ventures into rural Pakistan, the tighter is the grip of patriarchal tradition, and the lower the status of women. Although child marriage is against the law in Pakistan, 70 percent of girls are married by the age of eighteen, and 20 percent by the age of thirteen; the figures are especially high in rural areas.

"The feudal lords who occupy the corridors of power have enormous influence on the populations in their areas," a woman from northern Sindh wrote in a letter to a newspaper in 2010. When "women-friendly" legislation is proposed, they kill it or make sure those beneath them do not implement it. "Those ensconced at the helm of affairs don't know the agony of those girls given in marriage to men the age of their fathers and grandfathers." Forced child marriages, she added, lead to psychological problems, broken homes, economic burdens, and a "colossal increase in population."

Hardly exempted from toil, rural Pakistani women herd buffaloes, hack at stands of sugarcane, and mold bricks from raw clay alongside their husbands and brothers. They are also expected to produce and raise large numbers of children, often as many as eight, while running the home and serving the husband, his mother, and other relatives from his side of the family. Often they never leave their villages at all, except to attend family weddings or visit a Sufi shrine on the saint's annual day.

"In our society, women are supposed to stay home, keep quiet, and obey their husbands," said Sofia Abbasy, a teacher and activist in a town in northern Sindh. "They can be killed if dinner is late, and if they go out and meet people, they will be suspected of having wrong relations." In other words, any woman who ventures into the public realm except to buy groceries in the bazaar is assumed to have no legitimate social or intellectual reason for doing so, and her own neighbors will spread malicious gossip about her.

The grip of tribal tradition is especially strong in the northwest border regions, dominated by deeply conservative ethnic Pashtun or Afghan culture, and in the southwest desert areas of Balochistan and Sindh. These are semi-lawless realms where tribal feuds and violence have long been a way of life. The need to protect village women from the sexual predations of brigands and enemies has always taken priority, and opportunities such as allowing women to study or work have been regarded as dangerous luxuries.

While the law allows any woman in Pakistan to run for local office, the idea is anathema to many Pashtun, Baloch, and Sindhi tribes. In the spring of 2010, Mai Jori Jamali, an illiterate peasant woman and mother of nine, stunned the rural establishment by running for Sindh's provincial assembly. Just two years earlier, her home district had gained notoriety when five young women there were reportedly beaten, shot, and buried alive for "dishonoring" their families by seeking to marry men of their own choice.

Jamali, who campaigned against such abuses, received death threats during the campaign, and on election day she lost badly, with a scant 491 votes. Women's advocates in Pakistan called her high-profile candidacy an important breakthrough that challenged both feudal and patriarchal power. But the forces that defeated her were still inclined to the views of the Baloch legislator who staunchly backed the killing of the five wayward girls. "These are centuries-old traditions, and I will continue to defend them," he told his fellow members of Parliament at the time. "Only those who indulge in immoral acts should be afraid."

DURING THE PAST DECADE, successive Pakistani government leaders have publicly condemned honor crimes and violence against women, and national legislatures have passed a series of laws to protect them. In 2000, President Musharraf spoke out forcefully against honor killing, calling it unworthy of any religious or cultural justification. "Such acts do not find a place in our religion or law," he told a public gathering. "Killing in the name of honor is murder, and it will be treated as such."

Yet the Musharraf regime never aggressively pursued the issue, in part because the general needed the support of religious groups to stay in power and did not want to arouse opposition from other conservative and tribal segments of society. His liberalizing impulse was also overshadowed by the lingering legacy of General Zia, who had promulgated a series of harsh laws governing sexual misconduct as part of his "Islamization" drive that began in 1979.

These laws, known as the Hudood Ordinances, made all sexual activity outside marriage subject to Islamic criminal law, under an offense broadly referred to as *zina,* and made offenders subject to an array of harsh physical punishments including whippings and stonings. Such sentences were almost never carried out, because sex crimes such as rape were extremely difficult to prove and required four male witnesses to the act. However, laws against adultery were easily enforced against women, and if a rape victim accused her attacker, she often ended up imprisoned on charges of illicit sex.

In 2006, the Hudood laws were finally revised and replaced by a new Women's Protection Bill, which allowed rape to be prosecuted under civil instead of Islamic law and reduced the penalty for adultery from death to a five-year maximum prison term. Yet despite protests from Pakistani and international rights groups, the Hudood laws were never fully revoked because the legislature faced strong opposition by Islamic groups. Today, the majority of women in Pakistani jails have been incarcerated because of sexual offenses such as adultery and elopement.

In 2010, the National Assembly passed a sweeping revision of the Pakistani constitution that was touted as an effort to democratize the charter and remove the dictatorial influences of both Zia and Musharraf. But even with an elected government in place and the widower of Benazir Bhutto in the presidency, the lawmakers dared not touch what remained of the Hudood laws. This time the sponsors needed the support of conservative religious parties to pass the broader constitutional reform package, and they were reluctant to raise a volatile issue that could kill it.

IN 2010, I VISITED several districts of northern Sindh, where village boundaries were defined by clan and families had intermarried for four generations. The people were poor, sedentary, and deprived by any standard, with literacy rates that were among the very lowest in Pakistan, but they seemed generally content among themselves. (Villagers in southern Punjab told me the same thing: that as long as everyone in a village was from the same clan, life was relatively peaceful.)

On the other hand, they lived in a state of permanent hostility and mistrust with rival clans from nearby villages. There were frequent squabbles over traffic accidents, trespassing, and access to irrigation wells. The worst feuds, however, were over women, particularly illicit liaisons outside the clan, which were always referred to as kidnappings. Some of these fights had gone on for years, with much blood spilled. The habit of feuding seemed to satisfy a combination of frontier justice, blood lust, male pride, and a desire for entertainment.

During my visit, I met briefly with a few local lawyers, teachers, and other activists who were trying to keep track of abuse cases and prod local authorities to respond to them. But they were nervous and overworked, and they had very few sources of funds. They said area police officials had recently received special training in women's rights under a UN program, but that their ties to influential local clan leaders made them reluctant to challenge the verdicts of *jergas* to punish eloping couples or unfaithful wives. According to national statistics, that region of Sindh has had one of the highest rates of honor crimes and *jerga*-ordered killings.

Today, some community elders try to hold *jergas* in secret to avoid negative publicity, while continuing to mete out harsh sentences. In the spring of 2009, after two teenagers eloped and married against the wishes of the girl's father, a clandestine *jerga* in northern Sindh ordered the couple to be divorced and two sisters of the young man, age seventeen and ten, handed over for marriage to the girl's family to avenge its offended honor. A source leaked the story to the press, but local police said they knew nothing about it and did not intervene.

Activists say that with the right incentives and support from community elders, it may not take much to persuade even the most conservative villagers to send their daughters to school. In 2003, the U.S. Department of Agriculture and the Land o'Lakes dairy company launched a project in Jacobabad, the district with the lowest literacy rate in Sindh and female school attendance of only 19 percent. The concept was simple: every girl who appeared in school was rewarded with milk and a biscuit that day. By 2006, girls' enrollment was up to 47 percent; by 2009 it had reached 65 percent, and more than 200,000 students were getting the extra nutrition—along with basic information on health and hygiene such as how to brush their teeth.

Yet without that extra push, it was easy to see how the combination of traditional custom, economic need, and physical insecurity conspires to keep village girls sequestered at home. In one northern Sindhi village, when I asked community leaders how many children were attending school, they were both sheepish and defiant. A show of hands in a room of about twenty-five youngsters indicated that only half the boys and almost none of the girls were in school.

The elders offered a series of vague and complicated explanations. The roads were too dangerous, they said; the public schools were too far away; the private schools were too expensive. The girls were needed to work in the fields, but if they ventured beyond the village, strange boys could bother them, raising tensions among the clans.

"I have a little land and a big family. My children and grandchildren are my great source of happiness," said a beaming village elder named Jalaldin. He perched on a string bed in a dimly lit farmhouse while his entire extended family of about forty people, including three wives and countless progeny, crammed into the room to gawk at a foreign visitor. In a few words, the jovial, gray-bearded elder gave a coherent, logical, and tragic argument for why his community could not risk sending its girls to school.

"I want the girls to be educated, but it creates too many problems," he explained matter-of-factly. "There is no public school in our village, and if I send them to the private school in another village and a boy from another tribe teases or insults them, the men of our tribe will come out with guns. This is a very sensitive issue in our society. The police and the courts get involved. Cases drag on for years, everyone is disturbed, and life becomes a living hell. It is better to keep the girls at home."

The elder's urgent priority was to get all of his granddaughters engaged as soon as possible, because once they were "spoken for," no other young man would dare approach them. Three were already betrothed, including a girl of nine. "Some are promised before they are even born," the elder said. The arrangements were always within the extended tribe, and they served as a bond that was renewed and strengthened with each match. I dimly understood this logic, given the constant feuding that went on with the neighboring tribes, but I tried once more. Why could a girl, once safely betrothed, not then go to school once she became old enough to study?

This time, a woman answered. She was plump and smiling, a mother of seven in her late forties. Holding a bright purple scarf over half her face, she spoke with impatient politeness, as if explaining something obvious to a fool or a foreigner. "A girl here cannot get a job, so what is the use of her going to school?" the woman demanded. "If she goes out and gets an education, then she may get ideas and want to marry someone of her own choice. If I arrange to give her to my nephew and she refuses, I have to kill her."

The woman was still smiling as she said this, but she glanced sharply at me several times, and for a moment I thought she was exaggerating to gauge my reaction. Then I realized that we had finally come to the heart of the matter and that there was nothing more to say. On the string bed, a slender girl of about twelve was shyly fiddling with her hair. When her grandfather pointed her out to me as recently engaged, she lit up with pride.

THE ULTIMATE AUTHORITY IN the tribal or clan system of rural Pakistan is a man known as the *sardar,* or sometimes a *nawab.* The title is hereditary and carries enormous responsibilities. It obliges the titleholder to look after the interests of his clan, settle disputes, arrange marriages, and offer fatherly advice. It also entitles him to make decisions that carry all the force of a legal judgment and affect people's lives forever, such as formally declaring that a woman is *kari,* meaning she has committed adultery, or ordering that a girl from one family be given to another in payment for a crime.

The *sardar* system coexists, interacts, and sometimes clashes with the modern state administration of police and courts. In some areas, the government has made increasing inroads into the traditional system, but *sardars* often command extra authority as large landowners, and peasants naturally turn to them for personal counsel and intervention, especially in cases where the all-important honor of the tribe is at stake. Most often, that involves sex.

"My position came from my grandfather and it will pass on to my grandson. It is my responsibility to look after the traditions of the tribe," said Wahid Bux Bhayo, a *sardar* in Sindh and an astute, complex man who embodies many of the contradictions and competing influences between traditional values and modern institutions in Pakistani society today. Worldly and wealthy, he has studied at Oxford and skied in Wyoming; he wears expensive bifocals and speaks perfect English into his cell phone.

But at home, Bhayo plays the role of white-turbaned wise man, listening to endless, argumentative versions of intimate disputes. If a woman is accused of being *kari* by her husband or another male relative, he calls the leaders and sub-*sardars* from both sides. A date is set, people gather, witnesses are called, emotional and twisted tales unfold. At the end, Bhayo decides whether she is guilty of having an illicit affair and what the penalty should be. Often it is a monetary fine, but sometimes it is death.

"Our tribal tradition is not the same as Pakistani state law or sharia courts," he explains. "We do not let the state interfere in our affairs and vice versa." In the tribal system, "a woman may be eighteen or eighty years old, but she is never free to marry on her own, and nobody will tolerate it if she has an affair," he explains. "The honor of the clan and the village is called *ghairat.* It does not belong to one person. It is collective. If a wife has an affair and the man does nothing, everyone will keep hounding him. I don't like to declare a woman *kari,* but if I do not issue an edict against her, then I will be accused of being without *ghairat.*"

RUKSHANA'S STORY IS AN example of the long, unbending, and powerful reach of tribal rule—a reach that in her case extended across two decades and hundreds of miles. The facts, according to the couple and to various news accounts about the case, are these. About twenty years ago, when she was a toddler, her older brother accidentally shot a boy in his gun repair shop; the boy later died. The family accused him of murder and insisted on being compensated for their loss. Under tribal custom, girls are regularly pledged in marriage to settle such disputes, and the local *jerga* decreed that Rukshana should eventually be given to a man from the other clan, who was already in his twenties and married.

The little girl grew up and went to school, excelling in her studies. She became the first female member of her family to attend college, and even obtained a master's degree in sociology. But one day in 2008, her relatives came to her and said she must now honor the *jerga*'s decision and marry the man, who by then had daughters her age. She refused, infuriating her family and the entire community. Fearing she would be forcibly wed, she slipped away from a family gathering in another city and ran away with Amir, a friend and cousin who had agreed to marry her as a way out of her plight.

The family immediately filed a criminal case accusing Amir of kidnapping, and police began hunting down the couple, who hid in the city of Rawalpindi and sought help from various rights groups and government agencies. Eventually the police found them and brought them back to their village, halfway across the country, where they were denounced by tribal leaders as *karo-kari.* The terrified but resourceful couple managed to sneak away again and flee to Karachi, several hundred miles away, where they found a lawyer, went to a courthouse, and petitioned for help.

By pure chance, the chief justice of the Supreme Court, Mohammed Iftikhar Chaudhry, was visiting from Islamabad at the time. Chaudhry is a politically liberal jurist and a bit of a crusading grandstander with a penchant for personally intervening in cases that interest him. Upon learning of their plight, he presided over a hearing on their case, along with two other high court justices.

On April 6, 2010, the judicial panel issued a formal written ruling that stated that Rukshana and Amir were legally married and should be given official protection from harm. They were flown to Islamabad by court order and sent to stay in the government shelter near the capital. Meanwhile, they had befriended several local news reporters, who covered their case extensively without revealing their location.

Yet even though they were temporarily safe, with no less a power than the Supreme Court on their side, Rukshana and Amir understood the gravity and selfishness of their actions, which would have enormous consequences for their families. They came from a collective, densely knit society where the bonds within clans were often reinforced by multiple marriages, and where entire families were made to pay for the sins of a son or a niece.

They also came from a place where tribal leaders, landlords, and politicians were often related, land and debt disputes were constant, and economic motives were the frequent basis for false criminal accusations. In this intricate web, there was no room for individuals to make their own decisions. If they tried to escape, the strands always caught them and pulled them back.

THE GREAT MAJORITY OF sexual abuses, tribal punishments, and honor crimes remain hidden and their victims unknown, especially outside urban areas. A handful of women lawyers, rights activists, and politicians try to intervene in cases that come to their attention, but the real power still rests with the local networks of influential men—the landlords, tribal bosses, police chiefs, and politicians—who have always run things in rural Pakistan.

"Pakistan's dirty little secret is that feudalism is still alive and well as a state of mind and a way of life," said Marvi Memon, a young firebrand activist from a wealthy family and a recently elected member of the national assembly who has annoyed and alienated colleagues by bringing up individual abuse cases on the floor of Parliament. "Family problems and politics and land and partisan rivalries are all mixed up, and the people we elect give protection to the culprits," she said. "When I try to bring attention to these cases, they laugh and ask what's wrong with me."

In an open letter to officials of the Zardari government in May, 2010, Memon listed more than a dozen cases of killings and attacks by so-called honor gangs, including horrifying incidents in which they threw acid in women's faces. She also reported the kidnapping and rape of two dozen village women by local police as part of a crackdown on criminal activities by men in their families. Her letter noted that since 2004, Pakistan has enacted nine major laws to protect women and elected more than two hundred women to national and provincial legislatures.

"Why is it," Memon demanded, "that we have not been able to punish culprits with the same vigor?" Even in prominent cases, she added, there is a tendency to merely "take notice, condemn the violence and move on."

With aggressive media coverage, more cases are coming to light and provoking public outrage, but men continue exacting gruesome revenge for offended honor, often against their own sisters and daughters. In the summer of 2009, the newspaper *Dawn* reported that the male relative of a girl in Okara chopped off her leg and tongue, simply because her brother-in-law had married against the family's wishes. One year later, a college student in Chakwal shot his sister dead for daring to choose her own fiancé.

Gradually, under the glare of publicity and the advance of democratic institutions, the views of Pakistan's powerful men are beginning to change. Feudal landlords and tribal bosses know it is politically incorrect to admit the extent of their wealth and power over others' lives. Rural politicians profess to be horrified by honor crimes and cruel punishments for sexual misbehavior; police chiefs are now required to incorporate human rights material into their training programs. A small but growing class of lawyers and professionals in provincial towns are beginning to represent and speak up for victimized women.

But as a practical matter, the weight of long-standing relationships and customs is often still heavier than law, and both political and economic relationships come into play. Large rural landowners and tribal leaders often hold appointed or elected government positions and travel regularly to the capital at official expense, but back home they may still resist state intervention on their turf and ignore court rulings.

"Things are changing, but these are still complicated and sensitive issues," said Ghaus Bux Maher, a national legislator from one of the largest tribes in northern Sindh. "Men still kill over petty matters and call it honor. In all the tribes it was the custom for ages that if a man was declared *karo* he had to give his daughter or niece in penalty, even to an elderly man. It was a bad custom. The world has changed and sense should prevail. If someone kills, the law is there and he should hang. But girls should be responsible. In our society if a girl runs away with a boy it creates many problems. It can get villages burned down and people murdered," he said. "It is not accepted in the cities, much less in a village of 500 people."

Maher seemed to be debating with himself as he spoke, trying out and weighing different arguments. Asked about the case of Rukshana and Amir, who are from a different district but the same tribe as his, Maher expressed equally contradictory views. The main problem, he said, was that the families on both sides were now agitated and demanding revenge.

"There is nothing the authorities can do until the people are pacified," he said. "That girl has destroyed two villages. Now the courts say she is married, but the law also must have some respect for tradition. We cannot have the courts encouraging girls to marry whomever they want. The couple should let time pass until people calm down, and then they should go home and settle it."

A few miles away, in their barren little bedroom in the government shelter, Rukshana and Amir sat alone, totally cut off from their previous life. They were educated, mature, and thoughtful people in their twenties, being treated as wayward prodigal children.

The couple now faced an impossible choice. If they returned home and submitted to their elders' will, they would face community wrath, forcible divorce, and possibly an agonizing death. If they did not, they would have to live with the knowledge that their families would suffer endlessly for their sins, and bear the burden of long-term isolation that was bound to strain their relationship. In a society where kinship means everything, they would be condemned to social death.

Already, Rukshana's relatives had been arrested and their crops burned. Religious leaders had threatened to annul the marriages of her sisters, Amir's niece had been forced to leave medical school, and Rukshana's brothers had been taunted for failing to control her. Her three female cousins, married off young to elderly men who had since died, might now be condemned to widowhood for half a century. For months Rukshana had not been able to speak to her mother, the only relative who had supported her, and she had no idea if they would meet again. Was all of this an acceptable price for love, or for a lonely crusade against the seemingly immovable forces of tradition?

"Both of our families have suffered terribly because of us," Amir said with sadness and chagrin. "All our dreams have been reduced to the single wish to stay alive. But we cannot hide here forever. Sometimes I think we need to go home and face the consequences, even if they kill us. We are just two people against an entire system. Everyone is against us, and there is nothing we can do to change things. From now on, no girl in our family will be allowed to continue her education, because of what we have done. That will be the final result."

CHAPTER 4

HATE

THERE HAS BEEN ONLY one Nobel laureate in Pakistan's history, a theoretical physicist named Abdus Salam who won the prestigious prize in 1979 and died in 1996. But in a country desperate for national heroes, international stature, and role models in educational and scientific achievement, there are no monuments to Salam's achievements, no celebrations of his birthday, no biographies on state TV. In fact, most people in Pakistan have never heard of him.

In contrast, every schoolchild, peasant, and slum dweller knows the name of another Pakistani physicist, A. Q. Khan, who is proudly referred to as "the father of the Islamic bomb." Khan's career ended in disgrace and house arrest when he was discovered to have been peddling nuclear know-how to a series of rogue regimes. But many Pakistanis still view him as a hero who put their country on the world map—and on a par with archrival India—as a nuclear power.

The official shunning of Salam is a tragic example of how religious prejudice, condoned by the state and allowed to percolate through society, can eventually lead to the kinds of horrific atrocities against various religious minorities—some at the hands of frenzied mobs, others carried out by trained assailants—that Pakistan has witnessed in the last several years. In contrast to the official adulation of Khan, it is also an example of how rewarding and punishing the wrong heroes in the name of religion can be self-destructive for a country that urgently needs to train, inspire, and channel the energies of a vast and youthful populace.

Salam, a native of Punjab Province, was educated at Cambridge University and spent years conducting research in Italy. He was said to be a pious, modest man as well as a dedicated scientist. But he was also a member of the Ahmadi Muslim sect, a small minority that is reviled by many Sunni Muslims and legally ostracized by the state. To his homeland, Salam's achievements were an embarrassment and a glitch in the official narrative that Ahmadis are enemies of Islam— infidels to be avoided, mistrusted, and despised.

Ahmadis consider themselves Muslims but do not accept that Mohammed was the final prophet. They follow the teachings of a nineteenth-century religious reformist from India named Mirza Ghulam Ahmad, who claimed to be the Messiah and a prophet of God. Sunni Muslims, who revere Mohammed intensely, consider this claim to be heresy and Ahmad to have been a false pretender to prophethood.

Pakistan's founding father, Mohammed Ali Jinnah, was a secular-minded attorney who spearheaded the crusade to create an Indian Muslim homeland, yet who also strongly believed in the culture of tolerance and the right of religious freedom. In one of his most-quoted speeches, delivered on August 11, 1947, to Pakistan's constituent assembly, Jinnah outlined this vision for the new nation: "You are free. You are free to go to your temples, you are free to go to your mosques or to any other place of worship in this state of Pakistan. You may belong to any religion or caste or creed that has nothing to do with the business of the State."

But Jinnah's ecumenical vision has since been debated, distorted, and debunked as many Pakistanis, especially those from the Sunni Muslim majority, have become more conservative and defensive about Islam. Ahmadis in particular have been singled out for social,

legal, and political discrimination. The 1973 constitution provocatively labels them "non-Muslims," and a series of laws have banned
them from sending out calls to prayer, preaching in public, or dis-
seminating literature. Anyone applying for a Pakistani passport
must sign an oath declaring that Ahmad was an imposter and that
all Ahmadis are non-Muslims.

For years, the estimated 4 million Ahmadis in Pakistan have lived
as second-class citizens. They tend to cluster in insular, mostly
working-class urban communities, and they coexist somewhat un-
easily with their neighbors and colleagues, often facing personal harassment and workplace discrimination. Several years ago, as Sunni
extremist groups grew larger and bolder, and their belligerent message of religious intolerance and hate filtered through mosques in
poor urban communities, attacks on Ahmadis became more frequent, more violent, and more frenzied.

In January 2010, a white-haired Ahmadi school principal named
Mohammed Yusuf was gunned down by two young men on motorbikes in a shabby working-class district of Lahore. Several weeks
later, I found my way to the school on a narrow lane crowded with
bicycles and donkey carts. The building stood shuttered and silent.
On the wall was a hand-painted book and candle, with a slogan that
had been scratched over by vandals. It said, "Love for all, hatred for
none."

Inside, two of Yusuf's grown sons sat slumped on cots in a dark
room, looking glum and bitter. They told a tale of growing animos-
ity and hostility from their neighbors, of a new rabble-rousing cleric
who had built a mosque and seminary and stirred up sentiment
against them, of signs being put up that called Ahmadis infidels and
Satanists who deserved to be killed.

"We were here for thirty-five years, and many people sent their
children to our school because we provided a good education," said
one son, Fatehuddin. "Then this *maulvi* [Muslim cleric or teacher]
started holding meetings against us and telling parents to take their
children out. People we had always known started insulting us, even

spitting on us in the street. The hatred just came out of their hearts. In just three years, everything changed. After my father was killed, almost no one came to mourn him."

Much of the pejorative information seemed to have been spread by leaders of a newly built Sunni mosque, who erected an enormous sign at the entrance to the district that accused Ahmadis of devil worship, illegal proselytizing, and refusing to accept Mohammed as the last prophet. Their crusade, which soon gathered hundreds of local adherents, was called the Movement to Defend the Finality of the Prophet.

After Yusuf's death the sign was taken down and the leader of the mosque, Mohammed Faridi, was placed under arrest, but when my translator and I tracked him down at the local police station, he was serving tea to visitors in a comfortable, unlocked room, and seemed utterly unrepentant.

"I had nothing to do with this, but if someone got carried away with emotion, what can I say?" the cleric said with a sly smile. "The Ahmadis are bad people and blasphemers. They are the worst enemies of Islam." Several young acolytes nodded vigorously, trembling with nervous energy.

In longer conversations in tea shops and storefronts, older residents expressed more thoughtful, but confused, opinions. Many expressed sorrow at Yusuf's slaying and praised him as an educator; some had even sent their children to his school. Yet they were clearly struggling to reconcile their own experiences and mixed feelings about these longtime neighbors with the new warnings being spread that Ahmadis were an evil menace to their community and their faith. Only one man, a former student of Yusuf, said he had attended the funeral.

"Until two or three years ago, things were peaceful here. Then that new organization came, with its banners and signs. It raised our awareness as Muslims about the dangers we face," said one store owner. "We were all sad about the teacher's death. He was a man of good character and it was wrong to kill him. But if it's true what they say, that these people are trying to convert Muslims, then it is our duty to warn others," he said, growing more adamant. "Our own constitution says they are not Muslims. They should not be allowed to live among us. They should stay away and go somewhere else with their beliefs."

Half a dozen other men had gathered in the shabby storefront office, with a single dusty desk and sagging chairs. They were small business owners, a butcher, a college student, a real estate agent, a retired driver. The talk soon drifted to larger, more pressing problems—unemployment, corruption, government neglect of the common man. The decibel level rose. Everyone wanted to join in, add a complaint. There was a sense of resigned, impotent anger in the stifling room that seemed to suggest how ordinary Pakistanis, against their better judgment, might become caught up in a frenzy of religious scapegoating.

"There is no justice or security in this society. The whole system is corrupt, but if you complain you can get killed or thrown in jail," said the property manager, while the others nodded in agreement. There were a few more disparaging comments about Ahmadis, a few nervous jokes, then a glum silence. Finally the butcher, a hefty man with a look of permanent suppressed rage on his face, exploded in a litany of pent-up grievances.

"I'll tell you what the problem is," he said, standing at clenched attention. "I work from six in the morning to ten at night, just to make 600 rupees a day. It is not possible to make an honest living in this country. The police arrest you for nothing, just to get bribes, and they are behind all the crime anyway. We have no real leaders and we only see the politicians on election day." The others murmured in assent. "I remember when Bhutto spoke of bread, shelter, and clothing, but how can we afford them?" the butcher demanded. "If you try to live with respect and honesty, you get nowhere. The only thing that matters in Pakistan is wealth and power. The rest of us are nothing."

FIVE MONTHS LATER, IN a far more brazen and horrific incident, terrorist squads launched coordinated attacks on two Ahmadi mosques in Lahore during Friday prayers. The twin rampages killed at least seventy-four people, including a retired judge and a retired lieutenant general, and left more than a hundred injured. The attackers, heavily armed and wearing suicide vests, burst into both buildings and opened fire on worshippers with automatic weapons, shotguns, and grenades. Most of the assailants blew themselves up, but one, a teenager, failed and was arrested.

Equally alarming were the responses to the attacks by police, officials, the press, and the public. Police took more than two hours to reach the first site, in the heart of a major city, and failed to shoot down one gunman as he defiantly "pranced about on a minaret." The city's deputy mayor immediately blamed India. That evening, discussions on influential TV news-talk shows included suggestions that the Ahmadis deserved to be attacked.

Concerned Pakistani commentators suggested that the assailants had been emboldened by a growing climate of intolerance, deliberately spread by extremist Sunni groups with far too little official pushback. They noted that the Taliban and other groups had also threatened to broaden their attacks against other religious minorities, especially Christians and Shiites, who are much larger in number and occupy far more central places in Pakistani society.

The editors of the newspaper *Dawn* called the Ahmadi attacks a "tragic reminder of the growing intolerance that is threatening to destroy our social fabric." They noted that traditional practices and state policies had long encouraged mistreatment of religious minorities, from employers who make minority workers use separate eating utensils to antiblasphemy laws that are used against minorities to "settle personal scores," evade debts and forcibly grab land. Terrorism, they suggested, is the ultimate outcome of an "ingrained culture of intolerance" in a country whose "statute books are riddled with discriminatory laws."

Columnist Huma Yusuf went further. She called the attacks "the most terrible articulation of a widespread social sentiment" that Ahmadis are "lesser people," and she declared that all Pakistanis are thus "collectively complicit" in the attacks. The young men who

opened fire on the mosques, she noted, were "fed on the same rhetoric" that had recently led Pakistani authorities to ban Facebook after
it posted cartoons deemed offensive to Islam. The idea that anything
or anyone deemed sacrilegious or anti-Muslim should be "obliterated," she added, is the premise of a social and institutional intolerance that has Pakistan in a "death grip."

The most emotionally charged issue among Pakistan's Muslim
masses is blasphemy. Under Pakistan's blasphemy law, it is a capital
crime to say anything "derogatory" toward Islam, to "defile" the
Koran, or to take any action intended to "outrage" the religious feelings of Muslims. Such laws date as far back as British colonial rule,
but they were invoked very rarely until the 1980s, when General Zia
promoted the issue and added stricter punishments during his campaign to "Islamize" the country. According to one survey, there were
only nine registered cases from 1927 to 1984, but since then more
than five thousand cases have been filed and more than a thousand
people charged with committing blasphemy.

There have been many appeals by Pakistani human rights and
political activists to moderate or repeal the law, which is among the
most punitive in the Muslim world. However, as with the Hudood
Ordinances, no government has dared to touch it, in part because of
intense opposition from Sunni clerics and in part because of the extreme devotion many Pakistani Muslims have toward their faith. In
2002, General Musharraf promised to modify the law but then
backed off under strong clerical opposition. In 2010, Pakistan's national assembly approved a sweeping rewrite of the constitution, in
part to wipe out the repressive legal legacy of General Zia, but left
the blasphemy statute untouched.

Public sentiments are especially strong—and utterly humorless—
regarding the sanctity of the Koran and the Prophet Mohammed.
Islam forbids any image to be made or shown of the Prophet's face,
and public opinion polls show that three-quarters of Pakistanis believe anyone who blasphemes against Islam or the Prophet should be
put to death. When a Danish newspaper published cartoons of the
Prophet in 2006, Pakistanis were outraged, and when they were

posted on Facebook four years later, angry protests erupted in Lahore, Karachi, and other cities.

Accusations of blasphemy can be made, assumed to be true, and acted upon by eager or intimidated police for offenses as small as making a remark in anger, sharing a drinking cup, or leaving garbage in a mosque. In 2007, a group of Christian nurses were suspended from a hospital in Islamabad after being accused of blasphemy by female vigilantes from a radical seminary. The basis of the charge was that a water cooler with Koranic verses on it had been defaced. The students, armed with sticks, tried to attack the nurses' dormitory but were stopped.

In 2001, an English-language newspaper in Peshawar inadvertently published a letter to the editor that described the Prophet Mohammed as a philandering hypocrite. Police raided the paper and arrested half a dozen people, including the editor in chief. Most were eventually released, but an assistant night editor, who admitted he had sent the letter to press without reading it, was sentenced to life in prison and spent almost four years behind bars.

Although blasphemy is a capital crime in Pakistan, death sentences are extremely rare and no executions have been carried out. But dozens of defendants have been given life sentences, and some have been killed by enraged Muslims while awaiting trial. In 2004, a man was accused of blasphemy for leaving trash at a mosque. He was put in jail, where a police officer struck his head with a heavy tool and killed him. The officer reportedly said he acted because he "wanted to earn a place in heaven."

IT IS EXTREMELY EASY in Pakistan to arouse emotional frenzy against members of religious minorities, especially among uneducated people who have few sources of information other than Friday sermons and local gossip. False or malicious charges of blasphemy are often leveled at non-Muslims by leaders with religious, political, or personal agendas.

In a number of recent cases, the mere rumor that a Christian or other minority member had blasphemed sparked instant riots and lynch mobs. According to community leaders, local clerics with ties to radical or extremist Sunni groups—including sectarian militant groups officially banned by the government but allowed to operate in practice—have often spearheaded the accusations and galvanized community rage.

A frequent target of blasphemy charges and physical attacks is Pakistan's Christian community. Christians have been settled in the region that is now Pakistan for over a century, and they constitute the country's third largest majority. Today more than 12 percent of the populace is Christian, amounting to some 20 million Pakistanis. Unlike Ahmadis, they are not viewed officially as a deviant group or threat to mainstream Islam.

In fact, Christians have a long and honorable history in Pakistan, where Catholic missionaries established some of the country's finest schools and colleges before Partition. Since then, several generations of Pakistan's economic and political elite have sent their children to be educated at such prestigious institutions as La Salle and Sacred Heart high schools, the convents of Jesus and Mary, and Forman Christian College—clearly without fear of contamination or conversion. Graduates of Christian institutions in Pakistan include presidents, prime ministers, generals, jurists, and leading members of the establishment.

Yet for historical, social, and cultural reasons, intermingled with various forms of discrimination, Pakistani Christians have largely been relegated to the lowest rungs of society, where they perform certain menial tasks such as cleaning bathrooms, sweeping streets, and salvaging scrap. They tend to isolate themselves, clustering in shabby walled "colonies" at the fringes of urban areas. Many are from poor families who converted from Hinduism before Partition and have remained identified as lower-caste.

Because their religion permits alcohol use, Christians in Pakistan are often ostracized as drunks, even though drinking has long been widespread in affluent Pakistani society—especially in men's clubs and in the military. In private, even educated Pakistani Muslims sometimes refer to Christians as *juras,* or "sweepers"—a pejorative with the same connotation as "nigger."

Sporadic attacks against churches and Christian communities have taken place for years, but the recent rise of Sunni extremist groups has increased the number and ferocity of assaults, giving lower-class Muslim communities in particular a sense of license to go after their Christian neighbors. One of the most savage incidents took place in August 2009 in several villages of the Punjabi district of Gojra. It was sparked by a rumor that someone had torn up pages of the Koran at a Christian wedding. A frenzy of violence spread through the streets. Within twenty-four hours, more than fifty homes were set afire and destroyed, and seven people were killed in the conflagration.

When I visited Gojra at Easter the following spring, the charred homes had been preserved like shrines, and posters with photographs of the dead had been pasted on walls throughout the community. At the Roman Catholic Easter service on the lawn of the locked parish compound, several thousand worshippers listened to calls for brotherhood and reconciliation. But afterward, in the nearby warren of alleys where Muslims and Christians live in alternate blocks of shabby rowhouses, memories were still vivid and tensions high.

"A mob of thousands came, and we ran for our lives," recounted one man named Masih—a common Christian name, which means "messiah"—who saved his wife and children by barricading them inside a church. From the windows they watched flames rising above their neighborhood, and when they came back the next day, they found their home had been burned to the ground and their pet parakeets turned to ashes in their cage.

"We never saw such hatred until this happened," said the Reverend Shafiq Hadayat, the parish priest. He noted that Christians had been living in the area for more than half a century, without any major conflict. He said the charge of blasphemy was a "total lie" and that the issue had been deliberately provoked by a "certain group" of Islamic extremists from outside the area. He was reluctant to identify them, but local residents whispered the name of a radical Sunni militant party.

Hadayat said the Gojra attack had shaken the government; the prime minister personally visited the stricken community and pledged that the burned houses would be rehabilitated with government funds. "There are good Muslims, like the local traders, who have come to show their concern," he added. "Things are better than in the old days, when we couldn't even drink from the same cup as a Muslim, but it will take a long time for the mentality to change," he said.

Another man, a community leader with a high school degree, said several local mullahs had joined with extremist Sunni groups to enrage Muslims against them. "Our families have lived here since before Partition, but now these groups call us American dogs and Israeli agents and infidels," he said. " The extremist groups put down roots, and now they feel more power."

An accusation of blasphemy—however vague, unsubstantiated, or biased—has the power to sweep away reason and objectivity, even among officials charged with enforcing law and administering justice. As the religious right has gained political strength and popular support in Pakistan, police and judges have tended to side with the witch-hunting mob rather than fully investigate the facts, and senior officials can be reluctant to intervene for fear of aggravating religious groups.

The shocking persecution of a farm worker named Asia Bibi began with an argument in a Punjabi berry field in the summer of 2009, and gradually escalated to a national tragedy, the assassination of a public official who had defended her. Eighteen months later, the countroversy started when Muslim co-workers reportedly refused to drink from a water bucket Bibi was carrying to the field and taunted her because she was a Christian. The dispute grew heated, and the mob dragged her to a police station and accused her of blasphemy. The forty-five-year-old mother of five was thrown in prison for a year and a half, and when she was brought before a court in Lahore in November 2010, the judge quickly found her guilty and sentenced her to death.

The extreme ruling drew condemnation from rights groups around the world, and even Pope Benedict XVI called for the government to overturn it. But President Zardari, whose liberal party relied on religious allies to keep its majority in Parliament, faced strong domestic pressure from Islamic groups to let the sentence stand.

One of the few Pakistanis who dared to publicly criticize Asia Bibi's cruel punishment was Salman Taseer, an outspoken secular politician from the People's Party whom Zardari had named governor of Punjab Province. He visited the condemned woman in prison and then made several impassioned speeches against the blasphemy statute, calling it a "black law" that suppressed human rights.

On January 4, 2011, Taseer had just dined with friends at a café in Islamabad and was strolling to his official vehicle when a burst of gunfire erupted and the governor fell dead. The assassin was one of his specially trained bodyguards, twenty-six-year-old Mumtaz Qadri, who calmly confessed to the crime and told authorities he had killed Taseer because he was a blasphemer and an infidel.

What came next was even more stunning. Instead of being reviled, Qadri was lauded by much of the public as a religious hero. Lawyers threw wreaths on his neck when he was brought to court, and his modest home in Rawalpindi became a shrine mobbed by throngs of the faithful. Qadri became an instant emblem for the popular movement against modifying the blasphemy laws, and religious groups held boisterous street rallies featuring beatific posters of his face.

"There is no justice in our country for the common man, but Qadri's act against a blasphemer has made all Muslims feel stronger," said a shopkeeper in his neighborhood. "They can punish him, but what will they do with a million Qadris who have been born now?"

Taseer, instead of being mourned as a victim of extremism, was shunned as a non-Muslim. Policemen refused to move his body and clerics refused to officiate at his funeral. Sunni groups, including the moderate Berelvi sect, which had publicly opposed suicide bombings and the Taliban, joined forces with banned jihadi parties to condemn Taseer and demand full preservation of the blasphemy laws.

The outpouring of approval for Qadri's brazen crime left the Westernized ruling elite cowering in shocked silence, wondering if their cooks and drivers were closet fanatics capable of mayhem. Qadri was jailed and charged with murder, but the Zardari government, which had favored reforming the blasphemy law, hastily assured the public that not a word of it would be changed.

Overnight, the center of religious gravity in Pakistan shifted dramatically, ripping off the veneer of modern democracy and exposing the deep current of Islamic fervor below. The Sunni masses—marginalized from political power and resentful of Western encroachment—had suddenly found a common cause that channeled their grievances, swept away moral scruples and fear of the state, and replaced them with a cathartic chant for vengeful violence in the name of Islam.

THE GREAT SECTARIAN DIVIDE in Pakistan—the one that presents the gravest threat to domestic peace and regional stability—is not between Muslims and non-Muslims but between Sunnis and Shiites. This rift is violent and entrenched, with a history of tit-for-tat bloodshed that dwarfs attacks on other groups. It has been abetted by both Iran and Saudi Arabia, which have spent huge sums to build rival mosques, seminaries, and universities on Pakistani soil. It has spawned militant hate groups on both sides whose exclusive aim is to wipe out the other, and who have no scruples about gunning down hundreds of people at prayer.

Sunni Muslims are a majority in Pakistan, but Shiites are a strong and sizable minority, accounting for about one-quarter of the populace. The two sects disagree on several fundamental aspects of Islamic history and numerous smaller rituals. The central and most emotionally charged dispute is over the succession to the Prophet Mohammed as caliph or spiritual leader of Islam. Sunnis believe in four caliphs who immediately followed Mohammed's death, but Shiites accept only one of them, Ali, as the rightful caliph and his descendents as the only legitimate heirs to leadership of the faith.

For more than half a century, most Sunnis and Shiites in Pakistan have coexisted peacefully, and many of Pakistan's leading citizens have been Shiites. Mohammed Ali Jinnah, who strongly advocated religious freedom, was one. So were the Bhuttos, the landowning Sindhi dynasty that produced the country's two most charismatic prime ministers—Zulfiqar Ali Bhutto and his daughter Benazir. Her widower, President Zardari, is also a Shiite.

Tensions between the two Muslim groups sharpened during the tenure of General Zia, a fervent Sunni. Zia had Zulfiqar Bhutto hanged on murder charges in 1979, then took power and launched his crusade of Sunni-based "Islamization" that lasted a decade and remained an important influence on Pakistani society long after his death in a mysterious plane crash in 1988.

The stirring of sectarian biases was exacerbated by the Iranian revolution that brought a Shiite theocracy to power in 1979, at the same time radical Sunni clerics and organizations from the Wahhabi and Deobandi schools had put down deep roots in Pakistan under Zia's patronage and the shadow of the Afghan war. Seeking to thwart Shiites from being emboldened by events in Tehran, these clerics formed an anti-Shiite political party with a violent militant wing.

This militia, known in various incarnations and factions as Lashkar-e-Jhangvi and Sipah-e-Sahaba Pakistan (the Ranks of Companions of the Prophet), began attacking Shiite mosques and assassinating their leaders in the 1990s. Some of the worst violence took place in the northwest tribal areas, including a weeklong orgy of bloodshed among ethnic Pashtun tribes from both sects that killed more than two hundred people.

After General Musharraf took power, he vowed to stop the bloodshed and announced a series of crackdowns on sectarian groups in 2002. His aim was to halt strife among Islamic groups at home without undermining the militant, state-backed crusade against India—a distinction that would prove almost impossible to maintain. Among the groups he banned were Sipah-e-Sahaba Pakistan (SSP), Lashkar-e-Jhangvi, and later Jaish-e-Mohammed (Army of the Prophet Mohammed). He also banned the major Shiite militant group.

But the formal ban had little impact on their activities, largely because there was no concerted effort to stop them. Some groups had long-standing relations with the Pakistani intelligence services, which continued to send them mixed signals and often sabotaged or overrode police efforts to pursue them. Others went underground, changed their names, and reemerged in new guises. Several widened their targets to include foreigners and Christians, expanding their original sectarian aims to embrace a new, broader jihadist agenda of fighting the infidel West and building a theocratic Sunni state.

Within weeks of Musharraf's first announcement, militants from several of these groups, sometimes working together, carried out a series of horrific, high-profile crimes against international victims. They kidnapped *Wall Street Journal* reporter Daniel Pearl in Karachi and later videotaped his grisly beheading. They invaded a Protestant Sunday church service in Islamabad and threw grenades into the pews, killing five people including a U.S. embassy staffer. They bombed a bus carrying French technical workers to the port of Karachi, killing eleven.

The men behind these crimes enjoyed a degree of unspoken immunity because they had used their lethal skills and religious motivations on behalf of Pakistan's permanent guerrilla war against India. Both Omar Saeed Sheikh, who orchestrated Pearl's abduction, and Maulana Masood Azhar, who formed Jaish-e-Mohammed in 2000, had been released from Indian prisons in a hijacking hostage swap. Azhar, technically a wanted fugitive, was welcomed home in a large airport rally by his supporters, and Pakistan rejected a request from Interpol to arrest him.

Despite Musharraf's repeated vows to curb religious violence, the actual treatment of these and other militant leaders by Pakistani officials was a complicated game that mixed secret encouragement with public prosecution. High-profile arrests were followed by quiet releases. Charges were filed and then dismissed for lack of evidence.

Radical imams who called for holy war against the West were under house arrest one day, then back in their pulpits the next, fulminating against America and its Pakistani puppet leaders while police officers guarded the premises from a respectful distance.

In 2006, SSP was allowed to hold a huge public rally in Islamabad despite the ban, and it has since continued to operate openly from its base in Jhang, a gritty working-class city in southern Punjab. In a strategic bid for support, its leaders have run successfully for local office, cultivating the gratitude of the poor by defending farm laborers against landlords and by bringing sewage, gas, and electrical services to communities that once sweltered and stank in the summer and turned dark at sundown.

"There is a lot of feudalism here. Before Sipah-e-Sahaba came, the landlords had full control. But the *maulanas* raised slogans for the poor. They started delivering, so they started winning," explained Abdul Aziz, fifty, a locksmith in Jhang. "They got a bridge put in over the train tracks, where people used to have a lot of accidents before. They brought electricity to the villages. All the development in this area is due to them."

But there is no mistaking the SSP's sectarian agenda, and no hiding its bloody history. The maze of city walls leading to the group's mosque in Jhang are scrawled with anti-Shiite graffiti, and its offices sell posters with the faces of nine SSP leaders who have allegedly been "martyred" by Shiite hit squads. Maulana Haq Nawaz, the original SSP leader who won wide public support because of his constituent service, was gunned down in the 1990s. His successor, Azam Tariq, was elected to the national legislature from Jhang three times but slain in 2003.

"That's my father," said Moavia Azam, twenty-three, a slender and unsmiling young man in a white skullcap who greeted my translator and me at the SSP office and introduced himself as the organization's new "vice amir." He gestured to a poster of an elderly bearded man reading a newspaper, which was dripping in blood. "My father survived thirteen attempts on his life. The fourteenth time they put forty-five bullets in him, and it was fatal. Now I am the seventh prayer leader we have had in only twenty years."

Then Azam launched into a smooth, well-rehearsed speech on the evils of Shiism, the threat to Pakistan from neighboring Iran, and the suffering of innocent Sunnis. He accused Iran and its agents of trying to violently impose their religion—and that of Ahmadis—on Pakistan, which is 80 percent Sunni. But he insisted that the SSP had never responded in kind.

"We are peaceful and we do not believe in violence. Even though many of our activists and leaders have been martyred, still we do not pick up weapons to avenge them," Azam said. "We were banned by Musharraf under the pressure of his foreign masters in the West, but we have gone to the Supreme Court and we hope we will get justice."

THIS BLAND NARRATIVE BORE little resemblance to outside experts' descriptions of SSP, which has a long history of retaliatory violence against Shiites. It also promotes the conservative Sunni doctrines of the Deobandi sect, morphing its sectarian origins into a broader jihadi agenda. It is described by one expert as both "the Sunni sectarian army" and the "central nerve of Talibanization," bringing Deobandi groups together in support of terror against the state as well as its violent anti-Shiite crusade.

Between 1999 and 2009, official figures indicate that more than a thousand incidents of sectarian violence took place across Pakistan, killing more than three thousand people. Shiites bore the brunt of these attacks, many of which took place in mosques packed with worshippers. The major Shiite holidays have become frequent terror targets, especially the ten-day festival of Moharram, when Shiites mourn the suffering and death of Imam Hussain, grandson of the Prophet Mohammed and Shiism's holiest figure, who was killed in battle in A.D. 680.

The festival is full of color and passion. Elaborately decorated horses prance through the crowds, representing the steed Hussain was riding, and worshippers heap garlands around their necks. Special tents with free food and refreshments are open around the clock. But the climax is a bloody, highly emotional rite of public self-flagellation. On the last day of Moharram, known as Ashura, thousands of half-naked men and boys march through the streets of Peshawar and Lahore and Karachi, frenziedly whipping their own backs into a red froth with small barbed chains while onlookers weep and thump their chests.

Many Sunnis express commiseration with Shiites during their holy days, but such gory practices offend some groups and have become a lightning rod for anti-Shiite sentiments. Ashura processions are always guarded by police, but violence can erupt at any time. One of the worst ever Ashura attacks took place in Karachi on December 28, 2009. While thousands of Shiites solemnly paraded through the streets, terrorists exploded two bombs at different points in the procession, killing forty-five people and sowing mass panic.

"We were mourning peacefully. We were surrounded by police and barricades, and we could not even bring a cigarette lighter into the march. How could we think of such violence?" said one survivor, twenty-one-year-old Mohammed Hussain. The situation worsened when armed thugs, taking advantage of the chaos, torched and looted several city wholesale markets. Fed by cotton cloth and other combustibles, the fires burned all night in a spectacle of destruction.

Official investigators never determined who had planted the bombs or set the fires, but the possibilities were endless in the vast, brawling city that is home to numerous Deobandi mosques and seminaries, eternally warring ethnic gangs and criminal mafias, and a ruling party with its own shock troops that has vowed to stop the "Talibanization" of Karachi. Adding to the frenzy and confusion, militant Shiite and Sunni groups held joint protests blaming the Ashura blasts on Israel and the United States.

The attack was the fourth on Shiite gatherings throughout Pakistan in less than a week, and it aroused nationwide concern that a sectarian war could break out. Karachi shut down in an official one-day protest, and even its national stock exchange was closed for the day. Nevertheless, it was evident that the old habit of violence in the teeming metropolis, exacerbated by a new, more aggressive brand of proselytizing among Islamic groups, had contributed to an environment where religious prejudice could flourish—and terrorism aimed at destabilizing an entire community could easily masquerade as sectarianism. Two kinds of hate were becoming explosively commingled.

"Everyone in our market gets along well. There are Sunnis and Shiites, Pashtuns and non-Pashtuns. We have all known each other for so many years. Now they have destroyed everything," a clothing seller named Akbar al-Habib said disconsolately as he stood among piles of charred shirts and jeans in his tiny shop. He was angry, but he was even more bewildered and anguished. "I don't know why this is happening. I don't know what it means," he said. "Who would do this to us?"

CHAPTER 5

KHAKI

IN EVERY CITY IN Pakistan, there is a high-walled oasis of green trimmed lawns, watered flowerbeds, neatly lettered signs, and faded but stately colonial barracks, protected by barricades and uniformed sentinels.

These are the cantonments, or "cantts"—exclusive military precincts of order, privilege, and serenity that contrast sharply with the chaos and cacophony of impoverished urban life outside their gates, where sidewalk vendors jostle for space and streets are clogged with donkey carts, cargo trucks, and three-wheeled rickshaw taxis.

The cantonments contain barracks, training academies, officers' quarters, and other military facilities. They are the most visible and ubiquitous symbols of a vast enterprise, controlled by one of the world's largest and most privileged military establishments. Its style is neither ostentatious nor intimidating: there are no troops in the streets, no Soviet-style parades of tanks and artillery, no obvious trappings of a military state.

In Pakistan, though, the army is everywhere. It is in the fabric and lexicon, the psyche and assumptions of a society that has long become used to accepting the armed forces as a periodic antidote to the

foibles and failures of electoral politics and to seeing its flawed civilian leaders periodically swept aside by the orderly, efficient, and professional ranks of the men in khaki.

Historically, Pakistan's military has avoided launching unpopular
battlefield crusades, and its generals have been careful not to directly
intervene in politics without apparent provocation, such as violent
rebellion, collapsing civilian rule, or an attempted anti-military
coup. In 2009, when President Zardari banned a march by thousands of peaceful protesters heading for the heavily guarded capital,
the army chief called on him after midnight and the ban was lifted.

Instead, the army has assiduously cultivated public support and
sought to be viewed as what one general called a "mythical entity"
or "magical force" that would come to the country's aid in times of
need. The monsoon floods of 2010 offered a perfect opportunity to
reinforce this image, especially in contrast to the disorganized and
disengaged response by civilian authorities. While troops plucked
stranded families off rooftops, the president continued with his vacation in France. One opportunistic politician called on Pakistan's "patriotic generals" to step in and clean up the mess.

Meanwhile, over the past fifty years, Pakistan's military establishment has constructed a fortress of permanent influence in all spheres
of governance and society. Ever since martial law was first imposed
in the 1950s, through four periods of military control and several
short-lived attempts at civilian rule, this fortress has steadily expanded, while Pakistan's weak political institutions have scrambled
to keep up.

The army, the largest and most dominant of the three armed service branches, has established itself as the premier guardian of the
nation's interests and ideology, the pivotal arbiter in political crises,
and a major stakeholder in the economic fortunes of the nation.

"The paradox that hobbled Pakistan's political development was
that as the army grew in strength and size, it stunted the growth of
the political system," wrote Shuja Nawaz, a Pakistani American
scholar, in *Crossed Swords,* a voluminous 2008 book on the army's history. Successive civilian rulers "suborned and eviscerated" the profes-

sional bureaucracy, he wrote, ceding leadership and credibility to the military until the generals thought of themselves as the nation's true leaders.

Using the perennial threat of Hindu-dominated India, the army has commandeered a hefty chunk of the national budget, averaging about 5 percent of GDP each year since the early 1980s, while public spending has averaged 0.7 percent on health and just over 2 percent on education. With half a million men at arms, a fleet of fighter planes, and a nuclear arsenal—all ostensibly to ensure that India never attacks—the army never needs to justify its wealth, and few in Pakistan would dare call it to account.

Pakistan's military has a checkered history that includes the hanging of an elected prime minister on dubious murder charges in 1979, several aborted conflicts with India, and a confrontation with Bengali separatists that led to the bloody secession of East Pakistan in 1971. The army has never recovered from that humiliating event, which reduced Pakistan's population by more than half, created the new nation of Bangladesh, and represented a victory for the Bengalis' backers in India.

The military also operates a large intelligence agency called Inter-Service Intelligence, or ISI, which wields so much influence throughout Pakistani institutions and society that it is often described as a "state within a state." It not only spies on Pakistan's external adversaries but often plays a covert role in domestic politics and maintains close ties with Pakistani religious groups.

The military has faced periods of unpopularity, but these have been largely due to missteps or abuses by individual dictators. During the repressive rule of General Zia, from 1977 to 1988, Pakistan's intelligence services became the sword arm of his brutal campaign to "Islamize" Pakistani society by introducing harsh new laws and punishments against sex outside marriage, drinking alcohol, and other religious offenses. During the feckless reign of General Musharraf from 1999 to 2008, the army became unhappily identified with his political ambitions and failed counterinsurgency campaign against domestic militants.

Yet despite its temporary lapses and permanent darker side, Pakistan's military remains the strongest and most respected institution in the country. Year after year, even during periods of troubled military rule, the armed forces have remained highly popular with the public.

In 2009, a survey by the U.S. Institute for Peace found that 84 percent of Pakistanis viewed the army as doing a good or excellent job defending the country, and 66 percent thought it was doing a good job helping the nation's economic growth. A year later, the Pew Research Center reported that 84 percent of Pakistanis thought the army was having a "good impact" on the country and that the army chief was much more popular than the elected president.

"The army is always in sync with public opinion. You can take that for granted," said General Ehsan ul-Haq, a retired four-star Pakistani general who held posts as head of military intelligence, the ISI, and the joint services chiefs, told a group of experts in Washington during 2010.

Yet there is an element of prudent deference in the public praise. Pakistanis feel patriotic pride in the military, but they also fear it, and they harbor a permanent, nagging expectation that it will eventually be back in power. The press, though nominally free, often acts as a willing conduit for military propaganda and rarely criticizes the army or intelligence services. To critics, this view seems tragically self-defeating.

Shandana Mohmand, a Pakistani scholar based in England, pointed out in a 2009 essay that this so-called incorruptible savior often "rides roughshod over democratic principles" in pursuit of its own interests. "Why, after all these years," she asked, "are we not able to differentiate between the army's rightful role as defenders of Pakistanis, and its wrongful role as a political force?"

PART OF THE MILITARY'S enduring positive image comes from the sheer numbers of people involved in it. The force of currently serving soldiers, sailors, airmen, and special forces members, both active duty and reserve, is estimated at more than 800,000, which Nawaz notes is larger than the U.S. armed forces.

In addition, Pakistan's military world includes retired officers from all three service branches, thousands of people working in military welfare or corporate ventures, and hundreds of thousands of extended families where military service is a tradition and where military benefits and perquisites secure lifelong loyalty.

Theirs is a vast yet exclusive caste, a privileged and introverted subculture whose members tend to come from certain districts and ethnic groups.

Nearly 75 percent of all servicemen are natives of three districts in northern Punjab and two adjoining districts in Northwest Frontier, and more than 70 percent of senior officers are Punjabi. Recent efforts have extended military recruiting into southern Punjab, but there is still very little outreach in Sindh or Balochistan, the two provinces with the most rebellious leanings.

Retired army officers live in well-kept, subsidized military subdivisions, sometimes inside cantonments. Military families worship in military community mosques and dine with friends at subsidized social and sports clubs. Wives move up in status as husbands rise in rank and administrative grade, and officers' children often meet socially and marry. Their world is a bubble, an echo chamber that tends to distance its members from the rest of society, reward loyalty with lifelong perks and privileges, and reinforce the notion of military superiority over corrupt or incompetent civilian rule

Military-built residential neighborhoods command the choicest property in many cities; they are open to civilians but appeal to the tastes and ambitions of military families. "Live life club class!" beckoned a poster in a Pakistani airport, promoting a new development called Defense Raya Golf Resort. For men, the community offered an "18-hole USGA standard course"; for women, there were designer boutiques and spas to "pamper yourself after a day of shopping."

The fortress is also a successful moneymaking machine. Directly or indirectly, the military is involved in a long list of economic enterprises, adding up to a giant conglomerate with hundreds of subsidiaries and thousands of employees. Through four major welfare foundations linked to individual service branches, the military has invested in a wide array of businesses from cereal to cement, racehorses to real estate.

The Army Welfare Trust owns sugar and rice mills, fish farms and commercial banks, travel agencies and pharmaceutical factories. The Fauji Foundation (*fauj* means "soldier" in Urdu) owns security guard companies, plastic factories, a computer institute, and an experimental seed farm. Large attractive posters in Pakistani airports, featuring lush green fields, urge investors to "come grow with us" at the Fauji Fertilizer Company.

The Shaheen Foundation, linked to the air force, owns an airline and air cargo service, a radio station, and an insurance company. The Bahria Foundation, affiliated with the navy, owns construction and ship-breaking companies, a university, a bakery chain, and a number of large residential real estate developments, known as "town and housing schemes," located on some of the most desirable land in major urban areas.

Pakistani analyst Ayesha Siddiqa, in her painstakingly researched 2007 book *Military, Inc.,* lays out the structure and value of these enterprises in great detail. She also explains how the military has built this highly profitable conglomerate without significant civilian oversight or challenge—not breaking the law, but using its unique advantages to steer business, jobs, credit, and other economic opportunities toward its own community.

"The military's hegemony in Pakistan is a reality," Siddiqa writes. It has "penetrated the society, politics and the economy" and "grabbed the intellectual discourse and the imagination of the people." In the process, she adds, the military has "morphed into a dominant 'class' with its own rules and values, entry requirements and corporate culture, economic interests and financial autonomy." In other words, the military uses its might, money, and mystique to protect its members, market its indispensability, and advance its interests.

In addition to its public budget and private investments, the military has benefitted from large amounts of foreign aid, most of it supplied by the United States, first as part of the anti-Soviet fight in Afghanistan and recently as part of the war against terror. For years there has been little meaningful oversight of how that aid is used, and successive administrations in Washington have been reluctant to demand more accountability because of Pakistan's critical location and leverage in fighting these conflicts.

In 2009, when the U.S. Congress attached unprecedented controls and monitoring conditions to a new $5.7 billion aid package to Pakistan, the army's top brass reacted with a display of righteous indignation. In comments leaked by his aides, Pakistan's army chief huffily informed the senior U.S. regional military commander that the aid terms were "insulting" and "unacceptable." One of the aid bill's cosponsors, Senator John Kerry, had to travel to Islamabad to smooth over the dispute.

ANOTHER REASON FOR THE military's enduring stature in Pakistan is the relative weakness and poor reputation of its political institutions and leadership—even though repeated military interventions have contributed to these flaws. Pakistan's official and business dealings have long been riddled with corruption, and its political establishment has been dominated by an incestuous, feudal-minded elite. Often its governments have acted as protectors of the privileged few, rather than as a force to empower the development of its struggling majority.

Even during periods of civilian rule, the partnership between the civilian and military elite has ensured a steady flow of federal funds to the armed forces—almost always at the expense of social spending. For years the army invoked the permanent threat of India to justify its financial demands; recently it has cited the added costs of fighting Islamic insurgents.

In early 2010, despite receiving huge amounts of American military aid to help quash the Taliban, the Zardari government agreed to divert up to 30 percent of its social-sector budget, amounting to about 170 billion rupees, to security needs. The editors of *Dawn*, while careful to acknowledge the army's important role in the fight against Islamic militancy, suggested that by taking the money from social programs, the government was shooting itself in the foot.

"Unrelenting misery not only destroys lives but also contributes to the rise of extremism," *Dawn* pointed out. "When a man cannot feed or school his son, he may opt for a madrassa where the child would at least eat and receive instruction in religion"—and where he may also imbibe "a heavy dose of the ideology of hate."

Pakistan's civilian governments, weakened by corruption and hyperpartisanship, have all failed to make serious strides in the most urgent tasks of their time: to raise living standards and literacy levels among the poor majority, to unify a fragmented nation of multiple ethnic groups and cultures, to improve hostile relations with Pakistan's neighbors, to define the role of religion in a modern Muslim state, and to strengthen the immature democratic institutions that veered off course almost immediately after the death of Jinnah in 1948.

In Pakistan's political world, the concept of merit and honest competition is almost nonexistent. Obtaining a government job, a taxi license, a plot of land, or a bail bond often depends on a bribe or a personal reference from a politically connected person. The military also offers opportunities for graft and resists attempts at external oversight, yet it still projects an image of efficiency, stewardship and merit.

In the military world, connections count, but performance matters too. Soldiers and officers are tried and tested in a hundred ways and promoted on the results, not only because of their family ties to an influential general. The mantra of merit has created a certain arrogance that tends to blind military leaders to the advantages of civilian control.

"In the military, eight o'clock means eight o'clock. The environment is disciplined, and everything is based on merit," said General Ali Asghar, a retired general who directs the National University of Science and Technology near Islamabad. "In this institution, we have

no quotas," he said. "What matters is performance and professional-
ism. If you deserve it, the army moves you up." Asghar, a courtly and
white-haired engineer, clearly believed what he was saying. "The
main problem with our country," he declared, "is the violation of
merit."

Asghar's campus office of Spartan neatness and boardroom luxury
was appointed with a combination found in most military facilities.
On the morning of my visit, I was picked up by a sharp lieutenant
who arrived five minutes early. As soon as we reached the campus, a
white-gloved staff served us coffee and strawberries on fine china,
while an efficient and attractive young woman gave a PowerPoint
presentation about the university. There were new leather portfolios
and sharpened pencils at each place, and expensive gifts waiting
when we left.

The general and his staff were trying to sell a product that was
both worthy and long overdue: the importance of competitive scientific training in a country where public education had always been
sacrificed at the altar of defense. The presentation was intended to
persuade visitors that Pakistan's military-run educational institutions, long a coveted bastion of the uniformed elite, were throwing
open their doors to talented civilians at home and to peer institutions abroad. Both the general and the PowerPoint presenter mentioned a talented policeman's son who had received a scholarship, as
well as joint projects with Microsoft and Caltech.

Asghar professed great reluctance to see the army involved in politics, yet like every Pakistani officer I interviewed, he insisted that
sometimes there was no choice. "The armed forces will always play a
role. Not that we want to, but those are the ground realities," he
said. "Our officers are all professionals, and we want to keep our
reputation on a high plane. But Pakistan has many disasters, and the
army is always called in to help."

The political role played by Pakistan's army has usually been subtle rather than ham-fisted. Its officials have both courted and sabotaged civilian leaders, its takeovers have been largely bloodless, and
its clout has been used as a convenient cudgel by politicians against

their rivals. Its carefully nurtured image as the bulwark against the presumed designs of India has helped immunize it to criticism, and the de facto power of landlords, bosses and police in a weak democracy has conditioned the populace to the idea of authoritarian control.

As a result, military takeovers in Pakistan have tended to be greeted with resignation rather than alarm. When General Zia took power in 1977, the country was in the throes of social and political upheaval. The charismatic but dogmatic civilian leader at the center of the turmoil, Prime Minister Bhutto, was soon imprisoned and hanged. The public was stunned, but much of the establishment was relieved, and an era of potentially revolutionary ferment passed into one of cowed stability.

Similarly, when General Musharraf deposed Prime Minister Sharif in 1999, the country was veering from crisis to crisis and the civilian head of state had clumsily attempted to force the army chief into exile. Again the establishment accepted the army's intervention as a law-and-order necessity and a chance for a fresh start.

"Whenever the army has come in, it has been welcomed with open arms," said Mahmud Durrani, a jovial retired lieutenant general and former ambassador to Washington who lives in a well-appointed but not opulent home in a guarded and gated military community. "The reason is the weakness of political institutions, although you could make the opposite argument that if the army had not come in again and again, other institutions would be stronger."

As a young army officer in the 1980s, Durrani once served as secretary to General Zia, a stint serving an unsavory martinet that later caused him grief. "My relatives used to criticize me for working with a dictator," he recalled, "but when the civilian government can't deliver, the very same people say, 'Why doesn't the army come in and do the job?'"

Once in power, military rulers everywhere tend to suffer from a lack of legitimacy, isolation from the public, and a misguided belief in their indispensability that can lead them to abuses and blunders.

Even during periods of civilian rule, an enduring ethos of militarism in Pakistan has spawned a class of authoritarian-minded sycophants and reinforced the oligarchic tendencies of the ruling classes, creating what Siddiqa calls a three-way "predatory partnership" among political, economic, and military elites.

The partners, however, are not necessarily equal. Whoever heads the Pakistani army is always considered the most powerful man in Pakistan, able to create or solve problems for civilian leaders with a phone call. Today, the army chief is considered one leg of a ruling troika with the president and prime minister, a relationship one Pakistani analyst described as an "extra-constitutional arrangement for civilian-military consensus-building" on key issues. Even when the troops return to their barracks, the aura of permanent authority lingers and the levers of power remain.

THE OFFICIAL MOTTO OF the Pakistani army is *"Inam, taqwa, jihad fi sabilillah,"* or "Faith, piety, and struggle in the path of God." There is no mention of honor, duty, country, or military virtues. The army website, where recruits can apply by e-mail, is dominated by this motto and a discussion of its meaning, accompanied by a photo of a military squad in white parkas on a frozen mountainside— probably the Siachen Glacier—prostrate and praying in the snow.

It is a message with important appeal to young Muslims today, at a time when Islamic extremists are also heavily recruiting from the ranks of Pakistani youth, offering them a chance to join a glorious crusade in defense of their religion and denouncing the immoral ways of the country's "infidel" government.

But the army's definition of itself as a defender of Islam is not new. Although built by the British in India as a professional fighting force, the institution became imbued long ago with the mission of safeguarding Pakistan as a bulwark of Islam, not just a territory with borders. This mandate has been invoked as far back as the 1950s, and it was used as a rallying cry in both Pakistan's 1965 war with India and the 1971 conflict that led to the secession of East Pakistan.

Islam has also been used by the military, as well as by Pakistan's civilian leaders, as a miraculous glue to bind together a large nation of ethnic, geographic, and linguistic disparities that was born in bloodshed and confusion.

Yet in recent years, this identification with Islam has become excessive, counterproductive, and blinding. It has caused the army to rely too much on Islamist groups as proxy fighters and political partners. It has stood in the way of peacemaking efforts with India, and wedded a large professional military institution to violent jihadists who are international pariahs and no friend of the Pakistani state.

Now that the armed forces are being asked to fight Islamic militants, the institutional emphasis on religion has created schizophrenic tensions within the ranks. Groups of Frontier Corpsmen have quickly surrendered to Taliban tribesmen, ex-officers have been arrested in connection with terrorist plots, and two elite commandos were court-martialed after they refused to participate in the 2007 military siege of a mosque and seminary in Islamabad, which radical clerics had turned into an armed bunker.

For two generations, Pakistan's army has built its strength, wealth, and raison d'être around the idea of fighting India, with the disputed Himalayan border territory of Kashmir as the permanent focal point of that cause. In the 1980s, the Soviet-Afghan conflict offered a separate opportunity for the army to help defend Islam against the communist menace next door, although it was never seen as an existential threat to Pakistan in the same way as India.

Both the Kashmir and Afghan crusades generated ideological byproducts that have come back to haunt Pakistan in several forms. One was the official commingling of patriotism and religion, which led to the increasing Islamization of society and the army. The other was the enormous state investment in nurturing Islamic guerrilla and political groups. Military and intelligence officials believed they could deploy these groups abroad but control them at home, and for almost twenty years it worked.

Although Bhutto began trying to Islamize the military before his death, it was during Zia's rule that the army, intelligence agencies, and society at large became emphatically more Islamic. This phenomenon has had a profound and enduring impact on Pakistan, surviving a decade of civilian rule and proving far deeper than any imprint left by its more recent and liberal military ruler, General Musharraf. Not until 2009, after repeated atrocities, hundreds of terrorist attacks, and rising fears of a Taliban takeover, did military institutional thinking swing around to support a full-fledged army assault on Islamic militants.

On the day Zia came to power in 1977, he immediately declared himself to be a "soldier of Islam." Within weeks, he had reneged on his promise to hold elections and embarked on a course of domestic Islamization that was both petty and draconian. He issued laws that quashed women's rights and instituted harsh physical punishments for drinking alcohol and having sex outside marriage. He had school texts rewritten to enshrine Pakistan's status as a heroic bastion of Islam surrounded by infidels and enemies, especially India.

Similarly, Zia set about trying to "Islamize" the army. He changed its dress code so officers would wear traditional Muslim dress at formal dinners. He encouraged them to grow beards and participate in prayer groups or Koranic study sessions. He often gave speeches to soldiers and officers about their heroic duties as the guardians of Islam. He also greatly expanded the ranks and role of the ISI in the service of both his domestic and strategic agendas.

The Islamization drive dovetailed with Zia's major foreign policy endeavor, the massive covert support and training program for Afghan guerrilla groups fighting a "jihad" against the Soviet army. Thousands of military and intelligence officers were involved in that effort, and many came to passionately identify with it. Zia was killed in a mysterious military plane crash in 1988, abruptly ending more than a decade of absolute and transformative rule. After the Soviets were defeated a year later, the same religious rallying cry was easily transferred to Kashmir and the expansion of covert support for Muslim rebels fighting to free it from Indian control.

"Zia's iron-fisted rule . . . enabled the ISI, which by then employed tens of thousands of operatives, informants and contractors, to operate in the shadows in both controlling domestic politics and managing foreign operations," Husain Haqqani, a former advisor to Benazir Bhutto and Pakistan's current ambassador to Washington, wrote in *Pakistan: Between Mosque and Military*. The ISI's role in partisan dirty tricks, he wrote, was now "cloaked by the legitimate external function of fighting the evil Soviet empire."

The twin policies of promoting jihad abroad and Islamizing society at home had a second lasting consequence for Pakistan, allowing dozens of conservative and militant religious groups to take root and flourish. Some, such as Jamaat-e-Islami, operated within democratic rules and ran candidates for provincial and national office, but this was a strategic means to an ideological end: the creation of a pure Islamic state.

Others, such as Lashkar-e-Taiba, or "Army of the Pure," began as pro-Kashmir groups but later revealed themselves to be violent pan-Islamists. Still others, including SSP, had a virulent sectarian agenda that led to bouts of Sunni-Shiite bloodletting. All were politically useful to the military, but only up to a point. By the mid-2000s, many of these strategic assets would become domestic liabilities, and the armed proxies of the shadow state would turn against their handlers in pursuit of greater religious ambitions.

The legacy of Zia's religious indoctrination, which lasted a generation, made it extremely difficult for the army—and for society in general—to acknowledge the dangers posed by these groups. Some were officially banned as early as 2002, but they continued to operate with quiet official acquiescence. Even six years later, after home-grown militias launched a sustained terror campaign of suicide bombings and assassinations, it remained hard for soldiers and paramilitary forces to accept these fellow Muslims as enemies and obey orders to kill them.

"General Zia motivated the army on the basis of Islam, and that influence stayed for a very long time," Colonel Mohammed Basir, a retired official from the military public affairs office, told me in the spring of 2010. "Now we are supposed to fight the Taliban. It was difficult at first to tell Muslims they had to fight other Muslims. They did not disobey, but you could feel their discomfort."

THE AMBITIONS AND VIEWS of General Musharraf, who seized power on October 12, 1999, contrasted sharply with Zia's. Musharraf was a religious moderate with a worldly upbringing, who pledged to bring "true democracy" to Pakistan. Garrulous and charming, he championed a variety of liberal causes, from ending honor killings of women to modernizing the curriculums at Islamic seminaries. He often invoked Jinnah's democratic ideals and declared in an early speech that the "true jihad" should be against poverty, illiteracy, and other social ills.

But eventually Musharraf fell prey to the disease of dictatorship and came to see himself as indispensable. Determined to remain in office and poorly advised by civilian sycophants, he took unpopular measures whose only benefit was to protect his power. In 2001 he appointed himself president and indefinitely extended his tenure as army chief. In 2002 he held a referendum on his rule and then a nationwide election, both of which critics charged were manipulated in the regime's favor.

Despite his liberal image, Musharraf did not hesitate to make deals with right-wing Islamic groups when it suited his purposes. He pledged repeatedly to crack down on extremist militants, but then quietly released leaders after arresting them. He vowed to register all Islamic seminaries and balance their rote religious indoctrination with academic study, but then dropped this effort and formed electoral alliances with religious parties whose creed was to create a theocratic state.

As time passed and his desire for power grew, Musharraf abandoned the pretense of democratic reforms. He ordered fundamental changes in the constitution, fired the chief justice of the Supreme Court, and finally, when his political efforts failed, imposed a state of emergency rule.

Musharraf's image also suffered at home from his decision in late 2001 to side with the United States in the war on terror. This meant not only helping the West hunt down al Qaeda suspects but abandoning the Taliban in next-door Afghanistan, even though they had been nurtured by Pakistan's army, religious teachers, and intelligence services.

Musharraf defended his decision as a compromise that would allow him to protect Pakistan's two other major commitments—its nuclear assets and its crusade in Kashmir. He also tried to preserve a distinction between al Qaeda and local Islamist militants, keep his political balance by publicly banning some militant groups and arresting their leaders but then quietly letting them go.

But many Pakistanis viewed the fight against Islamic terrorism as "America's war" and resented Musharraf as kowtowing to Washington. Despite dozens of terrorist attacks, the public remained reluctant to blame fellow Muslims and Pakistanis and unenthusiastic about a series of punitive military forays into the tribal regions where local Islamic militias were based. After President George W. Bush welcomed Musharraf to the White House and praised his military cooperation, protesters in Peshawar city paraded twin straw effigies of Bush and "Mush" riding on a donkey.

By 2007, Musharraf had politically self-destructed and dragged the army's image to its lowest level in years. A bloody confrontation that summer between security forces and radical Islamist clerics from the Red Mosque in Islamabad, bunkered inside a compound with hundreds of students, paralyzed the government in an agony of indecision. Musharraf was under pressure from his Western allies to crack down on the defiant armed extremists, but he was reluctant to act against Islamic groups that once had been backed by the state and still enjoyed the sympathy of many in the security and intelligence establishment.

Finally, under strong pressure from foreign allies including Beijing, the government attacked, destroying the compound in a fiery conflagration and killing more than a hundred people inside. The mini-rebellion was snuffed out, but the siege became what one former ISI director called a "tipping point" in relations between the state and the militants. It spurred a wave of public sympathy for the victims and provoked a retaliatory terror war on the state by Islamist extremists that has taken thousands of lives and shows no signs of letting up.

Musharraf's regime never recovered from the Red Mosque debacle, but he has always insisted he made the right decision in attacking the compound. During a talk in Washington in 2010, where the former president was seeking support for a political comeback, he reacted sharply to a question about the event.

"I did nothing wrong," he said. "It was right in the heart of Islamabad. We were being humiliated and insulted. The government writ was being challenged . . . we had to take action." Musharraf said he had used all possible means to mediate with the clerics inside, but in the end had no choice. "We are not going to be called a banana state," he said irritably. "You cannot challenge the writ of the state, at least not under me."

Meanwhile, Musharraf's clumsy efforts to emasculate the Supreme Court unleashed an extraordinary protest campaign by Pakistan's dignified legal community. The campaign captured the nation's imagination. TV channels showed black-suited barristers marching in the streets, braving tear gas and police batons. With respectable citizens chanting, "Go, Musharraf, go," the commander in chief became a liability to his own institution. Ultimately he had no option but to step down as army chief, allow his hated civilian rivals to return from exile, and relinquish the presidency itself.

On November 29, 2007, a televised ceremony unfolded on a military sports ground near army headquarters. It was a nearly wordless ritual, inherited from the British era. General Musharraf and the senior military command strode onto the field, escorted by a goose-stepping honor guard. Commands were shouted, salutes exchanged. At the appointed moment, Musharraf presented his bamboo swagger stick, a symbol of army power, to General Ashfaq Kayani, his successor. The nation heaved a collective sigh of relief.

THE DARK SIDE OF Pakistan's military establishment is Inter-Services Intelligence, a parallel covert universe and center of power that employs thousands of people to spy on Pakistanis and foreigners alike. Officially, the ISI is managed by the army; its director is always a serving or retired army general, and many of its officers are military personnel. But its headquarters is an obscure, dun-colored building many miles from army headquarters, its agents are mostly disguised as civilians, and its operations are waged in the shadows.

ISI's role in both Pakistan's foreign and domestic affairs is pervasive, but its actions are publicly unaccountable; Parliament has no intelligence oversight committee and the cabinet has no minister to whom the ISI directly reports. Army officials bristle when critics call ISI a "rogue agency" and always insist it is fully under their control, yet they almost never admit its reported excesses. Periodic attempts to bring the agency under direct civilian command have been short-lived and sharply rebuffed.

In July 2008, the Zardari government announced that control of both the ISI and the Intelligence Bureau, which is the Pakistani equivalent of the FBI, would be transferred from the Defense Ministry to the Interior Ministry. But late the same night, after the prime minister reportedly received two "emergency calls from Rawalpindi," the government press office issued a "clarification" saying the original announcement had been "misinterpreted." Both agencies remained firmly under the military's aegis.

Four months later, after the shocking terrorist attack on the Indian city of Mumbai, Prime Minister Yousuf Gilani announced as a good faith gesture that Lieutenant General Ahmed Shuja Pasha, the new ISI chief, would travel to India to assist with the investigation. But the army interpreted the move as a summons from India, which would have been intolerable. Within hours, the army spokesman announced that no decision had been made, and that Pakistan would need a detailed invitation letter first. General Pasha never made the trip.

The heyday of ISI was the great Afghan jihad of the 1980s, when its agents trained and managed thousands of Afghan anticommunist "freedom fighters," with full covert backing from the Reagan administration and the U.S. Congress. The bilateral intelligence relationship went into hibernation after the war's end in 1989, leaving ISI as a full-blown spy apparatus without civilian oversight or Western partners.

The agency then turned its attention to Indian Kashmir, where Muslim dissidents were demanding autonomy and local guerrilla forces were ambushing and harassing Indian troops. ISI began training Pakistan-based fighters in more sophisticated tactics, including the first suicide bombings, and infiltrating them across the Line of Control, a militarized de facto border extending several hundred miles between Indian and Pakistani Kashmir. The agency was widely reported to operate training camps in the mountains of Pakistani Kashmir, a high-security area that foreigners are not allowed to enter without a government escort.

As ISI grew in size and ambition, it also broadened its activities inside Pakistan, acting as a covert political wing of the armed forces and their allies in the civilian establishment. It was used as a dirty-tricks gang to manipulate elections by spreading harmful rumors about some candidates, paying others to run for office, and creating and funding political alliances.

Pakistani officials now acknowledge that ISI worked covertly to generate opposition to Benazir Bhutto when she ran for office in 1988, basically because the army did not trust her. After Bhutto won anyway and became prime minister, Pakistani analysts say the same forces worked to undermine her credibility and power as prime minister until she was dismissed in 1990. Before the next elections, army officials reportedly set up a secret slush fund for ISI to funnel large sums to dozens of her opponents, from Nawaz Sharif of the Pakistan Muslim League to Liaqat Baloch of Jamaat-e-Islami.

In the years since, ISI has honed its reputation as a force to be feared by anyone who falls into its bad graces. Its acronym sends chills through people, just as DINA in Pinochet's Chile or SAVAK in the shah's Iran once did. The agency cultivates a reputation for omniscience, omnipresence, and impunity, and it floats rumors of horrific punishments in secret prisons, where men are said to be thrown into dungeons and tormented by rats, snakes, or starving dogs. When allegations of abuse surface, ISI officials rarely respond in public, adding to the chilling effect.

Yet ISI is a sophisticated professional institution that operates mostly in subtle and unobtrusive ways. It employs legions of people to follow and watch anyone of interest—foreign visitors, protesters, politicians, clerics, refugees, journalists, travelers from India—and report on their activities. Sometimes its observers tail visitors in cars or on motorbikes; sometimes they call a hotel room, without giving a name, to let a guest know they are aware of his whereabouts and activities.

Usually, when the intelligence services want to intimidate a foreigner, it is done through the person's local helper. Over the years, almost all my Pakistani translators have been questioned or bothered by their agents, either by phone or by subtle approaches in the street. I once went to the site of a suicide bombing near an ISI facility and stood among dozens of onlookers watching from the sidewalk. Out of nowhere, a plainclothes agent brushed past my translator and whispered in his ear. He turned white as a sheet and told me we had to leave immediately.

Pakistan's media tends to treat ISI with kid gloves. Television anchors and newspaper reports almost never mention the agency by name, instead using euphemisms such as "sensitive government agencies," which all readers and viewers understand. Few journalists dare to directly criticize the agency, and some are said to have been on intelligence payrolls for years. The rare reporter who delves into the dirty laundry of the military establishment can find himself in deep trouble with its shadow henchmen.

In 2010, Umar Cheema, an investigative reporter for *The News International,* wrote several articles about the military that cast disturbing light on its inner conflicts over the war on Islamic terrorism. One night his car was stopped in Islamabad by men in commando-style garb, who blindfolded him and drove him to a house. There, Cheema recounted later, he was stripped and beaten, hung upside down and humiliated, and threatened with rape. Early the next morning, he was dumped on a deserted road many miles away.

Cheema's captors were never identified and officials denied all involvement, but he said he was certain ISI, which previously had warned him to back off his aggressive coverage, carried out the operation.

Yet Pakistan's military and intelligence officials also weigh the strategic costs and benefits of shutting people up. They have ignored endless salvos by Kamran Shafi, a former army major and columnist for the *News,* whose essays often sarcastically denounce corruption and abuse. Shafi called Cheema's ordeal "another cruel and dastardly act by the Deep State," a term that was originally used to describe the permanent civilian and military establishment in modern Turkey. He wondered aloud why highway police could not identify the abductors' vehicle even though it had passed through tolls with cameras. "We will never find out what happened to poor Umar Cheema because the Deep State does not want us to find out," Shafi wrote. "No police force in the country dare stand up to it."

ISI harasses and bullies people for all kinds of reasons, and when the target is a Pakistani, the methods often include crude and violent thuggery. Sometimes the intent is to punish or compromise individuals who are already part of the shadow wars. Sometimes it is to quash investigations by other government entities, and sometimes even to carry out personal vendettas with mafia-like muscle.

In *Crossed Swords,* Nawaz relates the story of a retired eighty-year-old army brigadier—a winner of one of Pakistan's highest awards for military gallantry—who reported that one night, a dozen armed ISI agents forcibly entered his home, then proceeded to beat and abuse him, his daughter-in-law, and two grandsons, apparently on orders from an agency superior whose children had quarreled with the boys.

Shocked and mortified, the old brigadier wrote to President Musharraf, asking him to "restore my dignity as an ex-army officer" and bring the culprits to justice. The incident caused a scandal when it came out in the press, and the army spokesman said Musharraf had apologized to the decorated officer, but there is no evidence that any punitive action was ever taken against the agents involved.

THE TALIBAN TAKEOVER OF Kabul in 1996 put ISI back in business in Afghanistan, where the new leadership included many fighters it had trained for the anti-Soviet jihad. The formal relationship was tenuous and tense under two successive civilian administrations in Islamabad, but after Musharraf took over, Pakistan formally endorsed Taliban rule. For the next two years, ISI became its principal arm of influence in Kabul.

The 9/11 attacks changed all that, at least on paper. Musharraf was forced to abandon the Taliban and endorse Washington's war on terror. Two months later the Taliban regime fell, and thousands of its members and allies fled to sanctuary in Pakistan's tribal region. ISI, which had known and nurtured many of them, was put in a terrible bind. The war on terror had turned its assets into liabilities, friends into foes, and protégés into renegades.

There were also new rules and partners in Washington, demanding help in hunting down al Qaeda members and fugitive Taliban leaders. The first category was not a major problem; Pakistan had no reason to protect international terrorists, and its security agencies were useful in locating and handing over dozens of important al Qaeda suspects, including Khalid Sheikh Mohammed, the notorious 9/11 planner, who was found in a relative's house in Karachi.

But the long-standing relationships between ISI and a variety of Afghan, Kashmiri, and other militant groups, forged in ideological battle, were difficult to abandon or betray. Officially, American and Pakistani intelligence agencies worked closely together, sharing command centers and information that helped the CIA guide unmanned planes from bases in Afghanistan or the Arabian Sea to bomb suspected Taliban and al Qaeda hideouts in Pakistan, even though the government in Islamabad formally opposed such drone attacks.

Unofficially, ISI's role was much more complicated. Its new mission clashed with loyalties and beliefs forged in other wars. The country was under siege from Islamic terrorists, and the army was sending young soldiers out to die fighting them. Yet its shadow warriors were expected to maintain their old relationships, cultivate militant groups that could be useful as strategic assets against Indian influence in Afghanistan, and keep an eye on those it could no longer trust.

The situation unraveled further as these militant groups, based inside Pakistan and its semiautonomous tribal region along the Afghan border, began to splinter. There were Sunni and Shiite splits, ethnic and regional rivalries, pro-government and antigovernment stands, pro-Afghan and anti-Afghan factions.

According to Pakistani analysts, the army and intelligence agencies enacted what author Ahmed Rashid called a "pick-and-choose" policy toward these groups. They launched high-profile attacks on the Taliban, which brutally defied the writ of the Pakistani state, but they encouraged groups whose target was Afghanistan, maintaining covert contacts with them through retired agents or others. They assumed that Western forces would eventually depart from Kabul again, and they wanted to be prepared to pick up the pieces.

It is not clear how long Pakistan kept up this tricky double game, but it apparently went on long after senior officials in Islamabad adamantly denied it to numerous high-ranking American visitors. During much of this period, Pakistani observers noted, General Kayani was the senior official in charge of ISI.

In 2010, a series of bizarre events followed by a blizzard of leaked diplomatic and military documents suggested that the two-track policy had been in operation for several years. The documents described multiple contacts between Pakistani officials or their go-betweens and various militant groups, especially those who supported the Afghan Taliban. Husain Haqqani, by then Pakistan's ambassador to Washington, responded carefully that the information did not accurately "reflect the current on-ground realities."

One of these shadow warriors was a jovial-looking former Air

Force officer and retired intelligence agent named Khalid Khwaja. At fifty-eight, he wore a long gray beard and traditional Pashtun tribal clothing, a style he had cultivated as a field trainer of Afghan militia fighters for ISI in the 1980s. In April 2010, Khwaja was kidnapped in the northwestern tribal region, along with another former ISI agent, by a little-known Punjabi militant group called the Asian Tigers. Several weeks later, Khwaja's bullet-riddled corpse was found in the area.

The killing set off a barrage of speculation and conspiracy theories, involving numerous possible enemies from Khwaja's long career and shifting loyalties in the surreal and treacherous world of Pakistani spydom. The case is confusing and complex—not to mention melodramatic—but it is worth laying out here because it draws together many different aspects of Pakistan's muddled ideological and security aims, and connects the dots on many shadowy lines.

Khwaja's death also involved many intriguing characters from Pakistan's long-running, dangerous dalliance with Islamic militancy, including a former ISI chief, a television newsman, and a radical cleric who died in the army siege of the Red Mosque. It highlighted the respect and even appreciation many Pakistanis have for ISI, despite its history of political skullduggery and domestic espionage—in part because they identify it with the romance of the Afghan wars, and in part because they see it as an extension of the army.

After the flood of U.S. military documents released by Wikileaks detailed ISI's double-dealing with militant groups, Pakistan's media and opinion makers rushed to defend the agency. "On talk show after talk show, the ISI's accusers in the West were criticized for shortsightedness and shifting the blame to Pakistan for their doomed campaign in Afghanistan," noted Mohammed Hanif, a Pakistani writer. Suddenly, he noted, the spy agency's years of destructive, antidemocratic behavior were forgotten. "It is our ISI that is being accused, we felt."

But the pick-and-choose strategy, sometimes called the "good Taliban, bad Taliban" approach, had already begun to fall apart in

2007 with the military siege of the Red Mosque. The conflagration turned many militant groups against their former handlers and launched a campaign of retaliatory terror attacks against the state that continues to this day. On the ground, the web of plots and contradictory relationships between government go-betweens and their former allies in various "holy wars" began to violently unravel.

At that point, Khwaja had retired from the armed forces and become a self-proclaimed human rights activist. His orders or motives remain opaque, but he apparently became involved in efforts to mediate with the clerics bunkered inside the Red Mosque. One theory holds that his killing, three years later, was payback by militants who thought he had betrayed them there. Another suggests that he was targeted by a rising movement of Punjabi Taliban who viewed Khwaja, an ethnic Pashtun, as being too close to the Afghan factions.

Khwaja was a complicated man with a complicated life. He was a devout Muslim who publicly said he hated the United States for trying to destroy Islam but who was accused by his adversaries of being an American spy. He had trained Afghan mujaheddin under General Zia, who fired him for being too radical but allowed him to continue working covertly for his spy chief, Lieutenant General Hamid Gul. Although his métier was the Afghan jihad, Khwaja also admitted being involved in old covert plots against Pakistani political parties and leaders.

After his death, the plot thickened when it was reported that General Gul had sent Khwaja and a colleague, another former mujaheddin trainer known as Colonel Imam, into the tribal region to meet Afghan rebel groups. Gul, a relentless opponent of the U.S. war in Afghanistan, figured prominently in the leaked U.S. documents of July 2010, which depicted him as working tirelessly to revive his old contacts with pro-Afghan militants.

The picture grew even murkier when Hamid Mir, a leading TV newscaster in Islamabad with long-standing ties to ISI, was accused of conspiring to kill Khwaja in a taped phone conversation between him and Punjabi Taliban leaders. On the tape, a voice which sounded like Mir's angrily accused Khwaja of working for the CIA. Mir, who denounced the tape as a fake, was accused in turn of being a CIA agent by a right-wing television host.

It is not the details of this twisted tale that matter so much as the wider picture they paint of what can happen when an overdeveloped, military-backed spy apparatus outgrows its erstwhile mission and delves into personal, partisan, and ideological conflicts. Khwaja's story follows what columnist Kamila Hyat called the long "slimy trail"—a treacherous path running through a covert world where spies, guerrillas, clerics, and political figures maneuver and manipulate, play multiple roles, and change loyalties with the wind.

"Many secrets died with Khalid Khwaja," Hyat wrote, describing his career as a "dark indicator of the kind of state we have become. It is a state where plots and counterplots, often against elected governments, are hatched, where deals of various kinds are struck and where deep splits in ideology" spawn rival factions among former allies. "Within this world of conspiracy, it is often hard to know on whose side individuals are," she wrote. As to who killed Khalid Khwaja and why, she added, "we are unlikely to ever know the full truth."

THE GENERAL WHO REPLACED Musharraf as army chief was his institutional contemporary but stylistic opposite. Where Pervez Musharraf was impulsive, thin-skinned, and emotional, Ashfaq Kayani was taciturn, cool, and calculating. A former intelligence chief, he kept his counsel and plotted like a chess player. He was a native of Punjab, where the army's roots are strongest, rather than a Partition-era immigrant from India, a minority status that had always hurt Musharraf.

Kayani was ambitious even as a young officer in the 1980s, impressing colleagues with his shrewd institutional instincts and strategic silences at military meetings and conferences. He honed his reputation as a cool and apolitical soldier's soldier as he ticked off the benchmarks—battle service, military commands, and professional courses, including several at U.S. defense institutes—required to rise to the top.

The most important phase of Kayani's career, however, was opaque and shrouded in mystery. Under Musharraf's command, he ran ISI from 2004 to 2007, a tense period of growing terrorist threats and shifting covert relationships between the security establishment and its onetime militant proxies. The Red Mosque confrontation, which occurred during his tenure, placed extreme conflicting pressures on the Pakistani military—almost identical to those it had faced when Washington forced it to abandon the Taliban in 2001.

Kayani has never spoken publicly about the Red Mosque, but as ISI chief, he was presumably immersed in the frenzy of secret negotiations, arguments, promises, and betrayals that unfolded as officials tried and failed to resolve the standoff peacefully. When they finally resorted to a military siege, it ruined Musharraf's career, sharpened professional-religious tensions inside the army, and instantly turned a new jihadi generation against the state.

Four months later, when Kayani met Musharraf on the parade ground in Rawalpindi and took possession of his swagger stick, the new army chief instantly became the most powerful person in Pakistan—and grabbed his chance to wipe the slate clean. From the first day of his command, he used private political leverage when it counted, but shrewdly stayed out of the public limelight that had burned his predecessor.

Kayani knew his most urgent task was a nonmilitary one: to rebuild the tarnished reputation of the armed forces by extracting it from national politics, distancing himself from Musharraf, and putting his relationship with Washington on a new professional footing. He banned all officers from contact with politicians and withdrew hundreds of them from government posts. He told an audience of senior commanders, in a speech publicized by his aides, that the army "fully stands behind the democratic process and is committed to playing its constitutional role."

At the time, Pakistan was facing an eruption of terrorist attacks from Islamic extremists and territorial advances by the Taliban in the northwest tribal areas. It was also coming under increasing pressure from Washington to halt the spread of violent militancy and deny sanctuary to Taliban and al Qaeda forces. But a series of half-hearted military raids had produced heavy casualties and failed to dislodge the Taliban. Kayani was loath to take on the militants until he had secured full support from a skeptical public and could motivate his troops to fight an enemy they had been taught to admire as Islamic "freedom fighters" in Kashmir and Afghanistan.

"The military lost a lot of face when it went into Swat in 2007 and 2008. Nobody there trusted us," General Athar Abbas, the army spokesman, told me in 2009. "Now public opinion has swung the other direction, but we still have to deal with a lot of complexities and constraints. We can only deliver so much, and we can only go so far without hurting our long-term interests. We cannot afford a mass tribal uprising, and we cannot afford to alienate the public again."

The army and intelligence agencies had been intimately involved in nurturing and training the Afghan Taliban. Now they had great difficulty adjusting to the notion that these erstwhile Islamic freedom fighters and their Pakistani brethren—who hailed from interrelated tribes on both sides of the Afghan border, and who enjoyed strong local support within the semiautonomous tribal "agencies"—were now dangerous enemies of the state.

In short, the army had little stomach for a fight and every reason to avoid a major military clash with the Taliban. As a result, it attempted to play both sides of the fence, punishing outbursts of violence with limited air and ground raids while pushing for peace talks with tribal elders. The goal was to contain the militant threat to the rugged and remote tribal regions, and to reach a modus vivendi with extremist leaders who increasingly dominated the thinking and loyalty of the tribes.

Gradually it became clear that the militants had could neither be contained nor bought off. The campaign of terrorist bombings continued, targeting hotels, markets, police academies, and international aid compounds as well as military forces and facilities.

Repression worsened in Taliban-controlled tribal areas, and the militants began pushing their violent religious crusade closer to Pakistan's "settled areas" and the capital. Pressure mounted from Washington for the military to take decisive action, especially after the insurgents immediately violated a peace deal in which the Zardari government had given in to virtually all their demands.

Still, it took the army months to prepare for a full-fledged assault on the militants—preparations that had as much to do with politics and public opinion as with training and equipping a conventional army to face an agile and highly motivated guerrilla force. The generals refused to move until they were sure public opinion was behind them.

Once the army finally entered Swat in May 2009, however, what the troops saw with their own eyes convinced them they were doing the right thing. The Taliban were "digging up graves and hanging people in squares, doing things that were clearly un-Islamic," Colonel Basir recounted. "This made it much easier for commanders to motivate the men, to tell them, 'These are not your brothers. They are killing your brothers.'"

WHILE WORLD ATTENTION HAS been fixed on Pakistan's western border with Afghanistan, the Pakistan army's sites have remained trained on its eastern front. From the generals' perspective, neither the Afghans nor the Arabs present the same existential threat to Pakistan as India, its nuclear-armed, Hindu-majority neighbor.

Today, Westerners think of India as a benign tourist mecca of temples and gurus, a producer of zany song-and-dance films, and a fast-rising high-tech tiger. India has turned decisively from its Cold War–era fling with socialism to building a political and economic partnership with the West, and it has long sought a seat on the UN Security Council that would confer great-power status on the world's most populous democracy.

India has also won sympathy as a victim of terrorist attacks, often at the hands of groups based in Pakistan. In November 2008, terrorists besieged Mumbai for three days, killing 168 people including six Americans. As a result of arrests, confessions, and telephone intercepts, the attackers were conclusively linked to Lashkar-e-Taiba, the Punjabi jihadist militia, which had long received covert support from Islamabad to wage an insurgency in Indian Kashmir.

Nevertheless, Pakistan sees India as the aggressor—a permanent, next-door adversary that never accepted its need to exist. Schools across Pakistan, especially Islamic seminaries, teach children it is a dangerous and evil giant. Although most Pakistanis would like to see better economic and diplomatic relations with India, more than half view it as the greatest single threat to their country. In a 2010 opinion poll by the Pew Research Center, 74 percent of Pakistani respondents said they considered India a serious threat to their country, and 53 percent saw it as a "very serious threat." Significantly, both the Taliban and al Qaeda ranked much lower.

India is the prism through which Pakistan views every other aspect of its international relations, especially the war in Afghanistan. It is the perennial threat the military uses to justify its hefty budgets, its permanent demand for more weapons and equipment, the expansion of its nuclear capability, and its use of Islam to motivate the troops. When India accuses ISI of orchestrating attacks in India, Pakistan denounces India's military Research and Intelligence Wing as the "foreign hand" behind terror attacks in Pakistan.

Pakistani soldiers are taught to view India as a powerful and wily enemy with a huge army and an arsenal of conventional and nuclear weapons, against which they must never let down their guard. The Afghan conflict, by comparison, is seen as a skirmish in a backyard anthill, its cross-border fallout a containable problem of renegade ants. India is the rogue elephant that never leaves the room.

This fear is reinforced by a one-sided historic narrative of Indian ambition, aggression, and conspiracy. It began with Partition in 1948, then the 1965 war and the 1971 conflict and breakoff of East Pakistan—a stunning loss the army blamed on Indian interference rather than on its own excesses against Bengali dissidents. "We are one of the few countries in modern times to be divided by foreign aggression. That event cannot be easily forgotten," retired four-star general Ehsan ul-Haq told a Washington audience nearly forty years later.

The narrative of victimization continued through Indian nuclear tests in 1974 and war exercises in 1986, the Kashmir uprising of the 1990s, the Kargil border clash in 2000, and India's support for anti-Taliban militias in Afghanistan. Today, seen through the Pakistani prism, India is under every rock and behind every rebellion. If New Delhi befriends the Karzai government in Kabul, it is only to sabotage Pakistan. If India seeks membership on the UN Security Council, it is only to keep Pakistan off.

General ul-Haq, a onetime senior military and intelligence official, was clearly speaking for the army when he visited Washington in 2010. He described India as yearning to build a vast Hindu empire stretching "from the Straits of Malacca to the coast of Africa and the Red Sea," and Pakistan as the "first stumbling block" in its path. He also listed a number of points that were of "critical concern" to Pakistan, including India's "aggressive" involvement in Afghanistan.

Yet the core of his argument, the most inflexible and visceral cause, was Kashmir. As ul-Haq stated simply, Indo-Pakistan relations have been "defined for sixty years" by their dispute over Kashmir, and the "security paradigm" dominating their relationship will not change as long as the issue is unresolved.

Kashmir is a remote, bucolic region with a majority-Muslim population that was split between India and Pakistan at the time of Partition, but the terms remained in dispute and the region's official status was never resolved. To this day, under a temporary UN division that has lasted for six decades, the two portions are separated by the 340-mile Line of Control, along which Pakistan keeps more than 100,000 troops deployed.

The "Kashmir cause" has always been a centerpiece of the army's foreign policy, a patriotic rallying cry and justification for costly, permanent war footing. It is both a hook in the monster next door and a bond to unite a fractured and struggling Muslim nation that still has deep doubts about the legitimacy of its birth. To keep public emotions high, the state has spewed out endless propaganda about the struggle of Kashmiri Muslims for self-determination and the oppressive behavior of Indian troops there.

India and Pakistan have been engaged in intermittent talks for years about Kashmir and other issues, but every effort has collapsed, often due to hard-line opposition in both countries. The army's main concern, as General ul-Haq made clear, is to make sure negotiators do not barter Kashmir away in the quest for peace. He even criticized General Musharraf, his boss at the time, for taking a "totally one-sided" proposal to India in 2001 without consulting the army or the public. That effort, too, failed.

Meanwhile, since the early 1990s Pakistan has covertly trained and financed guerrilla groups to harass Indian forces in Kashmir. The most notorious of these is Lashkar-e-Taiba (LET), which introduced the extreme tactic of suicide attacks to the conflict. LET was banned by Musharraf in 2002, shortly after the United States declared it to be a foreign terrorist organization, but the militia continued operating with impunity under a new name and remained popular with the public. Pakistani officials arrested its leaders when things got hot but let them out after a cooling-off spell.

In the past few years, the "Kashmir cause" has metastasized into something much larger and more threatening. LET in particular has widened its aims, allying with foreign jihadi groups and launching attacks in other Indian cities, including a 2005 assault on the Parliament building in New Delhi and the 2008 commando siege of Mumbai.

Officials in Islamabad denied all involvement in the Mumbai attack and took weeks even to acknowledge the commandos were Pakistanis. They also denied LET's role until India provided a thick dossier of evidence, including the identities of all ten attackers and a commander named Zaki ul-Rehman Lakhvi, as well as transcripts of cell phone calls from Pakistan, made during the assault, with voices urging the young men to kill and die for the glory of Islam. Eventually Pakistani authorities arrested Lakhvi and six other LET members, though they refused to extradite them to India.

The state's investigation and prosecution dragged on for months, and even after two years in custody, none had been brought to trial. One possible factor in this foot-dragging was that lengthy investigations by Indian, American, and European law enforcement agencies, as well as statements by several arrested LET recruits, suggested strongly that ISI officers, some of whom had direct ties to the army, were involved in training and planning the attack.

A wealth of detail came from David Coleman Headley, a Pakistani American businessman who was arrested in Chicago in 2009. He cooperated with the FBI and testified that he had been recruited by LET to set up an office in Mumbai as cover for pre-attack scouting, which included making a plastic model of the famous Taj Hotel, which was to be a major target. In Pakistan, Headley said he reported to a Major Iqbal, apparently an ISI officer, and to a LET commander known as Sajid Mir, who Western investigators believe is a former Pakistani army officer with highly placed connections.

Another LET recruit from France described stints in mountain warfare camps, with army-supplied weapons and trainers (including Mir) who appeared to be army officers. American and French investigators said Mir wielded too much influence in Pakistan to be arrested, and a French judge said he "appeared to be protected at the highest levels of the state."

Lashkar-e-Taiba clearly enjoys semiuntouchable status in Pakistan because of its long years fighting in Kashmir as well as its widespread charitable and social programs at home. Even senior military officials express little interest in prosecuting the group, suggesting this would inflame public opinion, especially in northern Punjab Province, which not coincidentally is the main recruiting base for both the army and LET.

"Kashmir and LET are with the people's psyche. It is easier said than done to ban these groups," said General Musharraf in 2010, long after he had twice attempted to shut down LET during his years in power. "You can't rock the boat so much it capsizes."

Another senior army figure, when asked about the Mumbai attack, barely paused to acknowledge India's trauma before accusing

New Delhi of using it as a "pretext" to step back from peace negotiations. While insisting that Pakistan does not tolerate militant groups, he said coming down hard on LET would "distort our priorities." Pakistan's first priority, he said, is to "tackle the people doing suicide bombs in Islamabad and Karachi and Lahore. There is no evidence LET is doing terrorism in Pakistan."

Yet some Pakistanis see the army's enduring obsession with India as both shortsighted and self-destructive. By hitching its own fortunes to a costly, unwinnable conflict with a richer and more democratic country, they argue, the army will further isolate Pakistan from global sympathy and investment. By courting violent groups exclusively because of their anti-India stance, it is worsening Pakistan's reputation as a fount of Islamic terrorism and detracting from the fight against militant groups who want to replace the Pakistani state with a repressive theocracy.

"The military is still spending more money arming itself against India than it is spending to fight the Taliban," wrote Ahmed Rashid, Pakistan's leading expert on Islamic militancy. Unless there is a sea change in the army's "obsessive mind-set" about India," its aggressive drive for regional influence, and "its determination to define and control national security," Rashid wrote in 2010, "no real progress in Pakistan towards democracy, stability and peace is possible."

THE ARMY'S GENERAL HEADQUARTERS in Rawalpindi, known to all as GHQ, is an imposing modern fortress inside a sprawling garrison, surrounded by high brick walls with a single entrance that is guarded around the clock. Somehow, on the morning of October 10, 2009, a team of gunmen wearing military uniforms managed to storm the main gate and enter the compound, killing nine soldiers and taking forty-two other people hostage.

For twenty-two hours, the militants controlled the garrison. It was not until the next day that army commandos were able to quell the intrusion, free the hostages, and restore normalcy to the nerve center of Pakistan's military power. The incident was so embarrassing to the army and the nation that the next day's papers highlighted the bold, predawn commando rescue—waited for several paragraphs to explain exactly what had prompted the intervention.

Seven weeks later, another terrorist squad slipped into the Parade Lane mosque in a military neighborhood near GHQ, opening fire with guns and grenades during the crowded Friday prayer service. Forty people died in the mayhem, including a prominent colonel, a student who was about to be married, and dozens of other worshippers from the tight-knit military community. Some of the attackers blew themselves up; the rest were shot and killed as they tried to escape.

"My son died like a soldier to save his nephew. I feel pride in his martyrdom," said Nazim Riaz, seventy, a retired general, whose son Bilal had been praying next to the younger boy and shielded him from the gunfire. "These terrorists want to weaken the country and the resolve of the armed forces, but they will never succeed," Riaz vowed.

But the assault on two fundamental pillars of Pakistani society, the army and Islam, brought out both the strong religious bonds and the vexing internal contradictions of the military establishment. The attackers on both GHQ and the mosque were Islamic militants bent on defying and humiliating the army for its operations against the Taliban, but Kayani, speaking at a formal mourning ceremony for three of the military victims, framed the army's mission as a defense of Islam.

"Pakistan is our motherland. It is the bastion of Islam. We live and die for the glory of Islam," he told several hundred officers and victims' relatives standing in prayer rows before three pine coffins. "Our faith, resolve, and pride in our religion and in our country is an asset, which is further reinforced after each terrorist incident," the general continued, adding that the army "stands committed to defend, protect, and preserve Pakistan at all costs."

Elsewhere, in speeches to senior officers and in meetings with American officials, Kayani delivered a more nuanced message, distinguishing between moderate and extremist versions of Islam and describing the internal threat to Pakistan as more urgent than any external one. In a military academy speech in August 2009, he vowed to stop militant groups from imposing a "narrow and distorted" version of Islam on the nation.

Yet the military brass knows it must also remain sensitive to religious feelings in the public and within its own ranks, which have been deliberately imbued with religious fervor—sometimes by conservative mullahs preaching in cantonment mosques—and may not always make the same distinction.

Even after the attack on GHQ, which followed dozens of terrorist assaults on security forces and their facilities—offices of ISI in Peshawar and Rawalpindi, offices of the Federal Investigative Police and police training academies in Lahore—Pakistan's generals could not denounce radical Islamic groups too loudly. Many military officers today, not just the few who wear beards to signal their Islamic devotion, view Pakistan's Western partners as immoral and ill-intentioned toward the Muslim world.

To keep their troops motivated and their institutional prerogatives safe, the generals also need to keep Kashmir high on the agenda and Indo-Pakistani relations in the freezer, even if this means pulling rank on civilian officials and covertly supporting groups such as LET—international pariahs and violent terrorists whose domestic influence is contributing to the "Talibanization" of Pakistani society far more than the Taliban itself. Kayani, the former ISI chief, cannot simply sever the institutional ties of a generation.

All of this affects the other strategic balancing act General Kayani has to manage: his relationship with the United States. After the clumsy political machinations of Musharraf, Kayani was welcomed with relief in Washington as a professional "soldier's soldier," so he needs to avoid any appearance of meddling in civilian politics. The army's leverage depends in part on its ability to keep raking in Western military aid.

Yet the wily survivor has managed to come out on top, in part because of the unpopularity, ineptitude and corruption among Pakistan's civilian leadership. By the spring of 2010, Kayani had led two major operations against tribal militants in the northwest. He had gained added public sympathy from the attacks on GHQ and the Parade Lane mosque. He had kept his troops firmly in the barracks and acted with formal deference to Zardari while pushing back when he had enough public support.

The morning after Zardari relented and allowed the "Long March" to reach Islamabad, evidently at the eleventh-hour insistence of the army chief, the editorial in *The News International* bordered on reverential. "The role played by the army chief guaranteed the continuation of democracy in the country," it declared. "This step has also enhanced the image of the armed forces among the people."

On July 22, 2010, the Zardari government rewarded Kayani with the prize that mattered most. After a flurry of rumors about the president wanting to appoint a replacement for the army chief when his tenure expired in August, all speculation ended when Prime Minister Gilani appeared on late-night television and announced that Kayani's post would be extended for three more years.

It was clear that the government, struggling to survive amid relentless terrorist attacks, a free-falling economy, and a growing foreign perception of chaotic failure, hoped to send a message of national stability and institutional partnership that would last through its tenure. Gilani, speaking with evident relief and surprising frankness, declared that the four major individual "stakeholders" in Pakistan—himself, the president, the army chief, and the chief justice of the Supreme Court—were now in a "secure position" for the next three years.

Critics called the appointment political tampering with military promotions and a personal anointment that would give Kayani an excessive edge over all subordinates. Some suggested the decision had been made under American pressure, or called it a "silent coup" arranged to forestall an actual military takeover of Zardari's shaky and unpopular government. They predicted Kayani would honor the deal in the short run, but said it would weaken democracy in the long term and solidify the army's command of foreign policy.

Columnist Cyril Almeida, an articulate spokesmen for democracy, described Kayani as "our latest indispensable" in a pantheon of uniformed saviors. He warned that the army remained the "800-pound gorilla of Pakistan politics" and that its power had now been dangerously reinforced. Almeida conceded that the army knew when to "opt for strategic retreat and when to embark on unobtrusive encroachment," but he stressed that if Pakistan had any hope of building a strong democracy, "the army's political power and influence must recede."

No flowery prose was needed to make the same point in a late-night satire on Geo Television, which aired after the army's much-praised performance in the flood zones and the appeal by one exiled party leader for "patriotic generals" to take over. The pantomime skit depicted an array of Pakistani politicians as fruits and vegetables on a kitchen table, posturing and pontificating and pointing fingers. Suddenly an enormous unidentified figure in khaki trousers and black boots strode into the room and swept all the little apples and onions into a sack.

CHAPTER 6

TALIBANIZATION

A SEARCH FOR THE heart of Islam in Pakistan eventually leads to a Sufi shrine. There are dozens of them in cities and towns across the country—shady sanctuaries with cool stone terraces where people from all walks of life are welcome to enter, remove their shoes, and put down their burdens. There is no liturgy or leader or prescribed ritual; people may pray, read, beg, take a nap, hold a picnic, talk to their ancestors, play the harmonium, or sit in a trance all day, singing to themselves.

The shrines can be contemplative or carnivalesque, but they always have a magical feeling. They are human pageants where beggars and pickpockets mingle with pilgrims, poets, and penitents. Families bring their newborns in swaddling clothes and their newly dead parents in pine coffins to be blessed. Volunteers ladle out bowls of rice and lentil soup to lines of ragged families. Everyone watches his wallet, but no one is lectured or turned away.

The Sufis were mystics, many originating in Persia, who believed everyone should seek a personal relationship with God, free of liturgical rules or clerical hierarchy. Their followers believe they have special powers of healing and intercession, whether to cure a palsied limb, help a woman conceive, or rescue a wrongly accused person from the clutches of the law.

Many Sufis were famous writers and poets, inspired by their search for spiritual enlightenment to pen thousands of verses. They offered lessons for life that spoke in riddles rather than sermons, urging believers to shun material ambitions and physical temptations and seek only the love of God.

Each shrine is dedicated to a particular Sufi saint—Rahman Baba in Peshawar, Data Ganj Bakshs in Lahore, Sheikh Bahaddudin Zakria in Multan, Lal Shahbaz Qaladar in Sindh. Their tombs lie in small inner chambers, decorated with strands of tinsel, bright cloth and small tokens left by their followers. On special days, such as the *urs* or saint's death anniversary, shrines are mobbed with thousands of people, some of whom have traveled hundreds of miles to seek a blessing.

In my journeys across Pakistan, I have tried to visit as many Sufi shrines as possible and to understand what draws people to them. In the process I encountered much that was exotic—shrunken-headed children, whirling dervishes, a secret zoo with a full-grown male lion, and a roost full of gray doves that, if one listened closely enough, seemed to coo the name of Allah.

I also found an atmosphere of tolerance and welcome, even to a foreign woman and a non-Muslim. In many mosques, I was a self-conscious oddity that made male worshippers uncomfortable. In the shrines, I was an unremarkable visitor in a multitude of the faithful, free to seek opinions or just sit in the shade.

On a hilltop overlooking Multan, I beheld the shrine of a famous saint, surrounded by a carefree scene of picnicking families and children twirling sparklers long after dark. Up there, amid the evening breezes and the chatter of children, the threat of Islamic fanaticism seemed a distant phantasm.

In a densely crowded shrine in the Punjabi town of Pak Pathan, a uniformed policeman guided me to a grille in the wall of a dimly lit chamber, handed me a fistful of rose petals, and showed me how to push them through as an offering to the saint buried inside. Nearby

I met a boy who had come to get his father's new tractor blessed, and a smartly dressed college student who said she was praying to pass her exams.

An elderly woman rubbed warm oil on her arthritic legs. A large family had come all the way from Karachi, carrying big metal pots of rice. One of the daughters told me they had come to thank the saint for freeing their father from prison, where he had spent four years confined on a false accusation of murder.

"Our prayers were answered here, so we came to show our gratitude to the saint. Without his intervention, our father would still be in prison," the teenager, who spoke English, said with absolute conviction. A frail old man hovering nearby approached the group and held up his stained tunic like a basin. The girl smiled at him and carefully placed a scoop of steaming rice in the cloth. The ancient beggar backed away, bowing in thanks.

Many shrine visitors are poor and seem to know few facts about individual saints, yet their devotion is heartfelt and intense. For many Pakistanis, the Sufi saints appear to offer a last resort, a form of spiritual insurance, in a society where injustice is rampant and the common man can expect little relief from corrupt and politicized institutions such as the courts, the police, Parliament, or the bureaucracy.

Hundreds of Pakistanis are descendants of Sufi saints called *pirs*. They are accorded special reverence in the society, as are others, believed to be descendants of the Prophet Mohammed, who use the formal title *syed*. Some *pirs* wear the mantle modestly and take their hereditary shrine-keeping duties with a sober sense of duty. Others milk religious titles for political or economic advantage, straying from the pacific, austere Sufi way and becoming powerful politicians or corrupt officials.

The Hurs of Sindh, a Sufi clan with a hereditary leader always called Pir Pagaro, have a history fraught with violence and political vicissitude. The first Pir Pagaro was hanged in 1943 for leading an uprising against British rule. His son was a rival of Zulfiqar Ali Bhutto, and the Hurs were crushed after Bhutto came to power, then resurrected by Zia ul-Haq to gain a political foothold in Sindh and confront gangs of thieves. The current Pir Pagaro is known as a political kingmaker but spends much of his time on elite or occult hobbies such as horse racing and predicting the future.

Multan has also produced prominent politicians from the hereditary line of the Prophet, including both the current prime minister and former foreign minister of the Zardari government. There are hundreds of such *syeds* all over Pakistan, in every political party and profession. But even the hypocrites, bullies, and sybarites among them are viewed with a certain reverence and respect.

Pakistani audiences love nothing more than to spend an evening listening to languid Sufi music and verse. Often a trance seems to overcome them, and even middle-aged bureaucrats or matrons will start nodding, waving their wrists, and humming along to meandering melodies. In the contemporary music scene, the wildly successfully group Junoon has parlayed Sufism into a melodic jihad for world peace.

To most Pakistanis, Sufism is a benign cultural common denominator, a mystical bond that transcends politics, releases emotions, and simply allows people to be themselves. To Islamic extremists, however, it is direct competition and religious anathema—a form of spiritual hedonism that encourages personal indulgence, religious ecstasy and a personal relationship with God rather than militant discipline, vertical obedience to a leader, and undistracted devotion.

As a result, many Sufi leaders and shrines have come under threat or attacks from Sunni militant groups, as have Shiites, Christians, and members of Muslim minority sects. In 2008, the Taliban murdered Pir Samiullah, a Sufi leader in the Bajaur Tribal Agency who tried to champion a village uprising. After mourners buried him, the militants dug up his body and left it hanging in a village square for two days with a warning that no one should remove it—in part to prove he had no special spiritual powers and could not compete with their vision of Islam.

One old and beloved shrine is the mausoleum of Rahman Baba, on the outskirts of Peshawar. A cluster of low white buildings, painted with flowers and candles and couplets from the saint's pen, is surrounded by a wooded park. In years past, the shrine was often filled with people, including women who came to visit with their ancestors in a nearby cemetery. On Thursday evenings, there were lively cultural programs.

One night in the spring of 2009, someone crept into the unguarded sanctuary and detonated four bombs—one at each corner of a small pavilion where the saint's tomb rested—then slipped away again in the dark. No one was injured, but the warning was clear enough: another decadent saint and his so-called protective aura were no match for the true armies of God.

When I visited the shrine a few months later, it was nearly empty except for the official keeper and a couple of devotees napping by a small tiled fountain. The keeper told he had received cell phone threats in the weeks before the bombing. The callers had warned that women in particular should not continue coming to the shrine and that the popular weekly evenings of Sufi song and poetry should stop.

"I was afraid, but how could I tell the people to stop coming?" the keeper told me. He brought out a thick volume of Rahman Baba's poems, and I spent some time leafing through them. Many verses were about turning the other cheek to hostility and threats, tending one's spiritual garden, and respecting others' beliefs. "If we give in to these fanatics and let them drive us away," he said, "we are truly lost."

The fanatics struck against Sufism again in July 2010, but this time they went after a more challenging and symbolic target— a massive historic shrine that is dear to millions of Pakistanis, right in the middle of old Lahore and surrounded by a maze of police barricades. It has several long formal names, including the Darbar of Data Ganj Bakshs, the Bestower of Spritual Treasures, but Pakistanis affectionately refer to it as "Data Sahib."

The Data shrine was one of my favorite places in Pakistan. It was open twenty-four hours a day and always teemed with life, from wedding parties to weeping widows. Politicians in VIP caravans made pilgrimages there by day; pickpockets and heroin smokers gathered after dark. The alleys on either side of the immense open shrine smelled of hot oil and incense; volunteers ladled out bowls of rice and lentils to lines of people that never ended.

Once I met a man who had spent years begging on his knees at the shrine, after losing his legs in an industrial accident. He was living at a safer, more respectable place when we met at a vocational center for addicts and invalids, but I could tell he missed old Data Sahib. It was the shrine's wide welcome to respectable folk and lost souls alike, its spirited free-for-all atmosphere, that the violent purists were attacking.

IN ITS RELIGION AS well as geography, Pakistan has always been considered a South Asian country. Its center of spiritual gravity was mainstream and moderate, more a matter of cultural habit than obsession. Most men visited mosques to pray on Fridays, most people fasted during Ramadan, and everyone attended important religious and community rituals such as funeral prayers.

But there was no tradition of compulsion and no public obsession with religious conformity, let alone the kind of vigilante enforcement found in Saudi Arabia or Taliban-ruled Afghanistan. As one Pakistani columnist wrote with nostalgia, "We wore our religion lightly."

The Cold War introduced the first strains of punitive Taliban ideology into the tolerant Pakistani heartland. The Afghan conflict with the Soviet Union empowered conservative tribal militias, sent millions of refugees fleeing into northwest Pakistan, and spawned dozens of Sunni seminaries there. Many were funded by wealthy groups and individuals in Saudi Arabia and the Gulf, and they taught strict Wahhabi and Deobandi versions of Sunni Islam, imported from religious centers in Egypt and India.

In addition to sponsoring and launching Islamic mujaheddin to fight in Afghanistan and Indian Kashmir, General Zia's Islamization crusade cast a punitive pall over the nation's tolerant religious culture and affected every aspect of national life, including justice, education, politics, and social discourse. Saudi and Gulf money poured in to build Sunni mosques across the land, and the enormous ultramodern Faisal Mosque in Islamabad, a twenty-year project financed by the late Saudi king Faisal bin Abdul Aziz, opened in 1986.

The Zia era was defined by moral and religious zealotry that shifted the way Pakistanis thought as well as behaved. New school texts taught fifth-graders to make speeches about jihad. Army dress codes were changed so officers could wear Muslim garb to dinner. There were strict new laws against adultery, and public whippings of people caught drinking alcohol.

Although frightened by the harsh punishments meted out to offenders, Pakistanis, especially the young, also absorbed a new set of values and beliefs—religious dogmatism, submission to authority, and a paranoid worldview—that five successive governments since have either reinforced or preferred not to challenge.

"Zia used official coercion to promote religious orthodoxy as an instrument of policy and a basis for political legitimacy," said Hasan Askari Rizvi, a leading political scientist in Lahore. "There was an emphasis on the idea that the whole world was against us. It became an idiom, a frame of reference, a state of mind. No one questioned it or stuck their neck out. An entire generation was raised on the discourse of the state and Islam. Now, it will take another generation to change."

The largest and most successful of the conservative, Sunni-based political parties was Jamaat-e-Islami, founded in 1941, which worked within the electoral system but advocated the eventual creation of a full-fledged religious state. Its longtime leader, Qazi Hussain Ahmed, was a shrewd politician who gave fire-breathing sermons to excited followers but who also welcomed foreign visitors to his office, spoke good English, and always emphasized the importance of playing by democratic rules.

In the late 1990s, when I first started visiting Pakistan, I was impressed by Jamaat and its avuncular leader. The party was disciplined, organized, and pervasive. It operated low-cost hospitals and social programs in many cities. Its activists were often articulate, engaged middle-class professionals. Its female wing was a puzzling contradiction, full of educated women who covered themselves in black and adhered to a subservient notion of women's roles, but who worked actively to promote the party's goals.

Yet many in Pakistan's establishment continued to look down on these preachers as "barefoot mullahs" and fringe extremists who stood no chance of gaining a perch in power. Every time an election was held, candidates from Jamaat and the other national religious party, Jamiat-e-Ulema-e-Islam, won only a few seats in the provincial and national legislatures, and they appeared to present no serious challenge to the official order.

Outside the political arena, however, the religious agenda found more fertile ground. Jamaat's student wing, known as Jamiat-e-Tulaba, developed a large and aggressive presence on several major college campuses, especially Punjab University, where its activists battled with secular student groups for influence and spread conservative moral values. University officials, for the most part, did not resist. Tulaba leaders took over many campus activities and harassed male students to stop playing music or spending time with girls.

Religious enthusiasm was also spread through social movements such as the Tableeghi Jamaat, an organization of itinerant preachers who left their jobs or studies for a time, traveled on foot in groups, and slept in mosques. Another was al-Huda, a movement for female piety that drew thousands of young women. These popular organizations attracted the same kind of eager and idealistic young people who, in the West, might have joined the Peace Corps or attended summer church revival camps.

Meanwhile, the religious parties had quietly gained traction since the Zia era, in part by acting as useful political partners to establish governing coalitions, and in part by capitalizing on the rising awareness and anger within the Muslim *umma,* or community of believers, over what was portrayed as international aggression against Muslims.

In mosques across the country, Friday sermons became increasingly politicized. Instead of the usual reminders to pray and fast, clerics evoked the plight of Kashmiris and Palestinians, and denounced the West for supporting Israel and India. Soon they would be able to add the U.S. invasions of Iraq and Afghanistan to their narrative of Western aggression against the Muslim world.

Throughout the 1990s, the religious-military-political alliance grew stronger. Prime Minister Benazir Bhutto championed secular reforms, but she was not strong enough to defeat her enemies. Prime Minister Nawaz Sharif, a wealthy businessman who was a protégé of Zia and a conservative Muslim, nearly succeeded in passing a constitutional amendment in 1998 that would have replaced the state judicial system with Islamic laws and courts.

Musharraf, who detested civilian parties as incompetent and corrupt, also continued the political partnership with religious groups. Although he was a professed moderate Muslim with a liberal social agenda, and he formally banned the most violent extremist groups, Musharraf needed the mainstream religious parties for political support and formed a pact with their new alliance, the Muttahida-Majlis-e-Amal, or MMA.

In the 2002 elections, amid public unrest over the American invasion of Afghanistan, the MMA won control of the Northwest Frontier provincial assembly and a commanding number of assembly seats in Balochistan. In the northwest, the new religious leaders began banning all forms of entertainment. They harassed wedding singers and dancers, owners of popular cinemas in Peshawar that featured Indian action and romance films, and even craftsmen who carved traditional wooden instruments.

The MMA lost the next election in Northwest Frontier, but the chilling effect remained. By then the war in Afghanistan was raging again and tribal-based militants in the northwest border region were spreading Taliban ideology with armed enforcers. Their growing influence also penetrated Peshawar, the large provincial capital and a historic center of Afghan culture and entertainment.

Whenever I traveled to Peshawar during that time, it felt as if the heart of the old city had stopped beating. The cinema houses, usually filled with young men cheering Indian action heroes, were now empty. Beauty parlors locked their customers inside, and a hairdresser I interviewed was terrified of being identified. In Musicians' Alley, where craftsmen had fashioned instruments by hand for a century, I visited the last remaining carver of wooden lutes.

The trend took more subtle forms in other parts of the country, but the seeds of Talibanization fell on fertile ground there too. It was especially true in impoverished urban areas, where young men with few connections or prospects for the future now instantly learned of world events and plugged them into a scripted scenario of Muslim victimization and conflict.

The religious and nationalistic indoctrination of the Zia years was kept alive in Pakistani public schools, in part because successive governments found it a useful way to impart loyalty and patriotism. Students were generally taught by rote—whether memorizing Koranic verses or grammar rules—and both intellectual debate and analytical thinking were discouraged.

Pervez Hoodbhoy, a Pakistani physicist and political dissident in Islamabad, keeps a scanned copy of a 1995 social studies guide for public schools, which he shows when he lectures groups on the creeping "Saudi-ization" of Pakistan and the dangers of its nuclear weapons program. The guide stated that by the end of the fifth grade, all students should be able to "identify Pakistan's enemies," show "the fear of Allah," make speeches about holy war, and understand India's "evil designs" on Pakistan.

Hoodbhoy also copied a recent spelling book, probably used in a private seminary, that instructs children to recite, "A is for Allah," "H is for hejab," and "J is for jihad." The text, written after the terrorist attacks of September 2001, is illustrated with drawings of military weapons, twin office towers in flames, and a pile of what the authors viewed as offensive items—liquor bottles, satellite dishes, TV sets, musical instruments, and even kites—ready to be destroyed.

"An entire generation has been brought up on this garbage, and it has penetrated their minds," Hoodbhoy said. "We have created monsters from within."

I asked him why he thought the authorities allowed him to speak so freely. He chortled and shrugged, partly in resignation but also relishing his iconoclastic role. "In part it's because I have a public profile, but in part it's because I really don't matter very much," he said, acknowledging that many Pakistanis regard him as an obsessive crackpot. "I am like a dog trying to bite someone's ankles," he said. "I can annoy, but I can't change anything."

ON APRIL 8, 2010, Pakistan's national assembly passed a sweeping constitutional amendment that purged the name of General Zia from the national charter. The measure also reversed many of the constitutional changes that Zia, and later Musharraf, had made as military presidents to transfer various powers to themselves, the executive, or the armed forces during the two periods of military rule.

The removal of Zia's name was legally meaningless, but it was an important symbolic gesture and political achievement. It suggested that finally, across the political spectrum, Pakistan's establishment agreed on the need to renounce military quick fixes and strengthen its immature, easily abused democracy. *The News International,* suspending its customary skepticism, congratulated Parliament for wiping the charter clean of accumulated "dictatorial muck."

Yet Zia's impact on Pakistani society continue to endure. It outlasted the influence of all his successors and the violent deaths of Pakistan's two iconic secular leaders, Zulfiqar Ali Bhutto in 1979 and his daughter Benazir in 2007. Indeed, Zia's drive to Islamize Pakistani society—to equate national pride and identity with the unquestioning defense and pious practice of Islam—was experiencing a kind of revival.

Except for a small liberal elite based in a few large cities, the entire society seemed to become more religious and conservative. And even though new civilian government was dominated by the Pakistan People's Party, which had long championed social reforms and once ignited a socialistic fervor, the nation's values seemed to be turning in the opposite direction.

In public opinion polls, people gave high marks to the media and the courts, two institutions at the forefront of the struggle to build democracy, but they associated the new, secular-minded government with corruption. In contrast, they identified religiously minded politicians as having higher values, and a substantial chunk of the populace said they favored sharia law over the Western-style legal system.

Pakistanis were confused and conflicted. They feared the Taliban, but they viewed their political system as morally bankrupt and their society as under threat from Western libertinage. A majority felt that extreme, Taliban-style remedies were called for. A 2009 poll by the Pew Foundation showed that 79 percent of Pakistanis were worried about Islamic extremism, but that more than 80 percent believed women should be segregated from men in public and favored harsh punishments such as stoning for adultery and amputation of hands for theft.

Much of this heightened identification with Islam had to do with escalating tensions between the Muslim and Western worlds, especially after the 9/11 attacks and the U.S. invasion of Iraq. Even Pakistanis who were personally casual about their faith felt a new need to publicly stand up for it. People still prized visas to study or work in Europe and the United States, but a strong majority said they now felt threatened or oppressed by the West. In a 2008 survey by the U.S. Institute for Peace, 80 percent of Pakistanis said the U.S. military presence in the region was a major threat to Pakistan's "vital interests," and 86 percent agreed with the statement "The United States seeks to divide and weaken the Islamic world."

Affluent Pakistanis, many of whom had visited the West often, suddenly felt humiliated and tarred by the terrorist brush when they were taken aside for extra searches or questions upon landing at American airports. Yet some travelers also felt a new impulse to define and defend themselves as Muslims. A journalist from Karachi told me that her liberal, hard-drinking colleagues cautioned her not to drink alcohol at receptions during an upcoming visit to the United States, lest she give a bad impression.

"There is this general shift to the right, a heightened mixture of nationalist and religious feeling that one has to show one's credentials as a Muslim," she said. "A lot of middle-class Pakistanis used to be moderate or semiobservant Muslims. Now people feel it's all or nothing."

The English-language press nurtured a small stable of liberal academics, lawyers, and columnists, who regularly warned of a growing climate of hate and religious extremism. Columnist Kamila Hyat warned in 2009 that a "Talibanization of minds" was spreading across society, making Pakistanis more sensitive to religious pressure and reluctant to criticize any aspect of Islam. But their audiences were confined to the small Westernized elite, whose members were largely insulated from the anger and alienation of the struggling Muslim majority and who tended to underestimate the emotional appeal of militant Islam.

Liberal voices were also increasingly drowned out by Pakistan's burgeoning private TV channels, which often fanned the flames of the Islamic revival as they frenziedly competed for viewers. Several stations introduced twenty-four-hour religious programming and Koranic recitations. A new breed of talk show hosts gained rapid influence, and some won plaudits for exposing high-level corruption. But others pandered to the fears and prejudices of the Muslim masses. They offered conspiracy theories about terror attacks, found reasons to excuse hate crimes, promoted conservative guests, and ridiculed liberals.

The most infamous of these TV characters was Zaid Hamid, a security consultant who hosted a controversial but wildly popular show filled with satirical rants against India, Israel, and the CIA. The explosion of social media also advanced the religious cause, as Islamic groups created hundreds of websites and sent text messages to thousands of mobile phone customers. Commercial and media advertising took on a more Islamic emphasis as well, with more banks promoting interest-free lending services and more companies promoting and labelling products as "halal," or prepared according to Muslim ritual.

Pakistan had a long-established cottage industry of hawkish intellectuals, including some who were said to be on the ISI payroll. Their stock in trade had always been promoting national security issues, such as the Kashmir cause and Pakistan's nuclear program. But now they began commingling Islam and patriotism, and instead of condemning the Taliban, they framed its attacks as casualties in "America's war" against terror.

The doyenne of Pakistan's hawks, Shireen Mazari, was especially adroit at using sarcasm and sophistry to create the impression that Pakistan was being exploited and dragged into a needless conflict with Islamic militants solely to please the United States. She argued the case so well that she earned the nickname "Lady Taliban." Pakistan, she wrote in a typical column in 2010, had become little more than a "black comedy since we embraced the lethal US so-called war on terror."

To some extent, the Talibanization of Pakistani thinking was linked to the geographical migration of ethnic Pashtuns. The northwest had long been a magnet for Afghan Pashtuns fleeing conflict in their homeland. They were mostly impoverished Sunnis with conservative religious mores, and their gritty ethnic enclaves in Peshawar and Karachi became safe havens for radical Pashtun religious groups. Lahore, despite its moderate cultural history, was the home base and major recruiting ground of both Lashkar-e-Taiba and Jamaat-e-Islami.

In the secular world, important cultural figures also underwent religious transformations. A pop idol from the late 1980s, Junaid Jamshed, gave up his singing career, grew a beard, and began espousing conservative views. Several members of the national cricket team, once known for the playboy sprees of its superstar players began praying before games and preaching to their teammates. Another cricket star publicly converted from Christianity to Islam, reportedly in hopes that it would help him become national team captain.

Imran Khan, the handsome cricket champion of the 1980s who married a glamorous British woman, founded a political party in the

1990s that centered around his personality rather than any ideology. But during the Musharraf years he became increasingly religious and later began defending some aspects of the Taliban. In opinion surveys both Khan and Nawaz Sharif, another religious conservative, ranked higher than the president and other politicians on lists of popular national personalities.

On college campuses, there was a noticeable change in how students dressed and behaved. Longtime professors found themselves defending liberal views to students half their age. Many female students had adopted more fashionable clothing and gone bare-headed during the secular window of Benazir Bhutto's leadership in the 1990s. Now many came to class in tight head scarves, and some even wore face coverings with slits that revealed only their eyes.

Some of these changes were reflections of awakening religious feelings, like those that inspired young people to join the wandering Tableeghi preachers. Surveys of youthful attitudes suggested that "an affinity for religious identity is the new modernity," as Ayesha Siddiqa put it in 2010, in other words, Islam was becoming hip.

Siddiqa quoted extensively from a survey, conducted on private college campuses, that asked students about their religious and political views. The result showed that students strongly opposed terrorism but displayed a "great affinity for religious norms," a striking rejection of politics, and a generally conservative outlook. Fully 88 percent declared Islam to be their primary identity.

There was also a self-protective aspect to the more conservative feeling and look on campuses. No one wanted to confront vigilantes such as Jamiat-e-Tulaba, whose activists had become more aggressive in the new religious environment. In the spring of 2010, Tulaba shock troops beat up a dean at Punjab University who had taken action to expel some Tulaba activists, and they spread rumors that he met with female students alone in his private office. The faculty staged several protests, but Tulaba members continued to roam the campus freely, with tacit support from provincial authorities who had long cultivated relations with groups such as Jamaat-e-Islami and felt they had to appease the religious right.

A few days after the beating incident, I visited the campus for the first time in two years and was amazed to see how much power the Tulaba wielded. Several students I approached at random said they disagreed with the group's views but did not want to confront or provoke its aggressive proselytizers. That Friday, Tulaba members wearing beards and skullcaps were distributing pamphlets outside the campus mosque. When I approached a group of them with my translator, several turned and walked away. One student, a chemistry major from Multan, was silent at first when I asked about their motives and their goals. But then he changed his mind and launched into a passionate diatribe against modern society, Western values, and the corrupt secular state.

"We are good Muslims, so when on campus boys cross the limits, we have to check them," he explained earnestly. "Some of the values that come from the West do not belong in our society and we cannot allow them to be practiced on our campus."

I asked him to give some examples, which he quickly supplied. "Things like drugs, music, media, relations with girls. We are Muslims and we do not want changes in our culture to be imposed from the West," he said. "Our family system is getting destroyed because of television and media. When males and females mix, many ills can stem from it—intimacy, honor killings, elopements, even murder. Our values are being dangerously disturbed."

This argument came straight from the Taliban worldview, which essentially saw gender mingling as the root of all evil, with the added twist of opposing new technology that encouraged the evil to spread. But what about assaulting the dean and breaking his arm? I asked. What kind of moral example did that set? The chemistry major had a ready answer for that too.

"We respect our teachers, but the educational system is immoral," he said. "The curriculum has objectionable material, like one story about a sailor who fell in love with a beautiful girl. This makes students think such things are acceptable. I would never allow my sister or my daughter to sit with a boy. Why should I have to accept it on this campus?"

There were anecdotal signs that poor but pious Pakistanis felt more emboldened to correct errant Muslims of a higher class—and that rich Pakistanis were finding new religious justification to abuse those in their thrall.

A newspaper reported in 2010 that a Punjabi landlord ordered a peasant to be lashed two hundred times on charges of sodomy after obtaining a fatwa from a right-wing cleric; the victim's brother told police the charge had been fabricated because he refused to raise funds for a religious party. Writer Kamal Siddiqi reported that a friend shopping in Karachi was approached by a man with a pistol who warned her, "Next time you come in public, cover yourself from head to toe."

A university professor in Islamabad told me he had attended an annual scientific conference and was astonished when, for the first time ever, officials introduced every panel with a Koranic prayer. A writer in Lahore told me that a neighbor's small son, spotting a nude sculpture in her den, gravely informed her that the object was sinful and she should put it away. "It was the way he said it that shocked me," she recounted.

Then came the assassination of Governor Taseer in January 2011 and the stunning reaction by many Pakistanis, who celebrated the killing of the secular politician who had criticized Islamic blasphemy laws. While a handful of well-wishers gathered to lay flowers on the spot where Taseer had been gunned down, thousands of strangers thronged the gunman's home, praising him as a hero of Islam.

In the days after the shooting, some Pakistanis expressed great emotional satisfaction, as if the killer, a twenty-six-year-old policeman assigned to guard Taseer, had defended a besieged faith and rid society of a moral menace. Lawyers, policemen, and clerics joined in the chorus. Bloggers circulated snapshots of Taseer's wife and daughters in bathing suits at the beach, citing this as proof of "evil." Sherry Rehman, a liberal legislator who had sought to reform the blasphemy law, received death threats and was forced to retreat to her fortified family home in Karachi, guarded by police and privately urged by officials to leave the country.

It was a bleakly defining moment for Pakistan in its struggle for Islamic identity. A so-called moderate Muslim society was proving far more fanatical than either its political elite or Western backers had suspected, while its authorities were too intimidated to take on the religious mob.

DESPITE THE PUBLIC'S WILLINGNESS to endorse murder in defense of Islam, it seemed to be in a state of confused denial about the threat of Islamic terrorism. The overwhelming majority of Pakistanis told opinion polls that suicide bombings and mass attacks on civilians were wrong and un-Islamic, and despite all evidence to the contrary, many adamantly insisted that no fellow Muslims or Pakistanis could carry them out.

Even when Taliban leaders and others claimed responsibility for bombings in markets, schools, and bus stations, the public seemed to disbelieve it. This was in part because Pakistanis received a barrage of confusing messages from authority figures, including government officials, religious leaders, and media personalities.

When Taliban militants blew up the Marriott hotel in Islamabad in September 2008, killing sixty people, numerous commentators blamed "America's war" on terror for stirring up tribal forces along the Afghan border. When a commando squad opened fire on a Sri Lankan cricket team in Lahore in March 2009, officials suggested that Indian government agents might be behind the assault.

The policy of deliberate denial started at the top, where cabinet ministers hinted that "foreign hands" were behind suicide attacks, judges freed militant leaders for lack of evidence, and clerics blamed "America's war" in Afghanistan. The muddled message filtered down to millions of ordinary citizens who found it hard to believe their fellow Muslims and Pakistanis could be slaughtering innocent civilians. The difficulty of identifying the remains of suicide bombers made it easy to invent conspiracy theories, and a populace steeped in hatred of Pakistan's enemies found them easy to believe.

Even when the army launched major operations against the Taliban and described them as enemies of the state, nobody came out in the streets and protested against them. Fear was one reason, but lack of leadership was just as important. When demonstrations were held, they were usually sponsored by Jamaat or its affiliates, and the focus of their vituperation was always Israel, India, and the CIA. As a result, even victims and survivors of horrific attacks were perplexed about where to direct their anger and grief.

I didn't truly grasp the depth of Pakistan's collective denial until I spoke with people in Peshawar after a car bombing in a crowded bazaar that had killed some eighty people. Amid piles of rubble, I met survivors who had lost their husbands, brothers, and fathers in the blast. Several children had also died, and their bodies were buried under tiny mounds of earth. But the very cruelty of the attack seemed to reinforce people's opinion that no countryman or member of their faith could be responsible.

"I am certain the Taliban would never do this terrible thing," said Shah Zamin, thirty-five, whose cotton stall in the bombed market had caught on fire, engulfing his brother in flames while he watched, helpless to save the dying man. "It must be the foreigners, who want to give a bad name to Islam."

Later that day, in another part of the city, activists from Jamaat held what they called a "rally for peace" in a public square several miles away. They hoisted placards for TV cameras in neatly lettered English, denouncing the CIA and the U.S. security firm Blackwater for spying on Pakistanis. There was no mention of the Taliban, and no mention of the market bombing at all.

IN MANY WAYS, A war for Pakistan's soul is taking place today. It has been called a Manichaean struggle between liberal and obscurantist notions of Islam, a contest between Sufism and Salafism, an existential schizophrenia between South Asian and Middle Eastern ways. It is not only a war of violence, being waged by fanatics who bomb fashionable hotels or shrines where people come to pray for a saint to cure their cancer. There are also more subtle forces pulling the society in opposite directions. One set is pulling it forward toward a modern and internationalist era, the other back toward a traditional and ingrown world. One model is characterized by technology, analysis, and global immersion, as exemplified by Turkey or Bangladesh. The other is characterized by moral absolutism, emotion, and isolation, as exemplified by Yemen or Afghanistan under the Taliban.

In some ways this inner conflict has existed ever since Jinnah, a dapper, British-trained lawyer, founded Pakistan as a Muslim homeland in 1948. On paper it has been a democracy for sixty-three years; in fact it has never really been one. Its populace is fascinated by the lure of Western technology and freedom but more comfortable in the cocoon of tradition.

Pakistan's leaders are eager to claim a place in the modern global community but suspicious of foreign neighbors and allies alike. Its more than 170 million Muslims are proud of their religious roots but divided on the very definition of Islam. Its elite families send their children to study in the West but summon them home to marry an appropriate compatriot and fellow Muslim.

These tensions have increased as world events seemed to pit the Muslim world against the West and its allies. Whether after the latest Palestinian crisis or the terrorist attacks of 9/11, the Islamist propaganda juggernaut, quick to capitalize on religious sentiments, has consistently overshadowed the bureaucratic, caveat-laden message of Western governments.

While their opponents compose careful press releases and wait weeks to confirm facts, the jihadis go right for the gut, often using websites and electronic messages to take instant credit for attacks and broadcast their version of events first. They understand that in poor Muslim societies such as Pakistan, everything turns on emotion, and anyone who seeks influence must pander to it.

The episode that best captured the combustible mix of traditional Islamic sentiment, modern media technology, and Western misreading of the Muslim world was the great Facebook flap of 2010. This was an incendiary incident in which a single page posted on the social networking site sparked such an outpouring of emotion among

Pakistani Muslims that the state courts, scrambling to prevent violent unrest, ordered the state telecommunications agency to block Facebook from the entire country.

Several years before, a Danish newspaper had inflamed the Muslim world by publishing cartoons that showed the face of the Prophet Mohammed and caricatured Islam's most sacred and protected figure. Most Pakistanis never actually saw the cartoons, but many were upset by what they had heard, and religious parties staged protests denouncing the drawings as blasphemous.

In the new case, an artist in Seattle posted a page called "Draw Mohammed Day," inviting people to send in their own caricatures of the prophet on May 20. Later she said she had intended her contest as a spoof, but thousands of incensed Pakistanis took it as a personal insult. They launched an impassioned online protest, and demonstrators in Karachi and Lahore held up posters saying, "No to Internet Terrorism."

A group of Islamist lawyers went further, petitioning the Lahore High Court to ban the Facebook site. Within hours, a judge on the court, which had traditionally ruled in favor of religious groups, decided that the invitation page alone had "hurt the emotions of Muslims" and ordered a ten-day ban. All Internet service providers complied, and Facebook vanished from Pakistan.

Public reaction to the ban was more muddled than it had been after the original cartoon proposal. This ambivalence reflected both the tensions and the common bonds within a diverse and rapidly changing society. Pakistan in 2010 included a huge impoverished Muslim populace with increasingly religious preoccupations, a small Westernized elite with an awareness of civil rights and an addiction to the Internet, and a growing number of people who fell into both categories.

Responses poured into other, nonbanned Internet sites. Many writers praised the court decision as a victory for Islam against Western evils, expressed great love for the Prophet Mohammed, and urged that the site be blocked permanently. But some argued that the ban set a dangerous precedent and that Facebook users should have the right to decide whether postings were offensive or not.

Huma Yusuf, a commentator based in Karachi, noted with irony that just a few weeks before, she had logged onto Facebook to protest the bombings of two worship houses of the Ahmadi community. Now, she pointed out, the very same website had been banned for carrying blasphemous material.

"The attackers were fed the idea that some views, practices or people are anti-Islamic and blasphemous, and should therefore be obliterated," Yusuf wrote. "This basic idea is manifest in the sweeping ban on Facebook." Anything deemed offensive or different must simply be "snuffed out."

THERE IS ANOTHER WAY, though, to look at all of this confusion and tumult. It embraces a more complex view of Islam, and a more basic hope in human decency, than the starkly polarized scenario that pits highly motivated, obscurantist "fundos" in sandals and skullcaps against techno-savvy fashionistas who would be populating officialdom today if only Benazir had lived. Public opinion polls paint a more nuanced picture of Pakistani attitudes than a simplistic, into-the-future/back-to-the-past paradigm. Pakistan's identity crisis may be less a duel between two clashing visions of Islam than a still-evolving continuum of attitudes and choices.

In my travels across Pakistan, I met many people who saw the West as a fount of vulgarity and violence against Islam, yet who were appalled by terrorist bombings and ashamed to have their country associated with Islamic extremism. What they seemed to have in common was a quest to become better Muslims—the actual, original definition of jihad—in a society that had failed to live up to Muslim ideals.

One Friday in Lahore, I visited a small community mosque. There had just been another terrorist attack, and weekly prayer services were always useful places to gather Muslim opinion. After the prayers ended, the first few worshippers I approached immediately blamed America, India, and Israel for being behind the attack, but a thoughtful physics teacher said he believed all terrorism was wrong, "whether it comes from our land or others." A boy of nineteen told me he wanted nothing more than to "fight jihad in the name of Allah," but he also said anyone who killed another human being would "burn in hell."

The imam of the mosque, a gentle man in his fifties whose family lived in an adjoining apartment with a huge cage full of songbirds, told me he viewed Islam as a religion of peace and respect for "all God's creation," but that the violence had started when corrupt politicians became "puppets of a superpower" that sought to destroy Islam. Like many Pakistanis, he was especially incensed over the use of CIA drones to attack militant targets in the tribal areas.

Despite his ire at U.S. policies, the clergyman invited me home to have tea with his family. His two daughters were studying in their room—one for a master's degree in Arabic, the other for a master's in Islamic studies. They said they were afraid to go out because of terror attacks, but they echoed their elders' opinion that the violence would stop if the United States quit interfering in the Muslim world.

Then the conversation took an unexpected turn. The girls, both students at Punjab University, said they did not like the Jamiat-e-Tulaba students because they were too radical. They said they wanted to find jobs as teachers, but that public school administrators were biased against female applicants like them who wore full hejab, or head coverings, when they went out. "We are not so much modern or so much conservative," the older girl said. "We want our country to be in the middle."

Six months later, I found myself in the cramped, Spartan foyer of a new school in Barakaho, a gritty working-class suburb of Islamabad. Several fathers sat anxiously on adjacent couches, waiting to speak to the principal, a young bearded cleric, about enrolling their sons.

From classrooms upstairs came mingled choruses of young voices. Some were reciting the Koran in Arabic; others were practicing English grammar. Boys and girls sat in separate clusters, wearing blue uniforms and white skullcaps or head scarves. The atmosphere was orderly but not intimidating; the students seemed alert and eager.

"A clause is a part of a sentence that expresses one idea," said a solemn boy of about ten, standing at attention. The teacher nodded approvingly and wrote on the board: *Allah is great, and he created the universe.* "That sentence has two clauses," the boy declared promptly, and sat down at his desk. In another room two dozen tiny girls and boys, also wearing white kerchiefs and caps, watched a *Sesame Street*–style video of a puppet singing, "*L* is for love, *M* is for monkey, *S* is for strawberry." The children giggled, fidgeted, and tried to sing along.

The fathers in the waiting room below—a truck driver, a health care worker, and a property manager—shared a common, fervent wish. Each wanted his children, especially the sons, to have a strong Islamic education. Each felt that the state school system was grossly inadequate, and that academic study alone was not sufficient to develop a child's values and goals.

None expressed sympathy for the Taliban or Islamic militancy, but all three expressed disapproval over the secular and selfish direction of their society—and an almost desperate hope that their children could be inoculated against it. They were not wealthy men, but they were willing to pay 1,000 rupees per month in hopes that the little academy would mold their children for success in this world and the next.

"The public schools do not teach our children how to be true Muslims. The expensive private schools prepare them to be smart but not to be good citizens," complained the property manager. "Children need to learn to read and write and do math, but they also need to learn why we are here on this earth and what is our purpose from God. I want my sons to be educated and get good positions, but I want them to become pious men."

This discussion seemed to capture a vague but powerful current running through Pakistani society. It is the common man's search for a moral touchstone in a confusing and changing world, his need for a spiritual antidote to the corruption and vulgarity of public life, and his instinctive realization that the next generation will need help finding the right path between technical liberation and religious tradition.

These yearnings are not extremist, but they can be easy for extremists to distort and hijack. In a nation that is 90 percent Muslim, where memorizing the Koran is a prized feat and conservative cultural values are ingrained among millions of poor and working-class people, the search for piety can easily be twisted into a very different sort of jihad.

NOT ALL TARGETS OF Islamic terrorism in Pakistan fit into such easily explicable categories as luxury hotels, army barracks, and Sufi shrines. There is also a complicated subplot within the world of conservative Sunni Muslim establishments that pits the extreme against the not-so-extreme, the rigidly orthodox and vertical against the slightly more open and democratic, and the violent against the non-violent.

Some of this conflict has to do with personality clashes and obscure liturgical disputes, but it is essentially a form of competition for loyalty among the majority Sunni population, especially poorer and more conservative believers but also radicalized educated youth who are yearning for leadership and direction.

One of the most revealing attacks took place on October 20, 2009, during an especially intense period of terrorist activity across the nation. This time, two bombers entered the campus of Islamic International University, on the outskirts of Islamabad. One, wearing a shawl as a disguise, blew himself up in the cafeteria for women students; the other detonated in another building that housed the sharia and law departments. Six students and campus workers were killed.

At first glance, the attack made no sense. The university is a large institution, founded with Saudi money during the Zia years, that stresses both conservative Islamic underpinnings and high academic standards. It includes female students but segregates all classes and formal activities by gender. It attracts both pious young men from the radicalized Pashtun belt and middle-class achievers from the cities. The student body of 17,000 includes hundreds of foreigners from China, Africa, and elsewhere who are drawn to Pakistan as a mecca of religious and academic teaching.

But it was apparently this very mission—to combine "the essentials of the Islamic faith with the best of modern knowledge," as the university's website advertises—that the extremists found so threatening. To many Pakistanis, the university represented an innovative and promising path for young Muslims in the modern world. To the jihadis, it represented a betrayal of fundamentalist values, especially absolute female segregation, and a contamination of pure Islamic teachings.

Soon after the bombing, I attended a public speaking competition in a large auditorium on the campus. The contest was for male students, in English, and the topic was "He conquers who perseveres." There was a scattering of beards and skullcaps, but most competitors wore Western casual dress. About a dozen young men gave short speeches, and their choice of role models was extraordinarily wide-ranging.

Many spoke of their admiration for Pakistani leaders, especially Jinnah. Several mentioned Allama Iqbal, the late national poet, Mohammed Iftikhar Chaudhry, the crusading chief justice of the Supreme Court, or Dr. A. Q. Khan, the controversial nuclear physicist. "He worked day and night to make our Islamic bomb," one speaker said to applause. Another drew appreciative laughs when he mentioned the Pakistani cricket player who had recently married an Indian tennis star ("He had the Indian media against him, but he persevered and got the girl").

Others chose figures from Islamic history, including the Prophet Mohammed, the Shiite hero Imam Hussain, and the late Palestinian leader Yasir Arafat. Yet there were just as many references to Westerners and Christians who had struggled for freedom or ideas. Several speakers held up Martin Luther King Jr. as an example of courage under fire, and one quoted from his "I Have a Dream" speech. Others cited Nelson Mandela, Napoleon, and Thomas Edison ("His bulb failed, but it taught him a thousand ways a bulb cannot be made").

The most popular speech, though, was by a wisecracking student who pretended to lose his prepared notes and improvise. "You have to believe in yourself," he said. "Jinnah was terminally ill but he hid it, and kept up hope, and created Pakistan. Today we enjoy freedom and order as a result. I am no more a scholar than any of you, but I am serious," he added. "There is no genie to rub a magic lamp. You only need to say you believe in Allah and persevere."

For those two hours on the Islamic International University campus, I felt I was listening to the best and the brightest of a new generation of Pakistani Muslims, who were being taught to think as well as to follow, and from whom I wanted very much to believe the West would have little to fear.

Nine months later, another institution that symbolized the promising center of Sunni Islam was singled out for attack, and its longtime mentor was assassinated. A teenage bomber walked into the Jamia Naeemia seminary in Lahore and detonated his backpack in the office of Dr. Sarfraz Naeemi, killing them both.

Naeemi, sixty-one, had been a prominent religious scholar from the Berelvi school of Sunni Islam, which was slightly more moderate than the Deobandi and Wahhabi schools and competed with them for followers. The Berelvis, although theologically conservative, did not believe in the absolute authority of a single leader or amir, and they did not endorse violent jihad.

Naeemi was an unusually outspoken figure in the internecine struggle between violent and merely orthodox Sunni Islam. He had publicly opposed the Taliban and issued a religious fatwa against suicide bombing, saying it was contrary to Islam. He had close ties with the provincial and federal governments, and the day before his death, he had joined twenty fellow clerics in publicly endorsing the army's offensive against Taliban militants in the northwest Swat Valley.

The main Taliban spokesman took credit for the bombing that killed Naeemi, and the slaying unleashed a nationwide outpouring of grief and condemnation. But his place on the continuum of Pakistani Islam had not been simple to define.

Naeemi's opposition to the Taliban was partly a function of sectarian rivalry, and it did not stop him from being an equally outspoken critic of the United States and its allies, especially in Asia and the Middle East. The statement he had issued with the other clerics just before he died charged that the militants in Swat were acting as agents of India, Israel, and the CIA in a conspiracy to disintegrate Pakistan.

Eighteen months after Naeemi's death, when Punjab governor Salman Taseer was assassinated, the other leading clerics of the Berelvi school rushed to unite with their Deobandi competitors and jihadist adversaries in condemning Taseer as an infidel and a blasphemer, and all refused to officiate at his funeral in Lahore. Still, Naeemi's sect came closer than any other group to representing the moderate center of Sunni Islam in Pakistan at a time of defensive hyperreligiosity.

Jamia Naeemia, the mosque and seminary he had founded in the 1980s, looked and sounded a lot like the austere Taliban factories I had visited across Pakistan. The classrooms were full of barefoot boys in white robes and turbans, sitting on reed mats and rocking back and forth as they memorized the Koran. But Naeemi's son Munib, who took over as director after his father's death, was very different from the Deobandi and Wahhabi teachers who had been visibly uncomfortable in my presence and often refused requests from foreign journalists to visit their seminaries.

"My father was a modest man, but he believed strongly in his mission," the son told me. "I cannot fill his shoes; I can only try to carry on his goal to find the path of peaceful Islam in Pakistan." In the next breath, however, he launched into a passionate protest against American, Israeli, and Indian designs against Pakistan, echoing the contradictory views held by his father and many Pakistanis.

Later, when I met with several classes of students and asked their views, all condemned the Taliban, but some expressed a similar anger toward the West and a chilling wish to die for Islam. I realized, as I listened to them, that the Pakistani version of a Muslim middle ground might be impossible for Westerners to accept or trust—even though it might be the best they could hope for.

"We have no fear of martyrdom. It is an honor," said a slender boy of eighteen, who was clearly a leader in his class. "Both the Americans and the Taliban want to destroy our country. Whether we live or die defending our faith, we will be blessed."

CHAPTER 7

THE SIEGE

FOR YEARS, THE RED Mosque compound stood as a beacon of radical Islam in the heart of Pakistan's quiet and orderly capital city. Its classes drew thousands of impoverished boys and girls to learn the Koran by heart and imbibe the elixir of jihad. Its leaders gave rousing sermons every Friday, exhorting their followers to join the struggle to bring "true Islam" to Pakistan, a nation that was already more than 90 percent Muslim.

Often the crowd of worshippers overflowed the spacious carpeted inner rooms and spilled into the surrounding streets, where men and boys sat in orderly rows on the pavement, then knelt on cue and prayed as one, touching their heads to the ground.

Many worshippers came from the growing number of radical Sunni seminaries tucked in corners of the city, and every Friday hundreds of slim robed figures would stream on foot across the leafy capital, heading for the mosque. Women and girls, covered in black garments with small rectangular windows for their eyes, gathered outside a female seminary one block away, listening quietly.

Sometimes after the sermon throngs of energized male worshippers spilled out of the compound and held brief, boisterous rallies calling for holy war against Western infidels and hoisting posters of Osama bin Laden. Pakistani TV crews were allowed to film them, but if a foreign journalist tried to interview people in the crowd, a plainclothes security agent would invariably sidle up to listen and the interview would fizzle out.

The mosque was half a mile from the capital's diplomatic enclave and federal district, and just a few blocks from the unmarked head-quarters of the powerful ISI. But somehow, until the summer of 2007, no one in authority seemed to notice or worry that the Red Mosque—whose name originally referred to its brick color but later became a crusading symbol of spilled blood—was being transformed into a bastion of armed defiance against the state.

As the world later learned, the leaders of the mosque were busy all spring gathering weapons, digging tunnels, and creating a bunker-ized fort to resist government entry or attack. They were also train-ing students, especially young women living at the Jamia Hafsa seminary, to act as armed moral vigilante squads. In an especially provocative foray, one of those squads kidnapped several Chinese women from a spa and massage parlor in late June, drawing an out-raged protest from the Beijing government. When police tried to enter the seminary, they were reportedly stopped by girls armed with sticks.

The government, after months of attempting to cajole the Red Mosque leaders into stopping their objectionable activities, finally demanded that they turn over their weapons and surrender. Day after day negotiating teams came and went, deals were offered, dead-lines were postponed. Finally, with the talks going nowhere and the pressure becoming intolerable, Musharraf acted.

As the horrified nation watched on live TV, commandos attacked the compound on July 3, encountering heavy armed resistance. The battle raged intermittently for eight days, with gunfire and explo-sions echoing through the capital. Finally, in a do-or-die assault, se-curity forces quashed the last pockets of resistance as the compound went up in flames.

But the siege of the Red Mosque, far from quelling the threat of

Islamic militancy, fueled it further. The decimated compound became a symbol of Islamic martyrdom, with a bullet-riddled van deliberately left in the parking lot as a reminder of the deadly battle.
Abdul Rashid Ghazi, one of the two brothers who had run the
mosque for almost a decade, died in the siege; the other, Abdul Aziz
Ghazi, was held for two years under house arrest. But on April 15,
2009, he returned triumphantly to galvanize thousands of followers
with more fiery diatribes against "infidel" America and its official
Pakistani "slaves."

"We will continue our struggle until Islamic law is spread across
the country," vowed Aziz, who was carried on the jubilant crowd's
shoulders into the rebuilt mosque. Delivering a ringing sermon
while clad in long white robes and beard, he reminded the crowd of
his slain brother's "sacrifice" for Islam. Afterward, supporters chanted
slogans calling for a "revolution" nourished on the martyr's blood.

Instead of reinforcing the government's stature and demonstrating its will to crack down on Islamic terrorism, the standoff and
bloody siege exposed the failure of its ambitious plan to register and
reform thousands of Islamic seminaries. Instead of establishing the
"writ of the state," as President Musharraf told the nation, the assault turned these violent Islamists into sympathetic victims and the
decimated mosque into a shrine to their sacrifice.

Moreover, instead of dividing and intimidating the country's dis-
parate militant groups, the quashing of the Ghazis' revolt helped
unite and motivate a hodgepodge of groups that had been physically
scattered, ideologically distinct, devoted to individual leaders, and
divided among sectarian, anti-India, and pro-Taliban agendas.

Musharraf's strategic U-turn after the World Trade Center attacks
had already alienated pro-Taliban militias, as two attempts to assas-
sinate him in 2003 made clear. The Red Mosque debacle completed
that transformation, turning all but a handful of these groups against
the establishment that had given them birth.

By late summer, these groups had begun joining forces to launch
a sustained siege of suicide bombings and other terrorist attacks on
markets, hotels, mosques, military compounds, and other targets

across the country. From August 2007 to August 2010, more than five thousand people would be killed.

A few groups—notably Lashkar-e-Taiba in Punjab and several tribal Pashtun militias in the northwest—would continue to maintain a double posture of waging jihad in Afghanistan or India while refraining from violence at home. A few militant leaders would continue to be alternately coddled and scolded, launched and pulled back by the shadow state as it attempted to influence events in India and Afghanistan. None, however, would ever truly rejoin the fold.

The battle of the Red Mosque revealed "an ideological fault line whose reverberations are still being heard," wrote Amir Mir, a leading Pakistani journalist. The confrontation, he said, demonstrated that once-malleable militant groups were no longer willing to be "obedient tools" of a government they saw as a Western "stooge," and had now turned angrily against their handlers. Mir's book, *Talibanisation of Pakistan,* captured the phenomenon succinctly in three words. Its chapter about the Red Mosque is entitled simply "Monster Versus Creator."

IN THE BEGINNING THE monster had many heads—some created to fight Soviet troops in Afghanistan, others to harass Indian forces in Kashmir, and still others to combat Shiite influence at home. Over the years, their names and leadership shifted in a bewildering narrative of factional splits and alliances, real and fabricated dissident breakaways, geographic and ethnic divides, personal and ideological rivalries between various amirs and *maulanas,* assassinations and violent retaliations.

The history of this netherworld is complex and tortuous. One set of actors, the Pashtun tribal militants from the northwest border region who had fought the Soviets or alongside the Taliban in Afghanistan, later evolved into the Pakistani Taliban and became embroiled in a full-fledged war with the Pakistan armed forces. I explore their story in the next chapter.

This chapter focuses on the major Punjabi militant groups, some of whom turned against the state after the terror attacks of 9/11, and others of whom did so after the Red Mosque confrontation. One group, Lashkar-e-Taiba, still maintains strong ties to the state, despite its involvement in international terrorist activities including the 2008 Mumbai bombings, largely because it has remained faithful to the cause of liberating the disputed border territory of Kashmir from Indian control.

JAISH-E-MOHAMMED HAS ALWAYS BEEN one of the most violent and ruthless militant groups in Pakistan. It was formed with tacit government approval to fight Indian forces in Kashmir, but Pakistani officials were forced to crack down on the group repeatedly after it was linked to various domestic and international terrorist attacks. Their schizophrenic relationship illustrated the pitfalls of trying to manipulate charismatic and violent religious leaders who develop their own agendas and power bases.

The formation of Jaish in early 2000 was the direct outgrowth of a plane hijacking and negotiated hostage rescue in Afghanistan that led to the release of Maulana Masood Azhar, a veteran Pakistani militant and radical Sunni cleric, from prison in India. Azhar returned in triumph and was allowed to stage an exuberant armed welcoming rally at the Lahore airport. He then returned to his native town of Bahawalpur, where he built a new movement to "liberate" Indian Kashmir, reportedly with covert official support.

Within a few months, the group began staging the first-ever suicide attacks in Kashmir and then reportedly orchestrated a brazen assault on the Indian Parliament in New Delhi. The resulting international uproar led the Musharraf regime to arrest Azhar and ban his group in early 2002, but he was released by a court in Lahore that December.

Almost immediately, Azhar was implicated in the abduction and beheading of *Wall Street Journal* correspondent Daniel Pearl, but Pakistani officials refused to let international investigators question him. Musharraf banned Jaish again in 2003 after U.S. diplomatic complaints, and in retaliation the group reportedly launched the two suicide bombers who tried to kill Musharraf. Azhar claimed this was the work of a violent dissident faction, and his group splintered under conflicting pressures.

In 2007, Jaish suddenly reemerged under a new leader, Azhar's younger brother, to take up the Kashmir insurgency again. Meanwhile, another relative of Azhar's was arrested in Bahawalpur for allegedly training al Qaeda bombers in a plot to blow up British airliners, but he mysteriously escaped from police custody and vanished. Azhar continued maintaining a low profile, but as this account from a visitor to Bahawalpur in 2008 suggests, he had already transformed the town into an armed religious camp.

"The walls were filled with anti-West hate slogans" and the streets near the central mosque were full of "bearded men in white robes" chanting religious slogans, wrote Ahmed Bilal, a high-tech worker who visited his family in the summer of 2008 after several years away in the United States. He said Azhar's once-modest home had grown into a "multi-storied concrete compound housing 700 armed men," whom the police dared not touch. "This was not the Bahawalpur I knew," Bilal wrote. "I felt like a stranger in my hometown."

Azhar's name came up later in connection with the terror siege of Mumbai, after which he either was put under house arrest or went into hiding in Kashmir. Meanwhile, in a sign of the growing ties among a rogue's gallery of jihadi forces, Jaish militants were reportedly spotted by negotiators who entered the Red Mosque in July 2007, and later army officials said they had been seen fighting alongside the Pakistani Taliban in Swat. Azhar is now officially said to be either missing or living abroad.

LASHKAR-E-JHANGVI, FOUNDED IN THE 1990s as a militant Sunni sectarian group, expanded its anti-Shiite agenda to a broader anti-Western holy war after the 9/11 attacks, when the Musharraf regime joined the Western war on terror. It has since been linked to many violent terrorist attacks in Pakistan and abroad, and was a pioneer in the use of suicide bombers. Its founder was assassinated in the 1990s, and its latest leader, Akram Lahori, is in prison on terror charges.

Along with several other jihadi groups, Lashkar-e-Jhangvi was banned by the Musharraf regime in early 2002 but continued to carry out terrorist attacks. Officials blamed it for the deadly grenade and gunfire assault on a Protestant church in Islamabad in 2003, and for a series of bombings in Karachi that included the killing of eleven French engineers.

HARKAT-UL-JEHAD-UL-ISLAMI GAINED INTERNATIONAL NOTORIETY after Benazir Bhutto, in a book published after her assassination in late 2007, blamed the group and its leader, Qari Saifullah Akhtar, for orchestrating an earlier, horrendous suicide bombing in Karachi that nearly killed Bhutto and left 140 others dead.

But this group and its leader had a long militant history that stretched back to the anti-Soviet jihad in Afghanistan and segued into a close relationship with the Afghan Taliban. Akhtar also had a complicated, ambivalent relationship with Pakistani authorities that included repeated arrests and releases, and eventually his group turned violently against the military establishment.

After the fall of the Taliban, Akhtar fled to the tribal areas and then abroad. He was arrested in the United Arab Emirates and deported to Pakistan after the twin assassination attempts on Musharraf in 2003, yet he was never charged or prosecuted; instead he was kept in custody for nearly three years, then suddenly released just before Bhutto returned from long political exile.

Experts on militancy speculated that Pakistani intelligence agencies had played a catch-and-release game with Akhtar, depending on his usefulness. Eventually his group turned against the state, and it was linked to a series of terror attacks against military and police facilities in Lahore. Akhtar was arrested—and then freed again.

LASHKAR-E-TAIBA—later reincarnated as Jamaat-ud-Dawa—has always been the most officially favored and publicly active of all the jihadi militant groups. It has also been one of the most violent, and its fighters introduced the tactic of suicide attacks into the Kashmir insurgency. In recent years LET built connections with a variety of international militant organizations and broadened its attacks to major Indian cities.

Its founder and religious mentor, Professor Hafiz Saeed, a stooped and myopic man with a henna-dyed goatee, was always treated with exceptional deference by Pakistani authorities. This treatment continued long after LET was banned as a terrorist group in 2002 following the attack on India's Parliament, and even after the Mumbai siege was traced to LET handlers in Pakistan.

Whenever events heated up and Pakistan came under international pressure, Saeed would be placed under "house arrest" for a prudent period, but inevitably he would be released after weeks or months and head back to his pulpit in Lahore.

Whenever I was in Lahore on a Friday, I would huddle with my translator in an alley outside his mosque, listening to a loudspeaker and taking notes as Saeed thundered away. The building was always curtained off from the street and guarded by uniformed provincial police as well as bearded men on motorbikes, some carrying guns, who zipped around the premises and eyed me suspiciously. Women, clad in loose full-body covers and head scarves, worshipped in a separate curtained section where they could not be seen by the men.

Saeed's rambling messages ranged from primers on proper Muslim behavior to diatribes against India, Israel, America, and their puppets in Islamabad. He spoke in vague terms and never directly called for violence, presumably as part of a tacit agreement with Punjabi authorities and his intelligence handlers; in interviews he always insisted that LET no longer existed and that Jamaat-ud-Dawa was strictly a charitable and religious institution. But the aim of his diatribes was clearly to leave his followers in a state of belligerent emotion.

One Friday in April 2010, he began with a denunciation of profit-oriented economic systems as un-Islamic, then condemned the president and prime minister as superficial Muslims who slavishly followed the West. He particularly picked on Prime Minister Yousuf Gilani, who comes from a religious lineage of *syeds,* saying Gilani claimed to be a godly man but did not follow the "way of the Prophet."

Without specifically mentioning the Mumbai attack six months before, Saeed charged that every terror act attributed to Pakistanis was just an attempt to pave the way for the "nefarious designs" of the West.

"How much slavery will you accept from the West, and for how long?" he shrieked, his voice rasping as it rose. "Get out of this slavery and follow God! He will destroy all the evil forces bent on destroying Pakistan. . . . The time is very near when you will see America in hundreds of pieces, when jihad will not be equated with terror, when the prime minister sitting in Islamabad will also preach jihad. He will not be able to stray from the word of God, because it will be compulsory."

Among all the militant groups, LET had the most organized administration and the most politically agile strategy. It had a spokesman handy for press interviews and a website set up long before any other jihadi group. It operated charitable and social service projects, maintained recruiting and fund-raising offices all over the country, and changed its name when needed to preserve an air of legitimacy.

It cultivated close relations with civilian and police authorities in Punjab, where it built a vast campus for religious training in the village of Muridke near Lahore, reportedly with funds donated by a wealthy Arab businessman. Its annual convention drew thousands of followers to mass outdoor meetings, and the group directly recruited young men from poor families.

Visitors described the 200-acre campus as a religio-military academy, where students dressed alike, ate from a common pot, and underwent a rigorous schedule of martial and spiritual instruction. The group also developed the semirural area around the campus, including shops and mosques, creating a pious community where smoking and drinking were banned, taxi radios never played music, and women were rarely seen. Jamaat-ud-Dawa (JUD), wrote Amir Mir, "transformed the land between Lahore and Gujranwala cities . . . into an Islamic state."

The main source of LET's positive public image and official support was its undying hatred of India and its relentless mission to free "occupied" Kashmir, which meant sabotaging and if possible killing Indian troops. Although public opinion shifted sharply in 2009 against jihadi groups such as the Taliban, Pakistanis remained more sympathetic to LET even after international investigators found it had masterminded major terror attacks in India and Afghanistan.

This was especially true in northern Punjab, the heart of LET's religious and cultural terrain and also the longtime headquarters of Pakistan's largest and most influential religious party, Jamaat-e-Islami. The 2010 Pew survey of Pakistani opinion found that while 58 percent of respondents nationwide had unfavorable views of the Taliban and other extremist groups, they were evenly split on LET, with 34 percent expressing favorable opinions of the group and 34 percent unfavorable.

Yet unlike the original guerrilla movements in Kashmir, almost none of LET's fighters were of Kashmiri origin, and the group's agenda was always a wider, more ambitious crusade against India, which closely paralleled the army's worldview. Saeed, who founded the militia in Afghanistan in 1991, soon shifted his sights to India. When I visited the Muridke campus a decade ago, Saeed granted me a brief interview that focused almost exclusively on how his family had suffered at Indian hands during Partition, when more than thirty of his relatives were killed in the chaotic violence. The memory seemed to fuel his lifelong fanaticism.

Before the group was banned in 2002, foreign journalists were occasionally allowed to attend the annual convention, tour the campus, and meet young recruits, who were always identified by Arabic code names such as Abu Hafiz or Abu Majid. Even a decade later, I can still remember the chill that ran through me when one slender boy of about seventeen proudly described how, during a mission inside Indian Kashmir, he had planted remote-control land mines along wooded paths, hid himself until Indian soldiers approached, then pushed the button and watched them fly into the air.

LET also pioneered in the creation of fedayeen, or suicide forces, which radically changed the nature of the Kashmir conflict from a local "freedom struggle" fought by Kashmiri exiles to a hard-line, Punjabi-dominated religious jihad. As LET expanded its terror activities and drew international condemnation, it also went underground and officially ceased to exist. Although Saeed was widely regarded as the permanent godfather of LET, he insisted from 2003 onward that his only connection was with JUD, and that its only aim was to educate Muslims and help the poor.

This legal fig leaf was dutifully kept in place by the Pakistan courts, which repeatedly released Saeed from house arrest on grounds that there was no evidence to keep him detained. After the attack on Mumbai, Saeed was put under "preventive detention," while his spokesmen became impossible to reach.

But Saeed, who had denounced Pakistani democracy as an alien Western import that had no place in Islam, aggressively pursued vindication through its judicial system. In October 2009, the Lahore appeals court ordered him released him from custody. Its ruling was a masterpiece of legal hairsplitting, written in a tone of majestic righteousness. The judges noted that Saeed was "a citizen of Pakistan" and that JUD, even if listed as a terrorist organization abroad, was not banned in Pakistan; therefore the court saw no reason to detain him further.

"Notwithstanding any ramification of this matter in the context of terrorism, we cannot withhold from the petitioner what is rightfully due to him under the law," the ruling stated. "We cannot allow the concept of justice under the law to be brutalized or terrorized in the name of fighting terrorism."

By spring, Saeed and his organization had come charging out of hibernation. Suddenly young JUD activists seemed to be everywhere, wearing bushy beards and carrying banners. But instead of shouting for jihad, they were peacefully promoting safely distant foreign policy issues with mass appeal to Muslims.

In a shrewd bid for rehabilitation and respectability, JUD activists met with legislators and held rallies denouncing a proposed ban on minarets in Switzerland, a law against Muslim head scarves in France, and the publication of cartoons satirizing the Prophet Mohammed in a Danish newspaper. They also took up the issue of India's diversion of river water away from Pakistan and organized a photogenic protest of farmers on tractors.

One afternoon in 2010 I covered a JUD rally, where about a hundred men and boys in skullcaps and *salwar kameez* were milling boisterously outside the gates of the provincial assembly in Lahore, shouting slogans against the European cartoons. When I approached several of the younger demonstrators and asked if they had actually seen the cartoons, which were posted all over the Internet, they all shook their heads but said they had heard they were blasphemous. Two older men then appeared and took over the interview.

Later that day I met with Saeed's longtime spokesman, Yahya Mujahid, in the popular tearoom of a Lahore Hotel. He and other LET aides had been unavailable for months after the Mumbai attack, making no statements and not answering their cell phones. Now, with the court's blessing, they were back in business and apparently more popular than ever.

Mujahid, a mountainous man with a thick beard, was an instantly recognizable figure. As he entered the crowded café, everyone looked up and several diners nodded in salute. One waiter came over, bowed, and kissed his hand. Mujahid was in an expansive mood, and he handed me a copy of the court ruling with a triumphant grin.

"The Indians and the Americans tried their best to involve us in the Mumbai attacks, but the court said we are not terrorists, we are only a welfare organization," Mujahid said, munching on a pizza for which the waiter refused to let him pay. "We do not want to create unrest and anarchy in our country; we just want to spread God's message to the world. Thank God the people and the system are with us," he said. "Now we can be active again."

THE SIEGE OF MUMBAI began the night of November 26, when ten young men in two motorized rubber dinghies slid quietly onto an urban beach and crept up into the shadows. They were fit and ready after months of endurance training and warfare exercises in mountain camps. They were also mentally prepared to kill and die after intensive indoctrination by LET mentors who had convinced them their deadly mission was for the glory of Islam.

The young commandos carried powerful assault weapons, state-of-the-art communications equipment including computer-linked cell phones, and backpacks containing maps and dried fruit. They were dressed like college kids, in sports clothes and sneakers, with short fashionable haircuts. As dawn broke, they began moving into the city in pairs, heading for specific locations that had been scouted long in advance: the historic Taj Mahal Palace and a second luxury hotel, the fashionable Café Leopold, a hospital, a train station, a movie theater, and a center for Orthodox Jews.

Then they unleashed a systematic, two-day shooting spree through the seaside metropolis previously called Bombay—home to India's stock market, Bollywood film industry, urban beach resorts, and some of the world's biggest slums. By the time security forces regained control, nearly seventy-two hours had passed. More than 170 people were dead—including all but one attacker—and some 300 injured. It was the second deadliest terrorist incident in India's history after a 1993 bombing in the same city, also attributed to Islamic militants.

As the commando squads moved through streets and buildings, shooting anyone who tried to stop them and trapping terrified hotel guests, Mumbai became a war zone filled with police, ambulances, bodies, and screams. Ignoring the mayhem, the young men focused on the stream of live commands and pep talks coming through their earpieces. Their controllers in Pakistan, watching the conflagration on TV, exhorted the commandos to be bolder, to kill faster, and to resist being distracted by posh hotel rooms or weeping hostages. "God is waiting for you in heaven. . . . Fight bravely," one voice urged in a call intercepted by Indian officials.

Within days, Indian investigators had obtained solid evidence that the terror squad had been sent by Lashkar-e-Taiba. The lone surviving gunman, Ajmal Kasab, was a grade-school dropout from a poor family in southern Punjab. He confessed and later testified that he had been recruited by LET while trying to buy a pistol in a market in Rawalpindi, taken for months of intense physical and ideological training, and finally sent out on a ship from Karachi with his cohorts to attack Mumbai, five hundred miles down the coast.

Kasab, twenty-one, was eventually tried in an Indian court, where he retracted his confession but then pleaded guilty. He was sentenced to hang on charges of murder, conspiracy, and waging war against India. Indian officials identified the other nine gunmen by name and hometown; all were from Pakistan and all but one were from Punjab.

Officials in Islamabad reacted to the Mumbai assault as if they had been bitten by a poisonous snake. First they denied for an entire month that the attackers were Pakistani, let alone from LET. Finally they relented and arrested a group of LET members, including Zaki-ur-Rehman Lakhvi, the high-level military operations commander who had built a heroic reputation in Kashmir. They also put Hafiz Saeed back under house arrest for good measure.

But there was little hint of grief or compassion, just furious spinning and angling and contorted efforts to blame the victim. While the world looked on in horror, Pakistan seemed caught up in its own myths and conspiracy theories, so anxious to appease domestic anti-India sentiment that it could not react straightforwardly to a major human tragedy.

The full extent of LET's role did not come out until much later, through international investigations and revelations by several foreign recruits who were arrested abroad. The picture that emerged was of a sophisticated secret organization, with far greater ambition

Swept Away—Bannu Jawan, a villager from northern Sindh, lost her home, her son, and her daughter-in-law in the monsoon floods of 2010. Here she is waiting for help in a plastic tent on the outskirts of Karachi, with her orphaned grandson sleeping at her side.

Island of Mud—This farm family's possessions were hastily piled in a jumble after the monsoon floods inundated their fields and seeped into their hut near the city of Thatta. Hundreds of thousands of small farmers were wiped out by the floods.

Sea of Sugar—A boy with a scythe pauses from his labors in a stand of sugar-cane in southern Punjab. Sugar is a crucial source of energy for millions of Pakistanis and a very profitable crop for millers, whom critics accused of hoarding stocks when sugar prices skyrocketed in 2009.

Always Moving—This family of landless peasants in southern Punjab must wander permanently from town to town, with their worldly goods and animals tethered to their bullock cart, as they search for a few days' work and a temporary space to camp.

Soot-Filled Skies—A panoramic view of a brick-making valley in central Punjab, where the world is the color of clay and pack animals carry bricks back and forth all day between the dusty quarries and the ancient kilns that bake them around the clock.

Life of Clay—This brick maker squats barefoot on the floor of a quarry, molding row after row of construction bricks from raw clay and setting them out to dry. Entire families including small children work in the quarries, where they are often trapped in permanent debt to the owners.

Blur of Motion—Drivers load bricks into wooden cargo trucks that are vividly painted with nature scenes and dangle elaborate silver mudguards. Decorating these jingle trucks is a treasured national craft.

Chopping Block—A blood-spattered butcher in the Swat Valley cleaves meat on a tree stump in preparation for Eid, a time of rejoicing and feasting for Muslims. This was the first time Eid had been celebrated in Swat after the Taliban forces were driven out by the army.

Frills and Finery—These girls in Swat dressed up and ventured out for family picnics during Eid in November 2009, but the bucolic valley known as the Switzerland of Pakistan still resembled a war zone after months of fighting between army troops and militants.

Victims of Tradition—Rukshana and Amir, a couple from northern Sindh, were forced to hide in a government shelter from the wrath of their families and village elders. Rukshana defied tribal tradition and refused to marry an older man to whom she was pledged in payment for a family dispute.

Only Her Eyes—A young mother shops for bangles in an open market in the city of Rawalpindi. Some Pakistan Muslim women cover their bodies and heads with loose and modest garments when they appear in public, although others wear stylish fashions or even Western dress.

Shiite Ritual—Young Shiite Muslim men in Lahore whip themselves with chains and knives during the emotional religious rites of Moharram when Shiites commemorate the death of Imam Hussain, grandson of the Prophet Mohammed, in A.D. 680.

Law and Order—Police recruits at a training academy in Lahore, which was attacked by militant gunmen in 2009 during a spate of deadly terrorist assaults in the traditionally quiet city. Militants have attacked dozens of police, military, and intelligence facilities.

Lone Vigil—A Pakistani soldier guards a village in South Waziristan, a rugged tribal area that Taliban and other violent Islamic groups have long used as a sanctuary. This village was retaken by the army in 2009 and is now under government control.

Tribal Defender—Anwar Kamal Marwat, a wily tribal chief, politician, lawyer, and landowner, has led hundreds of his fellow tribesmen in armed posses to drive out violent Islamic militants from his semi-tribal region of north-west Punjab Province.

Bent on Revenge—Turbaned tribal elders carry Kalashnikov rifles as they discuss how to respond to a terrorist bombing that killed more than eighty people during an outdoor volleyball match in the village of Shah Hassan Khel. The village was divided between Taliban opponents and supporters.

Playing with Fire—Young boys in the Swat Valley play with toy guns during the Muslim festival of Eid. Residents returned to the valley in late 2009 after months of fierce fighting between army troops and Taliban forces, who imposed strict religious rules and killed those who resisted.

Suicidal Cause—These photographs of Taliban recruits, as well as large quantities of weapons and religious literature, were left behind after army forces recaptured a South Waziristan town where Taliban leaders had trained young men to become suicide bombers.

Fatherless Family—These three sisters were left as orphans when terrorists blew up an outdoor market in Peshawar in October 2009. More than one hundred people died in the blast, which was aimed at a warren of shops where women often took their children to shop for school.

Memorizing the Koran—Teenage students at an Islamic seminary in Lahore take a break between stints of committing the Koran to memory. The founder of the seminary, a moderate conservative Sunni scholar, was assassinated by a suicide bomber in 2010 after he publicly opposed the Taliban.

First Lessons—Village boys in Sindh, whose families fled areas flooded by the monsoon, study Islamic literature in a rudimentary refugee camp outside Karachi. The authorities provided minimal shelter and no classes or other activities, but an enterprising Islamic preacher brought copies of Koranic literature and began teaching them religious lessons in a tent.

Meditative Moment—A man reads alone in the serene setting of a Sufi shrine in northwest Pakistan. There are dozens of such shrines across the country, where all are welcome to pray, study, sing, picnic, or rest. Families seek blessings from Sufi saints who are buried there.

Feeding Souls—Pots of rice and lentil stew are prepared around the clock at the famous shrine of Data Ganj Baksh in Lahore, where tens of thousands of people visit each week and volunteers ladle out endless bowls of free food. The shrine was attacked by terrorists in 2010.

Studying Together—Young boys and girls share an English grammar class at a private Muslim seminary near Islamabad that combines academic with religious learning. Many parents say they want their children to become good Muslims, not just successful students.

Caught Up in a Cause—
These three boys were
brought by their fathers
to a mass demonstration
in Karachi, organized by
Muslim groups to show
support for Pakistan's
harsh laws against
blasphemy and for a
policeman who shot dead
a liberal provincial
governor who criticized
those laws.

Blaming America—Members of the Sunni political party Jamaat-e-Islami
demonstrate in Peshawar against U.S. military and intelligence actions in
Pakistan. The group blames the United States, India, and Israel for Pakistan's
problems and seeks a religious form of government.

Call to Prayer—Muslim men pray at an historic community mosque in northwest Pakistan. Women generally pray alone at home, but mosques serve as important social, religious, and political gathering places for men, especially on Fridays.

A Religion of Peace—A moderate Sunni cleric in Lahore, Abdul Rauf Farooqi, at home with his small son. He says he views Islam as a religion that respects "all God's creation" and has allowed his daughters to attend college, but he blames the West for trying to destroy his faith.

Subversive Saint—Abdul Sattar Edhi, who founded Pakistan's only free ambulance service, has been revered for his years of work aiding the poor but reviled for defying conservative social traditions. He is pictured in his office in Karachi, under a portrait of Pakistan's founder, Mohammed Ali Jinnah.

and reach than American officials had ever suspected, and far more closely connected to Pakistan's political and military elites than previously known. This was now a global jihad.

The attack had been planned meticulously and long in advance. One Pakistani American recruit, a globe-trotting businessman and former heroin dealer named David Coleman Headley, was arrested in Chicago and pleaded guilty to participating in the assault as an advance scout. He told investigators that LET had sent him to live in Mumbai, where he pretended to be a business consultant while he photographed the city and even made a plastic model of one of the hotels to be targeted. Lashkar had come a long way from detonating land mines on footpaths in the forests of Indian Kashmir.

BETWEEN THE FALL OF 2007 and the end of 2009, Pakistan endured an almost nonstop barrage of terrorist attacks. They included suicide bombings in village cattle markets and at volleyball games, and massive explosions that decimated luxury hotels and crowded urban bazaars. Terrorists assassinated government officials and politicians, blew up mosques and shrines, attacked foreign cricket teams and UN compounds, and assaulted the buildings or vehicles of army, navy, police, and intelligence agencies. At least once a week, a bomb exploded somewhere, taking human life.

During that two-year period, according to official Pakistani statistics, there were more than five hundred attacks. Overall, during the eight years between the beginning of 2002 and the spring of 2010, approximately 8,876 civilians and security forces were killed in terror attacks, and another 20,657 were injured.

The new wave of terrorism effectively began with the assassination of Benazir Bhutto on December 27, 2007. The former two-time prime minister had just returned home from years of exile to stage a political comeback, and she had narrowly escaped being killed at her massive homecoming rally in the streets of Karachi in October. She continued to campaign publicly, taking enormous risks to appear at rallies that drew huge, adoring crowds.

On the day of her death, she addressed a boisterous outdoor rally in a public park in Rawalpindi, then got into a sport utility vehicle with several of her closest aides and began driving out of the park. Eager to wave once more to the dissipating crowd, she poked her head through the sunroof and stood up. Two gunshots rang out, followed by a small explosion. The crowd panicked and stampeded, while Bhutto fell back into the vehicle, bleeding profusely from the head. Less than an hour later, she was pronounced dead at a hospital emergency room.

From that day on, Pakistan seemed to be under constant attack. Each week there were one or two more bombings or assaults, scattered across the country but endlessly replayed on Pakistan's competitive private TV channels, creating a psychological sense of siege. With each new attack, more blast barricades went up across urban boulevards, more policemen stopped drivers at checkpoints amid snarled traffic, and more sniffer dogs guarded the gates of government buildings.

Rising insecurity took an invisible toll on the economy as foreign investment dried up, nightspots closed for lack of customers, millions of rupees in domestic capital fled, and thousands of workers were laid off in the shaky private sector. One economic report in 2010 estimated that more than 40 billion rupees had been lost in potential investment and productivity as a result of the terrorist threat.

The Islamabad Marriott, long the capital's premier spot for society weddings and political tête-à-têtes, was decimated by a truck bomb that exploded at its front entrance one evening in September 2008, leaving more than sixty people dead and spectacular flames rising all night, silhouetted against the black sky.

The hotel reopened the following spring, and the management tried to re-create its air of casual polish. The uniformed doormen still smiled at the entrance to the marble lobby, and musicians still played the harmonium and tabla in the coffee shop, but the hotel was now an empty fortress, a fantasy encased in a massive concrete shell with narrow security slits. Room occupancy was down to

20 percent, and the tastefully refurbished eateries had few customers. At the Sakura restaurant, a dozen carp swam prettily in a shallow pool, but there were often no diners to enjoy them.

Sometimes the danger came very close. Two blocks from my house in Islamabad there was a small colony of tents set up in a grassy park. This was where a dozen paramilitary police officers slept, ate, and hung their laundry between shifts as community guards. A dirt footpath ran next to the camp, which we often used as a shortcut through the park. One night in March 2009, a teenager with a backpack stepped off the path and blew himself up, killing three policemen on the spot.

Another night, someone tossed a bomb over the garden wall of an Italian bistro where I had eaten dozens of times with friends. That evening I was out of town, but the garden was full. The bomb killed a Turkish aid worker and injured fifteen other diners, including several Americans and Chinese.

One of the worst attacks was the car bombing of the Meena Bazaar in Peshawar on the afternoon of October 29, 2009. It was a shabby but intimate warren of stalls where women often took their children shopping. Dozens of small shops sold blouses, makeup, sandals, and baby clothes. In the weeks before the attack, someone had put up posters and issued warnings to the merchants to stop using female mannequins, selling CDs, and displaying cosmetics.

The bombers left their vehicle packed with explosives right outside the market, next to a small blue-and-white-tiled mosque. The powerful blast toppled several levels of surrounding apartments and shops. At least 118 people were crushed to death, fatally engulfed by flames, or killed directly by the blast.

One of the dead was a middle-aged man whose family had owned a tea shop in the market since the 1920s. The building above collapsed on him and his brother, who survived with an injured eye and arm. Someone took me up a narrow flight of stairs to meet his widow and three daughters. Two of them were teenagers who stared like stones as I took their photograph; the youngest one buried her face in her hands. "Everything has changed now," the oldest girl said.

"Our father is gone, and our mother is so worried. Will we have to leave school? Will anyone marry us?"

But what shocked me most was neither the death of innocents nor the grief of survivors. It was not even the callous calculation of bombers who plotted to kill and maim the maximum number of people—virtually all of them Muslims—in a busy public place. It was the desperate and tortured logic that allowed the survivors to deny the reality of what had happened, and that permitted everyone in the community to distance their faith from such an inhuman act.

It was evident that the bombing was the work of Islamic fanatics, bent on forcing women out of public life and back into their homes, and on punishing a community that allowed unrelated men and women to interact with each other in public. And yet everyone I spoke to in the shell-shocked community seemed convinced that the bombing had been orchestrated by foreigners, probably Indians. There was no way, everyone explained earnestly, that a fellow Pakistani Muslim could have committed such an inhuman act.

THE MOLDING OF MINDS that leads young Pakistanis to embrace radical Islam often begins in a hushed and orderly world of strict Sunni seminaries or madrassas. They are austere but all-encompassing cocoons of faith, ritual and discipline, where stern clerics watch over cavernous rooms filled with students hunched over low lecterns on the floor. There is no sound but the murmur of voices and the swishing of robes as hundreds of bodies rock back and forth, memorizing the Koran in Arabic.

Since the 1980s, the number of madrassas across Pakistan had steadily skyrocketed, often assisted by wealthy individuals and institutions in Saudi Arabia and the United Arab Emirates that saw an opportunity to counter Shiite Iranian influence. Years after the Afghan jihad ended, many of these institutions were still churning out thousands of graduates each year, and it was not always clear what they taught inside their walled compounds. By 2002, according to government statistics, there were more than twenty thousand semi-naries in Pakistan, teaching more than 2 million students.

More than two-thirds of these religious academies, which at-tracted mostly poor students and enveloped them in a world of strict religious routine and indoctrination, were run by two factions of the Jamiat-e-Ulema-e-Islam party. Their leaders were pro-Taliban Pash-tuns whose Deobandi creed taught extreme piety, the complete seg-regation of women, an aggressive rejection of secular Western values, and a militant interpretation of the vague Islamic call to jihad, or "struggle."

The majority of madrassas were not registered with the govern-ment. Many closely guarded their privacy and resisted periodic at-tempts at official oversight. When President Musharraf announced an ambitious program to register all madrassas and reform their cur-riculums to require modern academic subjects, the initiative was so haphazard and encountered such strong resistance that officials only managed to register about five hundred seminaries. In a 2004 report, the International Crisis Group found that Musharraf's efforts to curb religious extremism and the promotion of "jihadi culture" in ma-drassas had failed badly.

Three years later, the International Crisis Group reported that ex-tremist madrassas and mosques continued to proliferate in Karachi, preaching jihad and "fueling sectarian hatred and violence." The re-port described Jamia Uloom Islamia, also known as the Binoori Town madrassa, as a "fountainhead of Deobandi militancy country-wide," noting that its leaders had helped establish both Jaish-e-Mohammed and Sipah-e-Sahaba Pakistan. While not all Deobandi seminaries directly fostered violence, the report said, they "promote an ideology that provides religious justification" for terror attacks.

Over the years I visited at least a dozen Sunni madrassas across Pakistan, but was turned away by others whose leaders were either suspicious of Western journalists, uncomfortable with foreign women, or both. Invariably, madrassa officials who did invite me in asserted they had nothing to do with the Taliban or terrorism, and that their only aim was to produce good Muslims and spread God's word.

Some of these dour and chilly seminaries were located in the same vicinity as Sufi shrines, but they seemed to be on another planet. On a hilltop in Multan, I found a group of teenage seminary students peeking through the gates of their dark, somber facility at a brightly lit shrine across the street, where families were enjoying picnics and children were exploring colorful pavilions decorated with blue and gold tinsel.

The seminary students said they were taking a break from their studies, but none were smiling or horsing around. I asked what they were studying, and the older ones said, "Holy Koran." Through my translator, I asked them for an example of one idea, one lesson, the Koran had taught them. The boys shrugged and looked at each other, not knowing what to say. "Be a good Muslim," one finally ventured. Then they all fell silent again.

In Karachi, I attempted to visit the notorious Binoori Town madrassa but ended up by mistake at a similarly named Deobandi seminary nearby, the Jamia Binooria. This was a large, yellow cement compound in a gritty industrial area, whose leaders purported to cultivate a more moderate image, allowed girls to study there in separate facilities, and were more welcoming to foreign visitors.

The director, Maulvi Naeem Mufti, proudly showed me the computer library donated to his school by the secular Karachi government, an online fatwa service to help Muslims seeking spiritual guidance, and a section of separate classrooms and dorms for girls. Eager to prove his moderate bona fides, he handed me a copy of a letter from an American diplomat vouching for his respectability. He also complained indignantly that he had been stopped and questioned at an airport during his last visit to the United States.

But as I was escorted through the complex, most students stared at me in silence, and a few hid their faces. Faculty members were reluctant to answer my questions, and I sensed they were distinctly unhappy with the boss's open-door policy. I tried to ask one teacher what kind of online advice he would give to young Muslims who asked whether suicide bombing was right or wrong, but he just grunted in annoyance and waved me away.

There was no doubt that this seminary was just as conservative, and only slightly less radical, than the more infamous one nearby, but Mufti kept pressing his case. The bespectacled, gray-bearded cleric offered to show me a controversial videotape of the other, harder-line Binoori seminary, made by a Western TV journalist, which claimed the school trained suicide bombers.

The tape showed several young boys who had been sent there by their Pakistani American parents to get an Islamic education. On tape, the boys were asked what they missed about America. One said he missed cheeseburgers and wanted to go home. Mufti sputtered with indignation that some viewers had confused the two institutions, and he said the tape had created a "wrong image" of his school.

"Everyone knows that suicide bombing is banned in Islam, that the Taliban are barbarians," Mufti said. "We do not teach Kalashnikov culture or fundamentalism. We teach modern education, and we have good relations with the Americans. People criticize us and say we are teaching American propaganda, so we are caught between both sides. The Taliban want to kill everyone, Muslims as well as infidels. If anyone here teaches their ideas, he will be fired or expelled."

I had a similar experience when I visited a smaller seminary called Jamia Mohammedia in Islamabad, a modest white building hidden in a grove of trees behind a parking lot. The school was among several seminaries in the capital that had just been raided by police looking for foreign clerics and students. The young *maulvi,* wearing a white turban with a long tail, was annoyed and agitated. He said the late-night search had disturbed the students and affronted the dignity of his institution.

"We have nothing to hide, and we have nothing to do with terrorism," he declared in an almost inaudible voice as barefoot students padded in and out of his office. "This is all baseless propaganda to please the foreigners. People come here to study and pray and receive counseling. Our aim is to produce good Muslims, to prepare leaders who can play a positive role in society in accordance with our religion."

I asked his opinion of the Taliban, and he answered sharply. "What they do is against the spirit of Islam. They wear beards but they misuse religion," he said. Then he bent over his writing desk and busied himself with some papers, signaling that the interview was over.

Even though these clerics knew exactly what I wanted to hear, I was far from convinced that they meant it. Denying to a foreign journalist that they had extremist ties was a form of political insurance, but there was very little liturgical space between the demands of the Taliban and the calls by other conservative Sunni groups for a total Islamic state.

I often got a strong feeling that these clerics were spouting rehearsed speeches, possibly dictated by some diligent handler from the shadow state. And no matter what the elders said, it was impossible to know what their obedient wards, rocking and murmuring and memorizing endless passages in Arabic, were really learning.

It was even more difficult to gain access to the female side of radical Islamic seminaries. I had often seen girls in black full-body and head coverings near the Red Mosque on Fridays, listening to the weekly sermon at a discreet distance from the all-male gathering, but when I tried to approach them they tended to murmur and shy away.

It was not until after the siege of the Red Mosque in 2007 that I realized these same timid girls were students at Jamia Hafsa, the companion seminary directed by the wife of one of the Red Mosque clerics. Girls from Jamia Hafsa had formed moral vigilante brigades and gone into the streets of the capital. Armed with wooden sticks, they hounded Chinese girls they believed to be prostitutes, and Christian nurses at a city hospital.

Most of the Jamia Hafsa girls were rescued unharmed from the siege, and afterward they were moved to separate dorms and campuses. I asked to visit them by making a formal request to Red Mosque officials, but the cleric's wife, who had a reputation for religious zeal and toughness, refused permission, saying the girls had received enough unwelcome exposure.

Whenever I had the chance, I went back to the Red Mosque on Fridays, and often I saw some of the Hafsa girls there, huddled a block away and trying to hear the sermon, most of them covered entirely in black except for those narrow eye slits. One day I saw a woman with two teenaged girls, and I went up to them to try and talk.

It was a mother with her daughters, all three of them covered from head to toe. One of the daughters spoke English, and she said both she and her sister had been there during the siege. I asked the mother, who also spoke a few words of English, why she sent them to Jamia Hafsa.

"I have little money, but I want my girls to be in a safe and proper environment," she said through her heavy veil. "I love Jamia Hafsa. I have sent all my daughters there. It is the only place I can be sure they will get the right Islamic values." She would have continued, but a plainclothes police agent strolled up and uttered a few words to her in Urdu. She nudged the girls and started to hurry away. I followed for a moment and asked the mother for her telephone number, but she shook her head and kept walking.

CHAPTER 8

THE GIRL FROM SWAT

THE ROAD WINDS UPWARD from the parched plains of north-west Pakistan, past apple orchards and eucalyptus groves and out-door cafés that serve fresh grilled fish to travelers resting on cushions. As the highway twists and climbs, the mountainsides fall steeply away, opening up breathtaking views of forested hills and rushing glacial streams below. As the slope eases and flattens into a high ver-dant plain, ancient stone Buddhist monuments, solitary and moss-covered, rise unexpectedly from ripe wheat fields. Beekeepers tend clusters of painted wooden hives and sell dripping jars of honey be-side the road.

This is the Swat Valley, a remote and bucolic region long known as the "Switzerland of Pakistan," which once attracted hardy Euro-pean trekkers and Asian tourists seeking their spiritual roots. Under British colonial rule, it was governed by a series of benign, heredi-tary royal rulers, each known as the Waali of Swat. The natives were mostly ethnic Pashtuns, conservative in culture and faith but less war-like than their brethren in the tribal badlands hugging the Af-ghan border. The more ambitious among them fled to construction jobs in the Middle East; those who stayed behind were described as dreamy and tolerant.

"There was something in the soil and the air that made us a soft people," Asad Khan, an orchard owner from Swat, told me over a leisurely picnic of fresh figs and yogurt at his rented house in Peshawar. "We grew dates and walnuts and apples. There was a system that worked, and tourists came to see the glaciers and the lakes. They felt so comfortable that some of them even married and stayed for years."

By the spring of 2009, when I met Khan, the valley was in flames and its pastoral image had been shattered by religious marauders and military mayhem. Air Force F-16s swooped low over farms and villages, dropping bomb after bomb. Taliban guerrilla fighters ambushed army convoys, attacked ferociously, and melted back into the densely forested hills. Hundreds of thousands of people were fleeing down the highway in trucks and buses, carrying beds and baby goats and cooking pots and electric fans, then crowding into makeshift camps on the sweltering plains.

The army had banned all foreign journalists from the combat zone, but we were free to wander among the displaced families who huddled anxiously in tents, sheds, and rented apartments across Northwest Frontier Province, with little to do but wait out the war. Their stories gave us a first direct glimpse of what life had been like under months of Taliban control. It was a far more ambivalent and nuanced picture than I had expected: a tale of hope and religious seduction, followed by dawning disillusionment and widening panic as a reign of punitive terror descended.

At first, people said, they had welcomed the bearded fighters who appeared in 2008. The strange men had approached local elders respectfully, urged the people to act as pious Muslims, and promised to bring full sharia law to the region, replacing the corrupt and indifferent government court system with swift and honest Islamic justice.

This agenda, however distasteful to Pakistan's urban elite and horrifying to its Western allies, had an undeniable appeal to the frustrated Muslim citizenry of this remote rural area. Swatis had felt increasingly neglected during the four decades since their region was formally annexed to the state of Pakistan. The Waali's power was reduced to an honorific title, and traditional Islamic judges had been replaced by a state court system widely criticized as slow, corrupt, and biased toward the wealthy and powerful.

Ever since, local religious leaders had been crusading to restore sharia law to Swat. The most determined was Sufi Mohammed, a white-bearded cleric who headed a group called the Tanzim Nifaz Shariat-e-Muhammadi (TNSM), or Movement of Mohammed's Sharia State. In 1994 the Sufi was imprisoned for starting an armed uprising; he was jailed again in 2002 after he led fighters into Afghanistan to confront American forces.

"People wanted justice. They wanted to go back to the old sharia system and they supported the Sufi, but that did not mean they were fundamentalists," explained Khan, who, like many affluent Swatis, fled with his family to Peshawar in the spring of 2009. "Then the conflict started in Afghanistan and the Sufi inspired people to go fight. There was an electric current in the air and things became more violent. After he went to prison, the men in black turbans came and the atmosphere changed. They made the people nervous. Girls started covering their faces."

It was hard to know what was really going on the valley, which was cut off for months from the outside world. The conflicting reports alternately bolstered arguments for appeasing and cracking down on the militants. Some fleeing residents, according to an account by Pakistani reporter Nahal Toosi, described thousands of bearded fighters, clad in flak vests, pajamas, and running shoes, "beheading and burning their way" through the valley. Other versions described them as pious preachers who promised to bring true Islamic justice to a society plagued by corruption and classism.

Half seduced and half intimidated, Swatis were gradually radicalized. Sufi Mohammed's son-in-law, a harder-line Sunni cleric known as Mullah Fazlullah, gained influence while the Sufi was in prison.

Fazlullah formed a militia of more than 2,000 black-turbaned fighters, who began patrolling towns and enforcing religious laws, while
their leader preached nightly sermons via shortwave radio, warning
the faithful against dancing, watching TV, or sending girls to school.

Many Swatis were initially inspired by Fazlullah's eloquent call to
achieve pure Islam through piety and sacrifice. Huge crowds gathered
to watch drug dealers and other criminals being punished. Families
dutifully dragged their television sets into market squares to be
burned in bonfires. Women donated their gold wedding jewelry—
a bride's only permanent possession in traditional South Asian
custom—to the cause of creating an orderly and just Islamic society.

The Taliban also appealed to issues of class and poverty, courting
support among farm laborers and other poor inhabitants, while many
landowners and members of the political and professional elite fled
to Peshawar, including lawyers who had practiced before the state
courts in Mingora that were now forcibly shut down. Most provincial and national legislators from Swat were too terrified to visit their
constituencies. More than 10,000 army troops remained stationed in
the valley, but they rarely ventured from their makeshift barracks in
schools or other buildings.

Gradually, however, the promise of an Islamic paradise gave way
to a reign of terror. By 2008, Taliban forces had gained sway over
most of Swat and began a brutal campaign to drive the state entirely
out of the region. Their goal was to establish a mini-theocracy. They
seized thieves and drunks and beat them on the spot, inspiring a
mixture of community dread and approval.

In January 2009, the turbaned Islamic enforcers killed a professional dancer named Shabana in the center of Mingora and hung her
body in a traffic circle, where no one dared touch it for days. They
dynamited schools and slaughtered policemen, mayors, and other
authority figures, jolting the populace from its religious reverie.

"When the militants first came to our village, we were happy because we all wanted sharia," said a haggard man named Hajji Abdul
Karim, who fled the fighting and made camp with his extended clan
of seventy people in an abandoned, dirt-floored stable a few miles

from the capital. But a few days after the Taliban appeared, he said, several bearded militiamen dragged a policeman from the street and tried to slit his throat. Horrified townspeople rushed to the spot, shouting angrily. The guerrillas finally left and the officer was saved, but the incident left the residents feeling stunned and betrayed.

"We all said to each other, 'What sort of people have come here? And what kind of sharia is this?'" Karim said bitterly. "Cutting off people's heads has nothing to do with Islam. We were all deceived. The people were filled with great rage, and great fear."

Later that week, I drove to one of the new refugee encampments in the Mardan District of Northwest Frontier Province, where thousands of families from Swat were huddled in plastic tents, some with a goat or cow tethered unhappily outside. Several men told similar tales of welcoming the militants, giving them the names of local criminals or even asking if they could join their movement—and then later realizing they had made a terrible mistake.

A night watchman told my translator that while making his rounds, he saw a slender young fighter, "no more than fifteen," take out a huge knife and sever the head of a white-haired elder. "I saw the blood gushing from his throat. He was squirming like a chicken," the man said. All night the headless body lay in the town square, with a paper pinned to it saying the man had been a spy for the government and that no one should move or bury his body. "No one did," the watchman said shamefacedly.

THE TALIBAN TERROR CAME from further north of Swat, in the wild and rugged tribal region that hugs the Pakistan-Afghan border. It is officially called the Federally Administered Tribal Areas, or FATA, but it has always been a political no-man's-land and a haven for criminals and refugees, inhabited by feuding Pashtun tribes that never accepted the border created by the British. Under the semiautonomous system set up during colonial rule, seven tribal "agencies" were allowed to govern their internal affairs through the tribal *jerga* system, but they remained partly under the government's thumb through powerful political "agents" assigned to each area.

For decades, Pakistan's tribal region has been among the most neglected and impoverished areas of the country. With few formal sources of employment, little outside interference, and a vast and inhospitable terrain crisscrossed with donkey and camel trails, the tribes became experts at smuggling, gun making, and other outlaw activities. During the Afghan wars of the 1980s and 1990s, streams of fighters and refugees moved back and forth across the porous border. When the Taliban regime was driven out of Kabul in late 2001, many of its leaders escaped into Pakistan and found shelter among their fellow tribal Pashtuns.

Despite the Musharraf regime's official decision to abandon the Taliban under U.S. pressure, the northwest tribal belt remained a de facto sanctuary for their Afghan leaders and fighters, Pakistani sympathizers, and foreign allies. American officials believed for years afterward that Osama bin Laden had fled across eastern Afghanistan's Tora Bora mountains into Pakistan, and until he was killed in a U.S. raid in 2011 in the Pakistani city of Abbotabad, many experts remained convinced he was still hiding somewhere in the tribal belt.

Pakistan's security establishment had few qualms about going after al Qaeda, and it was happy to comply with American requests for help in tracking down, capturing, or killing its members. The attitude of Pakistani authorities toward the Taliban and their tribal sympathizers, however, was both more tolerant and instrumental. Rather than seeing these militants as a threat, the army and intelligence agencies viewed them as a potentially useful reserve for future ventures into Afghanistan. Having nurtured the Taliban and backed their rule in Kabul, army leaders were extremely reluctant to go against tradition, law, and public opinion by sending their forces after these Islamist Pashtun fighters from both sides of the border. It would take almost eight years—from the winter of 2001 to the spring of 2009—for the army to truly change its mind.

Unseen by the world, off-limits to foreigners, avoided by the army, and rarely entered by most non-Pashtun Pakistanis, the remote tribal badlands became a hive of pro-Taliban militias. They were led by an array of scarred and bearded former mujaheddin commanders, who often fought among themselves but professed absolute loyalty to the Afghan Taliban's spiritual leader, Mullah Mohammed Omar. They almost never gave interviews and avoided being photographed for reasons of Islamic piety, but their reputations were fearsome and intimidating.

A rogue's gallery of these warlords included Jalaluddin Haqqani and his son Sirajuddin, who operated from a madrassa in North Waziristan and carried out dozens of suicide attacks in Afghanistan between 2003 and 2009; Hafiz Gul Bahadur, a Waziri tribesman and senior Taliban leader in North Waziristan, who remained loyal to the Pakistani government long after most Pashtun militants turned against it in 2007; Maulvi Nazir, an extremist cleric and Taliban leader in South Waziristan who became embroiled in violent disputes with other militant leaders; Qari Hussain Mehsud, who became notorious as a trainer of young suicide bombers; and Omar Khalid, an extreme Sunni fanatic whose forces in the Mohmand tribal agency captured a famous Sufi shrine in 2007 and turned it into a sharia court.

But the name that became synonymous with the Pakistani Taliban, along with its violent crusade to transform FATA into a parallel Islamic state, and its wider campaign of suicide bombings across Pakistan, was Baitullah Mehsud. Between 2004 and 2009, this ruthless, semiliterate fighter and religious fanatic would rise from tribal obscurity to world notoriety as Pakistan's "Public Enemy No. 1." He would be described by some as more dangerous than Osama bin Laden.

Mehsud was short and stocky, with a bushy beard and a Pashtun tribesman's pie-shaped wool hat, or *chitrali*. He had been raised with a rifle slung over his shoulder, steeped in the Pashtun code of vengeance, and seminary-schooled in the extreme Taliban interpretation of Islam. In his early twenties, he crossed into Afghanistan and worked as a Taliban religious enforcer, then fought alongside the Taliban forces until they lost Kabul in late 2001; during this time he earned a reputation for toughness, although he reportedly suffered from chronic diabetes.

Returning home, Mehsud clawed his way up the tribal pecking order and benefitted from the violent deaths of three more-senior militant commanders, one of whom was targeted and bombed by a pilotless American military plane controlled from afar. In 2004, he took command of the South Waziristan militant movement and began building a loyal army of black-turbaned, puritanically minded fighters, which ultimately grew to over 10,000 men. He also developed a reputation as a cruel and calculating leader in pursuit of his mission to create an independent Islamic emirate inside Pakistan's tribal zone.

At first, the Pakistani army was more than willing to reach a modus vivendi with the popular young commander. On February 7, 2005, Mehsud was invited to sign a truce in the old British army outpost in Sararogha, a South Waziristan village. In a ceremony that would come back to haunt them, senior army officials placed garlands around Mehsud's neck and called him a "soldier of peace." He agreed not to attack government forces, impede development projects in the FATA, or allow al Qaeda fighters into his area; in return, the army essentially agreed to leave him alone.

Even as the Taliban's predations continued, the army hesitated to attack and offered to negotiate. In May 2008, government forces pledged to withdraw from the tribal area if Mehsud would agree not to provoke them. But at a press conference in his hideout, the stocky fighter with disheveled locks told Pakistani journalists defiantly that his men would continue to wage "holy war" in Afghanistan until all Western troops had left, and would continue fighting Pakistani forces who helped the Americans.

The truce gave Mehsud a free hand to run amok across the Waziri region. His fighters killed any tribal leaders who resisted them, decimating the traditional power structure, and welcomed foreign militants into their sanctuary. Copying the Afghan Taliban, they issued strict religious edicts by shortwave radio, held sharia trials, and ordered thieves, drunks, and adulterers to be publicly stoned or flogged.

The truce collapsed by July, and Mehsud went back to killing soldiers as well.

"What is happening in South Waziristan is absolutely terrifying. They are creating their own religious empire by fear, and the traditional leadership has been wiped out," said Afrasiab Khattak, a human rights activist and Pashtun nationalist politician.

Khattak, whose political party had a secular/socialist philosophy, noted with alarm that the Talibanizing trend was also creeping into the provincial capital. Cinemas and music shops had been shut down since an alliance of Sunni-based parties won the 2002 elections in Northwest Frontier. Wedding entertainers and traditional Pashto singer-poets were threatened. "It's not only the writ of the state they are attacking, it's our traditional culture as well," he said sadly.

Over the next two years, Mehsud and his men consolidated their power, killing more tribal opponents and filling the vacuum with armed religious vigilantes. His relations with the military were tense and erratic, as armed raids into the FATA alternated with intermittent peace talks. In late 2006, tribal leaders in North Waziristan signed a pact with the government, agreeing once more to keep foreign fighters out of the region in return for significant reconstruction and development aid. By 2007, Taliban militias controlled three districts in FATA but were avoiding hostilities with the army, while Pakistani troops kept to their barracks in the border towns beyond.

Meanwhile, the Americans, impatient with Pakistan's selective pursuit of militant groups but barred from sending troops onto Pakistani soil, began launching more pilotless drones from bases in Afghanistan to target and bomb suspected militant hideouts in the tribal agencies. Between 2004 and 2007, they conducted more than a hundred missile strikes in North and South Waziristan, killing dozens of suspected militants. But the tactic, while quietly condoned by the Pakistani military, provoked growing public indignation and formal government protests as the air strikes produced repeated civilian casualties.

In the summer of 2007, the fragile bargain between the Pakistani army and the Pakistani Taliban fell apart. The deadly Red Mosque siege turned most militant groups against the state security estab-lishment that had tolerated, assisted, and used them for years.

Mehsud, vowing to avenge the slaughter of Muslim innocents, abandoned the Waziristan truce and turned against the army that had once praised him as a "soldier of peace." Fighting heated up again, as thousands of army troops moved back into Waziristan and militants blasted them with deadly ambushes. In September, Mehsud's agile guerrillas humiliated the army by overrunning a con-voy, taking some 240 troops prisoner, and decapitating three of them. The army lashed back with bombing raids and ground as-saults. In dozens of clashes, hundreds of soldiers and militants died.

That December, more than twenty militant leaders from across the FATA gathered in Peshawar. Drawn together by the Red Mosque debacle, they vowed to wage a unified jihad against the Pakistani state as well as the Western "infidel" forces in Afghanistan. They formed a new umbrella group, the Tehrik-e-Taliban Pakistan (TTP), and proclaimed Mehsud as their religious chief, or amir.

From virtually that day on, Pakistani militants unleashed a whirl-wind of terror across Pakistan, often using their newly developed art of suicide bombing. When Benazir Bhutto was assassinated in Rawalpindi on December 28, the government immediately pointed to Mehsud as the mastermind. The tribal militant chief denied hav-ing anything to do with her death, but several weeks later he taunted the army again by invading the old garrison town of Sararogha, where he had signed the famous cease-fire of 2005.

With his followers' zeal whetted by the siege of the Red Mosque and encouraged by the resurgence of Taliban fighting across the bor-der, Mehsud vowed to drive NATO forces out of Afghanistan and wage a "defensive jihad" against Pakistani troops, calling them slaves of the Bush administration. "I do pray that Allah will guide them back on the right path," he told Al Jazeera television in a rare inter-view, "but when the army soldiers come to this area to kill us, we will definitely kill them."

Now officially a wanted terrorist, Mehsud remained secluded in his Waziristan safe haven. The old Sararogha fort, once a nineteenth-century British outpost in the wild Afghan frontier, became the main TTP base for the next two years, serving as an indoctrination center for new recruits, a bomb-making workshop for terrorists, a courthouse for Islamic hearings and judgments, a venue for semi-clandestine news conferences, and a launching pad for terror attacks.

Working with their new allies among the Punjabi militant groups, the Pakistani Taliban became increasingly audacious and far-reaching. Over the next two years, there were hundreds of suicide bombings and attacks across the country, and Pakistani officials—including the new army chief, General Kayani—declared that Mehsud's forces were behind 80 to 90 percent of them.

ANWAR KAMAL MARWAT, A swaggering bantam of a man with a handlebar moustache, was just as formidable a Pashtun chief as Baitullah Mehsud. But he and the Marwats, a powerful clan that controls a large chunk of land bordering North Waziristan, were on the other side of the conflict, and they mounted one of the earliest, most aggressive, and best-organized efforts to beat back the Taliban menace.

The invisible war raging in the tribal territories was far from a straightforward contest between uniformed soldiers and turbaned guerrillas. It was also a war within and among the dozens of Pashtun tribes that inhabited the border region. All of these tribesmen had been raised on the same immutable codes of vengeance and honor, all of them were territorial and feud-prone, and many were veterans of the Afghan wars.

Although fellow Muslims and Pashtuns, many tribal leaders were furious when Taliban commanders began moving into their turf, enticing their sons to join jihad, ordering them to close girls' schools, extorting Islamic taxes, or kidnapping affluent residents for ransom. Some opposed them because of prior enmities with the Mehsuds or other allied clans; some were Shiites singled out for special persecution; others were pressured by the government into forming local anti-Taliban militias.

A handful of leaders across the FATA and in the surrounding semitribal belt decided to put up a fight. Usually this meant raising armed community posses, or *lashkars,* to chase the Taliban out of their territory, kill them, or turn them over to the security forces. But those who resisted paid a heavy price. Their districts were relentlessly attacked and their followers slaughtered.

Marwat, a wealthy politician and large landowner with a law degree as well as hereditary tribal powers, was not an easy man to scare. He kept a small but formidable arsenal in his sprawling compound in Lakki Marwat town and an entourage of fearsome tribal bodyguards, including fugitives from murder raps who owed him their lives. The grizzled chief, who spoke perfect English, relished regaling visitors with the story of how he and his *lashkar* had laid down the law to Baitullah Mehsud's men in 2008.

"We were the first to challenge them," Marwat told me during one of several long conversations. "I went up to Waziristan with 300 men for a *jerga.* The Taliban wanted to make a deal, and said they would only attack U.S. and NATO forces if we left them alone. But I drew a line with a stick and I told them, 'If you try to come into Marwat lands and do any operations, we will arrest you or kill you.' We were a united tribe, and we could raise a *lashkar* of 5,000 men anytime. For a while they behaved, and we made Lakki Marwat the safest district in the Northwest Frontier."

The short-lived peace soon disintegrated into a series of running battles between marauding Taliban and Marwat fighters, punctuated by killings, arrests, attempted kidnappings, and suicide bombings. At the same time, Marwat and other tribal elders recounted, Taliban commanders were using other methods to seduce aimless young men from poor Marwat villages, offering them money and weapons to join what they painted as a glorious crusade for sharia and "true" Islam.

The tragic events that unfolded in the remote village of Shah Hassan Khel illustrated many lessons from the Taliban conflict: the power of religion to divide a close-knit Muslim community, the aggravating effect of military pressure tactics that forced residents to

choose sides, the self-destructiveness of a young generation manipulated by zealots to betray its elders, and the deadly impact of violently retributive Pashtun tribal culture on the clash between Taliban
forces and their opponents.

In 2008, when Taliban emissaries first appeared in the village,
they seemed well-intentioned and nonthreatening. "They asked if
we wanted a true Islamic system, and they caused no problems," recalled Mushtaq Ahmad, one of a dozen village elders I met at Marwat's compound. Like the others, he had hawkish features, piercing
black eyes, and a worn Kalashnikov rifle cradled in his lap. "Then
they started asking why we had girls in school, why we allowed vac-
cinations. They started influencing some of our boys and converting
some families. We were all related by blood, but a great gulf grew
among us," he said.

In the summer of 2009, the disintegration worsened when the
army relocated all the anti-Taliban families out of Shah Hassan Khel
and bombed the homes of those who remained. When it was safe to
return, the tribal elders formed a posse and arrested a group of Taliban fighters, hoping to persuade their sympathizers to leave so that
normal village life could be restored.

But on January 10, 2010, while hundreds of villagers were gathered on a weekend afternoon to watch an outdoor volleyball match,
a man driving a Pajero sport utility vehicle charged wildly onto the
field. The vehicle exploded, hurling burned and bloodied players
and spectators across the ground.

Officials suspected the bombing was an act of Taliban retaliation
against the recent arrests, and spectators who glimpsed the driver
recognized him as a troubled local teenager who had been rejected
by his parents for joining the Taliban. More than 105 people died
that day, including two of the bomber's brothers and dozens of his
childhood friends.

The grief-stricken village was quickly blanketed with army
troops, but its elders—all veterans of the Afghan wars—began plotting their revenge. Two weeks later they gathered in Marwat's court-

yard, sipping tea but keeping their Kalashnikovs within arm's reach. It was Marwat's job as tribal chief to goad his followers to action, to keep them united and motivated against the Taliban. He could play senator and businessman in another city on another day. The mood of the meeting was cold-blooded and dry-eyed.

"Every one of us has lost a cousin or a nephew, but none of us is weeping. We are Pashtuns, and vengeance is in our blood," Ahmad declared. Marwat, who had invited me to meet the villagers, nodded approvingly, and the elder continued. "The army comes and goes, but we are here forever. These Taliban are criminals and cowards, not Muslims," he said. "Once the time of mourning is ended, we will sit and decide whether to arrest them or kill them, but we will not let the fire cool in our hearts. We will hunt down every last Talib, even if it takes a hundred years."

FOR TWO YEARS, THE government of Pakistan tried to avoid a violent confrontation in Swat. Even as tales of atrocities spilled out of the valley and the surrounding tribal region, federal and provincial officials clung to the hope that they could somehow negotiate an end to the crisis, satisfy the Swatis' demand for sharia, and co-opt the Taliban into giving up their armed crusade.

One reason for their hope was their principal interlocutor, Sufi Mohammed. Unlike his more overtly fanatical son-in-law Fazlullah, the Sufi was a disarming and avuncular figure who disguised his latest religious crusade as an innocuous "peace camp," in which he led thousands of cheering supporters through the towns of Swat, often accompanied by sympathetic Pakistani journalists and camera crews.

By 2008, there was also a new political regime in Islamabad, headed by elected civilians rather than men in uniform. General Musharraf had been forced from office, and a government dominated by the liberal Pakistan People's Party was installed. The army, smarting from years of unpopularity under military rule, was eager to rebuild public confidence and loath to send in troops to fight their countrymen. After years of ineffectual grappling with the problem of Islamic militancy, the country's new leaders were desperate for a peaceful solution.

In Northwest Frontier Province, the governing religious alliance had been badly defeated and the Awami National Party (ANP), a bastion of Pashtun politics, had won power. Despite their historically secular stance, worried ANP leaders were also anxious to make peace with the Taliban. They were physically close to Afghanistan, where Islamic insurgents were putting up a fierce opposition to NATO and American troops. They were even closer to the FATA, where armed militias had murdered numerous ANP activists.

Feeling vulnerable and cornered, the party swallowed its objections and took the lead in negotiating a deal with the Sufi. Its leaders gambled that by agreeing to install Islamic law and sharia judges, the state could pacify Swat, contain the local Taliban's ambitions, and keep the war next door from spilling into their poorly protected province. If the ANP succeeded in brokering peace, its political fortunes would skyrocket.

My old friend Afrasiab Khattak, now a senior provincial official, became a key figure in negotiating with men whose beliefs and actions he had always abhorred. Critics charged that the ANP was selling out, but Khattak's argument was simple and pragmatic. "We don't have any choice," he told me bluntly. "If we don't find a way to solve this, there will be no end to the bloodshed. Everything will be stuck, and nothing will be able to move ahead."

Pakistani society was appalled and frightened by images of terrorist explosions, shrieking survivors, and body parts scattered on the roads. Yet to most Pakistanis, the Taliban's demand to install full sharia law in Swat did not seem wrong, alien, or especially threatening. Sharia was, after all, the legal and moral framework of the Muslim faith, and many people did not realize that the Taliban version of sharia was harsh, arbitrary, and punitive. The dark days of public floggings under General Zia were a distant memory, while everyone could share stories of fresh injustices or humiliations at the hands of the country's state courts.

Sharia is the Arabic word for "pathway." It points the way to God-liness, but it is much more than a list of dos and don'ts. There are five basic duties for every Muslim: praying, fasting, giving to charity, performing the hajj pilgrimage, and waging jihad—a concept that traditionally means struggling to perfect oneself as a Muslim, but which also can mean taking up holy war against those who oppress Muslims. Beyond this, Islam through sharia offers a comprehensive guide to life. It is an all-encompassing framework of faith that lays out a clear moral vision, shields believers from the temptations and assaults of the secular world, and prescribes punishments for those who stray.

In a theocracy such as Iran or Saudi Arabia, sharia law and reli-gious judges called *qazis* are the only source of justice. Because sharia prescribes extreme physical punishments such as stoning, flogging, and amputation for crimes including theft, adultery, and drunken-ness, Western societies have come to associate it with cruel and bar-baric excess. During the five years of Taliban rule in Kabul, executions were carried out in sports stadiums and people who failed to obey edicts on beard length or head covering were beaten by religious vigilante squads, shocking the world.

In a constitutional democracy such as Pakistan, however, the sharia justice system coexists with the regular state court system, and its jurisdiction is generally limited to religious offenses such as blasphemy and sexual offenses such as adultery. Harsh physical pun-ishments based on sharia have almost never been carried out since the Islamization crusade under the Zia regime of the 1980s, although in theory they can still be applied. Also, Pakistani Muslims follow various schools of Islamic thought, including Shiism and several va-rieties of Sunni Islam with views ranging from moderate to ex-tremely strict, so no single interpretation of sharia prevails.

For years, a number of religious groups in Pakistan, including the two major Islamic-based political parties, Jamaat-e-Islami and Jamiat-e-Ulema-e-Islam, have been advocating the establishment of full-fledged sharia law. They have never gotten very far, and until recently they had not been perceived as a threat by the elite. They have also participated peacefully in electoral politics, forming coalitions with nonreligious parties and couching their aims in moderate and tolerant terms in order to broaden their appeal. Jamaat-e-Islami, the largest Sunni-based party, has worked within the political system for decades.

As a result, the Taliban proposal to bring a full system of sharia law to Swat rang few alarm bells outside the small echo chamber of Westernized intellectuals and rights activists. To the rest of the county, Swat seemed a safely remote pocket in the conservative Pashtun belt whose own leaders had been calling for a restoration of the sharia courts. Was that not a small price to pay for peace?

On February 15, the government capitulated to the Taliban's demand and agreed to the so-called Nizam-e-Adl, or Order of Justice regulation, which would establish full sharia law across the greater Swat region and replace all state courts with *qazis*. The government also agreed to gradually withdraw all military forces from the area. In return, the militants promised to turn over their heavy weapons and shut down their training camps, stop harassing barbers and music sellers, cooperate with the police, allow women to work, and cease denouncing polio vaccination, which the Taliban viewed as a stealth form of sterilization or AIDS infection designed to reduce the Muslim population.

In Peshawar, provincial leaders immediately declared the agreement a victory for the citizens of Swat. Provincial chief minister Haider Khan Hoti, a longtime leader of the secular ANP, asserted that the new Islamic courts would fill a legal "vacuum" in the region and assured journalists that the result would be "nothing" like the Afghan Taliban. "The people demanded this and they deserve it," he said.

In Swat, TV footage showed crowds of people cheering with happiness, but the inhabitants were also exhausted and desperately hoping the agreement would bring an end to months of violence and tension. Some local leaders expressed doubts, including Afzal Khan Lala, an eighty-three-year-old Pashtun nationalist, former federal minister and sometime ANP member. Lala had fought to end Swat's princely rule in the 1960s, spent three years in jail as a dissident in the 1970s, and formed breakaway parties in the cause of secular rule and ethnic autonomy. After the Taliban takeover in Swat, he survived an assassination attempt in which his driver and a servant were shot dead, but still he refused to leave his village.

"We are not sure what is going to come of this. The only thing clear is that the people of Swat want peace," Lala told me by phone from his home in Bara Drushkhela. "But if the Taliban want political supremacy with their own writ, I don't see how peace can come." He said Swatis were confused and had not been consulted by officials in Peshawar who made the deal, while Taliban vigilantes were already starting to make arrests again and occupy homes. "The people support Nizam-e-Adl, but they have suffered too much," Lala said just before the connection cut off. "Everything here is destroyed."

Less than two months later, the national assembly in Islamabad ratified the peace accord with virtually no debate. The Taliban spokesman had warned that the life of any legislator opposing it would be in danger. The ANP was pushing hard for the deal, and everyone else was anxious to put the issue to rest. President Zardari quickly signed the pact.

"The problem wasn't Nizam-e-Adl, it was who would be enforcing it," Sherry Rehman, a liberal legislator who raised questions about the Swat accord, told me several days after the vote. "How could we allow a rabble with guns to be interpreting sharia? The people in Swat were demanding speedy justice, not a culture of impunity. They wanted law and order, not girls being covered from head to toe." Rehman said some of her colleagues were afraid to object, and others were reluctant for religious reasons. "This is a direct and open challenge to our survival as a state," she insisted. "It is not about sharia, it is about the advance of terrorism, militancy, and extremism in Pakistan."

Across society, reaction to the enactment of the Swat accord was both impassioned and deeply divided. Some people congratulated Swatis on their liberation from a corrupt secular state; others accused lawmakers and generals of "surrendering to a handful of illiterate barbarians." Many Pakistanis said they supported sharia, but not in Taliban hands. Some denounced critics as shills for India or part of a foreign conspiracy against Pakistan; others dared politicians from the secular PPP to move to Swat and see how their wives and daughters fared under Taliban rule.

A few intellectuals and establishment figures warned that the government was making an enormous mistake and treading on a slippery slope to theocracy. Maleeha Lodhi, a veteran diplomat and journalist, charged that the Swat accord signaled the "retreat of Jinnah's Pakistan" and the "bankruptcy" of the ruling elite. Lodhi and others warned that appeasing the Taliban menace would set a dangerous precedent and embolden the extremists to push for even more sweeping control.

It took only a few weeks for the Taliban to prove these critics right. After agreeing to a unilateral cease-fire for ten days, the militants made new demands for a faster and broader replacement of judges. A spokesman said the Taliban's religious agenda meant they did not need to lay down their arms. There were reports of fresh killings and abuses in tribal areas, and the peace agreement began to crumble.

On April 19, the true nature of the Taliban's agenda became clear. In a speech broadcast live on most national news stations, Sufi Mohammed, the diminutive white-bearded peace broker, stood before a crowd of supporters on a grassy field in Mingora. Instead of praising the accord as expected, he bluntly denounced the constitution and the federal judiciary, vowing that no appeals to government courts would be allowed once sharia judges were installed in Swat. "The Koran says that supporting an infidel system is a great sin," the Sufi declared, adding that now "all un-Islamic laws and customs" would be abolished across the region of 1.5 million people—and, in time, beyond.

The defiant address stunned Pakistan's establishment. A flurry of efforts ensued to save the peace deal, amid recriminations that ANP leaders had capitulated to the fundamentalists. The editors of *Dawn* blamed the government for failing to put religious savages and murderers behind bars.

"It is now clear that the Taliban will not stop until they have their way," the editors wrote. They described the Taliban's goal as a nation "armed with nuclear weapons" and "jerked back to a medieval age," where men are whipped for not growing beards and women are shot for dancing. "That is where we are headed," they warned. "One is wrong if one thinks this can't happen in Pakistan."

THE NAIL IN THE coffin of the Swat accord was a blurry three-minute videotape that presented the confused and divided Muslim nation with horrifying evidence of what a Talibanized Pakistan would look like.

The tape, obtained by a human rights activist in Islamabad, showed a teenage girl being held facedown on the ground by two bearded men and writhing in agony while a third man whipped her thirty-four times with a leather cable. As she shrieked and begged for mercy, another man ordered her captors to hold her down more firmly. The girl was unidentified and covered in a burqa, but the incident was said to have taken place in Swat.

The flogging video appeared on the Internet on April 3. By the next day it had been shown on television hundreds of times, provoking a storm of national and international outrage. The prime minister characterized the incident as a shame on the nation and called for an investigation. The chief justice of the Supreme Court ordered the girl brought to his courtroom, along with provincial officials. Protests were held in major cities; newspapers were flooded with outraged letters. "This is not our Islam," protested one anguished reader. "If Jinnah were alive today, he would have been flogged by the Taliban," said another.

But the video revealed as much about the hypocrisy and cynicism of Pakistani politics—and about the murky, malleable nature of truth in a society full of spies and plots and conspiracy theories—as it did about the barbarity of the Taliban.

Because the tape came to light just as Parliament was preparing to take up the Swat accord, politicians and officials who had invested heavily in the accord's success—even leaders of the liberal ANP—either played down the significance of the incident or denounced the video as a fabrication that had been circulated in order to sabotage the deal. There were also persistent rumors that Pakistani intelligence agents had produced the tape, possibly in order to strengthen public support for the army's offensive against Taliban militants.

Even after a Taliban spokesman stated that the girl had indeed been punished—and properly so—for being in the company of an unrelated male, peace deal advocates continued to challenge the veracity, timing, and motive of the video. Some said it didn't "count" because it had taken place before the agreement. Some offered the medical opinion that it had to be a fake, because the girl could not possibly have gotten up and walked away after such a severe beating. Conservative bloggers and talk show hosts repeatedly referred to the incident as the "alleged" flogging.

Samar Minallah, a documentary filmmaker and activist in Islamabad who originally circulated the video, later said she was appalled and shaken by the accusations, and hurt by the callous reactions of people she knew. "I felt completely alone and ostracized," she told me several months later. "Friends told me I had been a fool to stick my neck out. Nobody seemed to care about the girl at all. It was as if the only thing that mattered was how this affected politics."

The real story of Chand Bibi, the girl in the video, was never told. There were reports that she had been caught having an affair, or that the Taliban had mistaken her father-in-law for a boyfriend, or that she had been punished for rejecting a Taliban suitor. But she made no public statements, and her family kept her in seclusion on grounds of Islamic modesty.

The incident did not stop Parliament from endorsing the peace deal, and in other circumstances the concerted effort to discredit or shrug off the video might have worked. Pakistanis were long accustomed to living with a brutal police culture that routinely involved beating confessions out of prisoners; a domestic spy apparatus that used slander, lies, and espionage techniques as political weapons; and a tradition of tribal codes that mandated harsh physical punishments for moral offenses such as elopement. The Taliban's behavior was not that far out of line.

But this time, the damage was cumulative. The shocking video brought back repressed memories of Zia-era horrors and crystallized people's doubts about the Taliban as their demands and ambitions kept growing. As human rights activist Asma Jehangir put it, the lash had also fallen on every woman and man in Pakistan. Once the militants snubbed the long-awaited peace deal, those who had trivialized a girl's suffering in order to appease them seemed like callous hypocrites. And once the call for a "sharia nation" had echoed from the field in Mingora to the Red Mosque in Islamabad, the threat of Talibanization seemed much closer to home.

IT WAS THIS CONFLUENCE of events—augmented by strong pressure from Washington—that finally gave the Pakistani army the institutional resolve to unleash a full-fledged war against the Taliban. For the armed forces, the road to Swat had been a long, reluctant journey, a disastrous four-year march littered with soldiers' bodies, broken truces, failed raids, and tribal tensions. Politically, it was fraught with conflicting loyalties, contradictory priorities, deep ambivalence about confronting fellow Muslims and Pakistanis in battle, and equally strong reluctance to embark on any military mission that did not have significant public support.

Despite its size, firepower, and influence on Pakistan's affairs, the army in 2009 was beginning to look like a paper tiger. It was smarting from its recent association with the unpopular Musharraf presidency, an era marked by ineffectual military rule, multiple political blunders, grudging obeisance to Washington, and a vacillating policy toward the growing extremist menace.

By spring of that year, however, Pakistan's political scenario had changed. Musharraf and the onus of military rule were gone, Bhutto's widower was the elected civilian president, and a new general with a reputation as a tough professional soldier was in charge of the army. The security forces were being outclassed by a few thousand tribal fighters, and public opinion was finally beginning to turn against the Taliban.

Pressure from Washington for Pakistan to take decisive action also intensified, especially after the Taliban expanded their grip from Swat into the neighboring district of Buner, which bordered on Punjab Province and was only 60 miles from the capital. The fighters had occupied government buildings, looted international aid vehicles, and turned a famous Sufi shrine into a command post. With public opinion turning against the Taliban, the shocking video of the girl being flogged gave General Kayani all the cover he needed.

On April 26, the security forces launched a massive offensive, code-named Black Thunderstorm, to clear insurgents from Swat and three adjacent districts in the Malakand region. This time there was a full-fledged assault by conventional forces. More than 30,000 infantry troops, Frontier Corps, and special commandos were deployed on the ground, while helicopter gunships strafed insurgent hideouts and F-16 planes rained bombs on village after village. Taliban fighters came down from the hills to attack security checkpoints and reportedly shot at government troops from inside a web of emerald mines.

The offensive began in Lower Dir and moved to Buner, where security forces attacked with both airpower and stealth. Military spokesmen in Islamabad reported that army commandos had swarmed down ropes to drop behind Taliban lines, and villagers in one insurgent-infested community described warplanes bombing house after house. The army never released civilian casualty figures, saying the number was unknown, but villagers in Buner reported by telephone that numerous people were injured by artillery fire and had no way to get to a hospital.

Tens of thousands of civilians had already fled the area in trucks, buses, tractors, and on foot, streaming down the Swat highway toward the plains of Mardan and other communities where tent encampments were set up. Military curfews were imposed and roads were sealed, trapping many people overnight at highway roadblocks. In all, more than 3.4 million people were temporarily displaced—

the largest human exodus since Partition—and hundreds of buildings were bombed, shelled, or destroyed by heavy crossfire.

By May 5, the security forces had entered the Swat Valley and begun a new phase of their operation, called Rah-i-Rast. Despite the overwhelming superiority of government numbers and firepower, the insurgents had the advantage of high mobility and motivation, and the fighting lasted more than a month. In Mingora, the Taliban prepared for a bloody urban battle, laying mines and digging trenches. The military, in turn, vowed to besiege the area and crush the Taliban "even if the fighting resembles that of the Battle of Stalingrad," declared the military spokesman, Lieutenant General Athar Abbas.

On May 23, state forces entered Mingora and commandos fought insurgents in close combat through the streets and shops of the abandoned city. The next day, the army captured Green Square, the notorious traffic circle where Taliban vigilantes had hung their victims. Then they took back the airport, the technical college, and the suburbs.

By mid-June the entire valley had been cleared of insurgents, but at a high human cost. Official figures tallied more than 150 Pakistani forces killed and more than 300 wounded, with more than 2,400 Taliban fighters dead. None of the top Taliban leaders had been killed or captured, and many insurgents had melted away into the hills and forests to the north. But the battle of Swat was over.

Three months later, a friend and I drove up the meandering highway, past the autumn fields and orchards and streams, into the heart of Swat. It was Eid, the three-day festival after Ramadan, the month of fasting, and Swatis had come out to celebrate for the first time in three years. Little girls in pastel dresses were playing on swings, vendors were selling ice cream, and families were chatting in parks.

But although the army had declared it safe for the inhabitants to return home, Swat still resembled a war zone. Makeshift roadblocks of tree trunks and metal bed frames remained in place. We passed dozens of buildings flattened to rubble, including houses shelled by the military and schools destroyed by the Taliban. The military curfew had been lifted for Eid, but people said they were still fearful to be out after dark, lest the insurgents return.

Opinions about the Taliban were mixed. Some villagers said they had cleaned up communities by punishing drunks and thieves; others complained that their daughters had been forced to stay home from school and their wives could not shop. Some had been waiting many weeks for promised government help to repair their damaged homes; several said their sons had been arrested by mistake and never reappeared.

"It doesn't really feel like Eid, because we cannot forget so soon," said Sadiq Khan, who was selling grapes and apples in the town of Batkhela. He and his family had spent the summer in a sweltering tent in Mardan, and one of his female relatives had given birth beside the highway as they fled the fighting. "There is too much shame and sorrow for us to celebrate," he said. "And they are still finding bodies in the river."

HOPING TO BUILD ON its victory in Swat, the army turned to South Waziristan, the stronghold of Baitullah Mehsud. Months before, authorities in Peshawar had endorsed the Swat accord as a victory for justice. Now the governor of Northwest Frontier gave the army full cover, calling Mehsud "the root cause of all evils" and announcing that the federal government had called on the armed forces to launch a "full-fledged" operation to wipe out his forces.

The battle for South Waziristan was a much tougher fight for the army than Swat. Now, they were facing a much larger guerrilla force that moved easily in a vast, 2,000-square-mile area of parched villages and jagged hills. Many of Mehsud's fighters were veterans of the Afghan jihad, highly trained and seized with religious fervor. The area was so isolated that it was almost impossible to verify official battle accounts or casualty figures. The fighting continued on and off for months, while American drone strikes pounded the border area.

Then, sometime in August, a drone missile killed Baitullah

Mehsud. His death was initially denied by the Taliban and remained unconfirmed for several weeks, until his associates called the BBC to say he had died of injuries from the initial strike. Mehsud, who had recently married a second wife, was reportedly visiting her and his in-laws in the Orakzai tribal area when the CIA's aerial tracking system homed in on his location. No one predicted the Taliban would collapse, but his death threw the insurgents into temporary disarray, briefly muted Pakistani opposition to the drone attacks, and gave the government the first significant kill in the domestic war on terror.

In November, the army destroyed what remained of Mehsud's headquarters in Sararogha, coming full circle from the ceremony there four and a half years earlier, when military officials had lauded the tribal terrorist as a man of peace. One morning shortly after that, military officials flew a group of journalists there for a glimpse of what life had been like in the nerve center of the Pakistani Taliban emirate.

From the portholes of an old Russian military helicopter, the terrain looked windswept and desolate. Sararogha was a ghost town, with half its rooftops collapsed from bombing raids. We landed next to a dirt field, where expressionless crew-cut soldiers had laid out a picnic of hot, crunchy *pakoras* and tea. Neatly arranged nearby was an impressive arsenal of confiscated rifles, machine guns, and stacks of ammunition.

Other items, some far more revealing, were jumbled in piles or stuffed in cobwebbed corners of the vacant compound. There were hundreds of disassembled cell phones, scavenged to build remote-control bombs. There were chemistry texts and military engineering manuals, typed in English and Arabic, with margin notes in Pakistani Urdu.

Inside an abandoned classroom, we found videotapes whose covers depicted young holy warriors on glorious missions, and many clues to the existence of a parallel Islamic state. There were tablets of stationery with embossed headings in Pashto script that read "The Central Office of the South Waziristan District of the Islamic Emirate of

Pakistan." There were printed decrees ordering that families could not be forced to pay exorbitant wedding dowries, and handwritten orders by religious judges referring to cases by number.

"This place was a fountainhead of terrorism," Major General Abbas declared as he stood on the roof of a mosque that overlooked the rubble of a market, a school, and the old military fort, all destroyed during five days of fighting. "The Taliban leaders even had press conferences here."

Below, unfinished wooden coffins and damaged copies of the Koran had been collected in an unsettling display. Finally, there were the ghosts of the Taliban fighters themselves: boxes full of scuffed snapshots showing young men with guns roughhousing or posing in formation like boot camp recruits, and several dozen Pakistani identity cards, each with a name and a number and a face staring grimly into the camera.

I looked at those faces for a long time, wondering what had led these men to join the Taliban and take up arms against the government of their Muslim homeland. Perhaps they had been convinced they were creating a purified Islamic society and would automatically go to paradise if they died. Perhaps the slow grind of poverty had goaded them to powerful rage against a corrupt, indifferent state. Perhaps they had been enticed by money and weapons that offered a brief thrill of power. Or perhaps they were merely superfluous, vulnerable souls with little to live for and nothing to lose.

The army was so pleased with its performance in Swat and South Waziristan that it did more than show a few journalists and camera crews around a ruined guerrilla camp in the tribal wasteland. It also invited us into the army's general headquarters, the nerve center of the Pakistani armed forces in Rawalpindi, for a rare meeting with the notoriously taciturn and press-averse army chief.

The general's presentation was a blow-by-blow account of the military war against Islamic militancy, set within a broad overview of the army's strategic concerns. Kayani spoke in fluent, husky English, illustrating his points with slides full of statistics. There were detailed descriptions of the Swat and Waziristan operations, lists of troop deployments and casualties (2,273 Pakistani forces killed and 6,512 injured in two years), and dramatic photos of soldiers making high-altitude helicopter drops onto steep snowy hillsides.

"The myth had to be broken," Kayani said, referring to the general perception that Pakistan's conventional army, trained to fight Indian troops, could not defeat guerrillas on their own rugged turf. The militants were "strongly prepared to defend themselves, but we changed tactics, we took the ridgeline approach, and we unhinged them," he declared with a brief grimace of triumph.

For well over an hour, the general spoke with unhurried confidence, dragging on his cigarette holder. It was a smooth and persuasive performance, aimed at winning over foreign skeptics and making clear that the army was acting in the best interests of Pakistan.

It was also clear, though, that Kayani felt the army's greatest achievement had not been on the battlefield. When he gave a list of his strategic concerns, high on his list were "fragile public opinion" and the "shallow political consensus" for military action. "How many numbers you kill or capture, how much area you control—all that is meaningless without public support," he said.

CHAPTER 9

JUSTICE

JUST OFF A FAST boulevard in Rawalpindi, beyond a narrow gate with a metal detector, lies a warren of alleys and cubicles and tin-roofed sheds. There is a purposeful hum of activity, a milling of shabby and official traffic, a murmured drama playing out in every corner. Scribes peck out petitions on old metal typewriters, police lead prisoners chained together by the wrist, clerks scurry about with frayed files, and black-suited lawyers confer with bewildered villagers in turbans and sandals. Shoeshine boys dart among the crowd, and tired women wait outside an iron door with baskets of food for their detained husbands and sons.

Hidden at the heart of this shabby legal bazaar is a block of hearing rooms with peeling paint, sagging benches, and languid ceiling fans. Inside, judges listen to mumblings from nervous petitioners, interrupting every few moments to translate their words into English. Dozens of relatives, witnesses, and neighbors wait outside the doors, gossiping, and arguing about the case in hushed, urgent tones. Almost always the case is continued for another hearing. Often it may not be resolved for years.

This is the Dickensian world of Pakistan's district courts, which

deal with the range of human conflict and crime—from cattle rus-
tling to wife-beating to murder. The issues are intimate rather than
earth-shattering, petty rather than precedent-setting. But there is no
better place to learn how the legal system works in Pakistan: how
little truth and facts matter, how money and influence decide who is
accused or set free, how political pressure is brought to bear on the
smallest dispute, how entire families can be dragged into a case for
years and plunged into debt for life, and how everyone becomes complicit in a warped and broken system.

After even a brief foray into this world, listening at random to
cases and complaints, chatting with lawyers, clerks, plaintiffs, and
defendants, it becomes painfully clear why so many Pakistanis say
there is no justice in their country. It also becomes clear why the
pledge by the Taliban and other Islamic extremists to install full
sharia law has such powerful appeal, and why when Pakistanis are
asked to list the causes of terrorist attacks in their country, the one
they mention most often is "injustice."

"Here justice is a business, just like any other. It is bought and
sold. You have to pay something to get a paper filed, a court date set.
The clerks will lose documents until your client delivers them something. The police and the lawyers and the judges have relations and
collaborate. The judges are overburdened and the delays are terrible.
A simple criminal case can take ten years to complete. People's whole
lives are ruined, even if they have done nothing. But if their family
has political connections, a single phone call can get the case thrown
out. I am an honest man, but in this system you cannot survive honestly; even I cannot. So we all become part of the problem."

That comment was made to me by a veteran attorney and law
professor in his fifties, a man who had spent his entire career in Pakistan's legal world. It was a sad and cynical indictment of his own
profession and milieu, both a protest against an unfair system and a
confession of participation in it. Jurists in a country such as Pakistan
face a particular burden: that of knowing what is right and wrong, of
having vowed to uphold the law, and of realizing that everything
around them conspires against it.

Listening to stories in and around the district courts in Rawal-pindi, Islamabad, Peshawar, and Lahore reveals how malleable and irrelevant the truth seems to be, and how casually people hurl false legal charges at each other from pure malice.

To be involved in a case—to have charges filed against you or a near relative—can turn into a nightmare that lasts for years and wipes out a family financially. Police routinely charge a defendant's brothers, cousins, and other relatives, using them as human collateral to speed the case along and expand the opportunity for bribes. A hotel worker I knew spent months in prison because his brother had run away with a young woman; her family filed kidnapping charges against the brother and police detained half a dozen of his relatives when they could not locate him. During my friend's months in jail, he lost first his job and then his house, because he could no longer pay the mortgage.

Becoming party to a legal case, even as a witness, can be crush-ingly expensive. Every time a hearing is postponed or continued, it means another long bus trip for half a dozen family members from village to city and back. Lawyers' fees are low by Western standards but higher than most Pakistanis can afford, and bribes can double the cost. People sell their livestock, crop shares, and wedding jew-elry to meet the expenses. If a defendant has no powerful patron to support him, he may have to borrow thousands of dollars to bribe his way out of jail.

Issues of class, clan, and political alliance are intimately bound up in the legal process. A fellow journalist told me his servant's sister, a street sweeper, was knocked down by a public bus, breaking her leg. Because she had no one of consequence to speak for her, the police refused to register her complaint unless she paid a huge bribe worth six months' pay. On the other hand, I was told by people throughout the system, if an accused criminal came from an influential family or tribe, he could count on local, provincial, or even national politicians to intercede—often resulting in police reports being changed, evi-dence lost, and cases dismissed.

"The ordinary perception in Pakistan is that our criminal justice system is a rotting monstrosity that needs immediate overhaul and correction if the promised contract between state and citizen is to have any meaning," wrote Babar Sattar, a lawyer and legal analyst. His comments were prompted by allegations that a judge in Lahore had offered to protect a fugitive murderer in exchange for lavish gifts and entertainment. The public belief that Pakistan's "power elites" are above the law, Sattar added, "breeds contempt amongst ordinary citizens" who are forced to seek "personal patronage" from those elites to gain access to justice. "This state of affairs where men rule, and not law, must change."

AN OLD MAN IN a turban, leaning on a cane, was explaining something to a patient clerk behind his typewriter. It was the story of a property case going back to Partition, when the Hindu farmers had fled and his ancestral land was given to some new Muslim settlers. They sold it to another owner, who allowed the old man and his family to live there, but they he had been trying in vain to regain title through the courts for years. In the meantime, the real estate market boomed and the little parcel near a major city suddenly became very valuable, so the title fight heated up.

"We already got one court ruling in our favor, but our rival is still pressing. He knows people, he has influence, he is a front for the land mafia," the old man said, thumping his cane and waving an old handwritten court petition. The clerk listened politely, but he had stopped typing. "We are just farmers trying to protect our ancestral lands, but he is greedy and he has important politicians on his side. Now we are afraid we may lose the land again."

In a cramped cubicle, a young man named Akbar Khan was talking to a lawyer. His younger brother had been accused of robbery and put in jail. Khan, a butcher from Mansehra, said the charge was fabricated by his brother's boss after they had an argument, and the boss persuaded one of his relatives to file a false case. The lawyer said such things happen all the time—criminal charges are made up out of whole cloth from personal spite.

"There is no law in this country. A person with money can do whatever he wants, and a poor man ends up in prison," the butcher said bitterly. "My brother did nothing wrong, and we finally persuaded the relative to withdraw his charge, but the case is still dragging on. We had to spend 40,000 rupees on the lawyer and the courts, I had to take the bus all the way here twenty times, and my brother is still sitting in jail."

Around the corner, in another cubicle, a law clerk snorted at my question about justice in Pakistan. "You want to know about justice? I'll tell you." He said his previous employer, a lawyer whose wife works for a women's charity, asked to borrow his daughter's government ID card, then filed a criminal case against the daughter's husband for abuse. The lawyer told the clerk not to worry, that after they pried some money out of the charity he would withdraw the case. "My daughter is perfectly happy, and I had no idea that lawyer would bring such a shameful charge," the clerk said indignantly. "Now we want to take him to court. I quit my job and he still owes me 60,000 rupees, but he doesn't answer his phone anymore."

Hunting for a case with more gravitas, I came upon a courtroom with dozens of people swarming outside. A slight man in coveralls was standing before the judge with his head bowed. As he murmured inaudibly, the judge kept interrupting to translate his testimony into English. It turned out the laborer was not a defendant but a witness to a complicated murder case. He had originally testified that he had gone with a friend to steal cattle and ended up in a shootout, but now he said he had made that statement under pressure. Actually, he now declared, they had gone to confront a man about an old murder, but found him waiting with a gun. "I swear what I am saying today is true," the laborer mumbled.

Outside the courtroom, I was surrounded by a crowd of relatives and other villagers. All talking at once, they recounted the story of the original murder case and how the killer had friends in politics, so his family was able to bribe the police and a doctor into changing their reports. "We had to sell all our cattle to pay the lawyer, but the other side has money and political connections," said one friend of the victim. "This whole case was changed by one phone call from the MNA's [member of the National Assembly] office. Two people were shot in broad daylight and the killer is free. We are from a poor family. We do not expect justice."

There was another side to the story, of course, with which I was bombarded later while squeezed into a cubicle with a lawyer, a fat policeman, and six or seven village men who identified themselves as witnesses and defendants in the shooting. They were all relatives of the killer, a man named Afzal, who they insisted had shot two intruders in self-defense because they were attempting to kidnap his teenage niece.

This was yet a third version, which if true would constitute a defensible "honor crime" in Pakistani culture, if not in law. Afzal was apparently in hiding, but eight of his relatives had also been charged, a common police tactic. Everyone in the crowded lawyer's office heaped contempt on the dead victims, saying they had been habitual thieves and murderers. A fifteen-year-old witness was pushed forward to recount what happened, which he did, in a breathless recitation that seemed both implausible and rehearsed.

"I was asleep and so was my cousin Amina," he began. "My mother was in the kitchen making tea. These two men came in with pistols and they told me to give Amina to them. I said 'This is the honor of our family and I cannot do it.' They grabbed me and beat me and threw me in the woods. Then my uncle Afzal came. He smashed the door and got one of the pistols and shot them." The police officer guarding the men seemed on friendly terms with them, and it turned out he was from their clan, as the plaintiffs had said. I suddenly realized that Afzal would never be caught.

These random cases played no role in Pakistan's national life and had no special significance, yet they all contained elements that reinforced what critics of the justice system charge: the side with the strongest clan or political connections usually wins. The facts are endlessly revisable to fit the prevailing version of a crime. No case is too petty or grave for a politician to weigh in on. The police have enormous power over those below but are easily suborned or intimidated by those above. No one is necessarily rewarded for telling the truth or penalized for lying, and everyone tries to manipulate the system.

A young lawyer named Abdul Qureshi, who comes from a family of educators and attorneys in the northwest, succinctly and candidly explained to me the three powerful factors working against justice in Pakistan. "One is the *baraderi* system. If you belong to a certain clan, all the influential people in that clan will come to help you, even if you are a murderer. If my brother kills someone, even I will go to the police and ask them for a favor," he confessed.

"The second is politics. If people know someone up high, in the army or the bureaucracy or the national assembly, they will usually try to influence the case. The politicians have to go back for votes, so they support criminals with large families who will all vote for them. The third is fear. All of us are afraid, and none of us has the courage to say this is wrong. It comes from sixty years of military influence, and it comes from greed. Every lawyer has his own clients and interests. We all need help from the system, so we all go along with it."

As I sat in his cubicle, I noticed that across the alley, a group of people in another tiny law office were holding up their palms in prayer. When I asked what was going on, I was stunned to learn that the prayers were for Nahida Mahbooba Elahi, a lawyer in her early fifties who had recently died of a brain tumor.

I had not seen Elahi in years, but I had once gotten to know this quiet, determined crusader when she represented a village woman whose jealous husband had carved off her ears, eyes, and nose with a butcher knife. I had visited Elahi's stuffy, cluttered law office in Rawalpindi, five flights up in a dark building with no elevators or air-conditioning. I had gone with her to the woman's village, and to the husband's trial in a town where local officials begged me not to harm the community's image. I had watched Elahi lead the blind and disfigured victim into court to testify, and watched other men shake the husband's manacled hand as he was led into a prison van, sentenced to five years for assault.

I had always admired Elahi, and stumbling on the prayer ceremony for her was an unexpected reminder that not everyone in the system was cynical and jaded. Her husband, also a lawyer, and a young woman in a stiff black suit told me they were carrying on Elahi's important cases, including one in which a man in northern Sindh had murdered his niece and her lover. "We have their engagement papers, and we have footage of the bodies," the young lawyer said quietly. "They were both seventeen."

PAKISTAN'S JUDICIAL SYSTEM, ESTABLISHED under the British raj, wears all the dignified trappings of that colonial inheritance. Its lawyers use terms like "barrister" and "high court advocate" on their business cards; they address black robed justices as "milord." The judicial system is huge and hierarchical, with hundreds of civil and criminal courts across the country and appeals courts in each province.

In an impoverished country with high illiteracy rates and a wide gulf between rich and poor, the legal world occupies a unique niche of respectability, regulated social values, and academic knowledge. Pakistan has more than a hundred thousand lawyers, including some of the country's best-known political activists. Its legal codes are modeled on British law from the Roman tradition, wrapped in a religious constitutional framework that declares no law shall contradict the principles and values of Islam.

At the pinnacle of judicial authority is the seventeen-member Supreme Court, established in 1956 and one of the most respected institutions in the country. It is housed in a majestic modern edifice in the capital, where bewigged senior judges hear eloquent arguments in English by black-robed senior advocates, and justices issue rulings that include long passages in Latin.

Under a constitutional system of checks and balances, the Supreme Court has specific powers to veto presidential and parliamentary orders, and its members are accorded enormous public respect. For half a century, leading members of Pakistan's most distinguished families have served on the high court. Some, such as Muhammad

Rustam Kayani, chief justice of the West Pakistan High Court in the 1950s and 1960s and an outspoken opponent of martial law, were courageous advocates of freedom and eloquent, witty intellectuals.

One of the last surviving members of the idealistic, Jinnah-era generation of Pakistani jurists is Javid Iqbal, now in his eighties. A Cambridge-educated lawyer and scholar who rose through the judiciary to become a Supreme Court justice in the 1980s, he is also the son of Mohammed Allama Iqbal, a liberal philosopher-poet and one of the leading figures in Pakistan's history. Even as an old man, the retired justice clings fiercely to the torch of Jinnah's dream for a nation that was modern, democratic, and Muslim. His wife, Nasira, is a retired Lahore high court judge.

"In the beginning, Pakistan was created as a new and strange experiment, based on the idea that Islam could mean democracy, human rights and the rule of law," Iqbal told me during a conversation in his backyard in Lahore. "The problem was that conventional Islam is not modern or democratic. After Jinnah died, we deviated from the course and our idealism was lost." The recurrent military interventions that followed, especially the Islamization campaign of General Zia, distorted the relationship between religion and governance, he said. "It was not the Islam that Jinnah wanted. We all became its hostages, and we are still fighting it today."

The courts, like all Pakistan's civilian institutions, have had great difficulty maintaining their independence in the face of feudalism and militarism, the two great antidemocratic forces that have derailed the country's political development for decades. They have repeatedly had to cope with extended periods of martial law, military rule, and suspended constitutions, during which the Supreme Court has been forced to concede many of its formal powers in order to survive, but has often sought to act as a limited check on executive excess.

Both civilian and military leaders in Pakistan have used the higher courts as instruments of policy and political handmaidens, manipulating the judicial appointment process and pressuring judges to conform to their views. In some cases this has provoked institutional and even physical confrontations, such as the mob attack on the Supreme Court by supporters of Prime Minister Nawaz Sharif in late 1997 that ended in fistfights and clouds of tear gas.

In other cases, Pakistani judges have functioned as willing partners of military regimes, lending an aura of legitimacy to dictatorial rule and setting a subservient tone for the lower courts. Forced to make difficult moral choices, they succumbed to sycophancy and survivalism. Appointed to positions of public trust but operating in a milieu of corrupting political influence and pressure, they took the path of least resistance. Others sided with military rulers for reasons of ideology, class, or kinship, especially after a period of nasty partisan conflict or civil unrest.

One of the darkest moments in Pakistan's history, the conviction and execution of deposed prime minister Zulfiqar Ali Bhutto on vague murder conspiracy charges, was the product of a court system that had been emasculated and co-opted by a military dictator, and of senior judges who had been poisoned by ideological hatred and professional grudges against Bhutto. Sheikh Anwar ul-Haq, the Supreme Court chief justice who wrote the final judgment denying Bhutto's appeal and condemning him to hang on a 4–3 split decision, had been handpicked by General Zia and was said to be a member of his Punjab *baraderi*.

Two decades later, the relationship between General Musharraf and the Supreme Court started out as a pragmatic modus vivendi, but it deteriorated as the general attempted to remove its dissident members and manipulate loyalists to strengthen and extend his rule. His two-year war with Chief Justice Mohammed Iftikhar Chaudhry spawned an extraordinary public protest movement by Pakistan's legal fraternity that became a major factor in forcing Musharraf to abandon power.

Upon seizing control from Sharif in 1999, Musharraf demanded that all Supreme Court and appeals court members take new oaths of office under a provisional constitutional order. He then dismissed and replaced eighteen judges who refused. Six months later a more

conciliatory Supreme Court ratified his coup on both legal and political grounds. It invoked the "doctrine of state necessity," blaming
constitutional meddling by Sharif, and the "consent of the governed," based on widespread public support for the bloodless takeover. The ruling attempted to stake out a middle ground between
abject surrender and principled opposition to military rule. The justices asserted the right to review Musharraf's decrees and gave him a
two-year deadline to hold elections.

The tenuous relationship began to sour after Musharraf pushed
through a constitutional amendment in 2003 that transferred key
powers from the prime minister to the presidency. Chaudhry was
named chief justice two years later. A heretofore unremarkable judge
who had quietly voted to endorse Musharraf's coup and subsequent
decrees, Chaudhry began to publicly challenge the president on a
range of issues, from questionable privatization deals to secret deten-
tions.

Embarrassed and enraged, the general lashed back, gathering reports of high-handedness and misconduct by the chief justice. On
March 9, 2007, he summoned Chaudhry to his military residence
and asked him to resign. When the chief justice refused, he was suspended from office, prevented from entering the court, and held
under unofficial house arrest until a replacement could be sworn in.
Musharraf pressed further, convening the Supreme Judicial Council
to hold hearings on a list of charges against him.

The accusations had mostly to do with personal abuses of stature,
protocol privileges, and influence. They included driving a
government-owned Mercedes instead of a smaller car, insisting on
more police escorts than a justice was entitled to, and pressuring officials to help his son get into medical school. Chaudhry had also
been accused of improperly using his influence to obtain for his son
a job with the federal investigative police. This was common behavior in Pakistan, but it damaged the judge's credentials as a crusader.

While this petty drama unfolded behind closed courtroom doors
all week, something profound was stirring outside. The humiliation
of the chief justice had crystallized growing public anger against

Musharraf's rule and galvanized the staid legal community. Suddenly black-suited lawyers in Islamabad, Lahore, Karachi, and Quetta were boycotting court sessions, pouring out of meeting halls, and marching through the streets. Activists from the liberal left and the religious right converged outside the Supreme Court, chanting antiregime slogans.

All spring the protests continued. The movement acquired a name, the "Black Revolution," and a leader, Aitzaz Ahsan, the eloquent silver-maned barrister and longtime People's Party legislator who had represented Chaudhry before the judicial council. The rallies grew bigger and bolder, while BBC images of well-dressed lawyers being tear-gassed and dragged off to jail gained sympathetic notice from legal groups around the world. Retaliation took other forms too: in Karachi, a violent mob attacked supporters waiting for Chaudhry's plane, and rioting left forty-two people dead and eight hundred arrested. In Islamabad, armed men broke into the home of a Supreme Court official close to Chaudhry and shot him in the head.

But four months after he had been dismissed, a Supreme Court panel cleared Chaudhry of all charges and reinstated him as chief justice. The stunning vindication further energized the lawyers' movement, which broadened its agenda to a blanket rejection of Musharraf's "illegal rule." Flushed with the heady momentum of change, Ahsan led caravans through the streets and told cheering crowds that states based on dictatorship instead of law and rights would be "destroyed."

Instead, the iron fist crashed down. On November 3, Musharraf imposed emergency rule, suspended the constitution, and ordered the arrest of sixty judges who refused to take an oath under the new provisional constitutional order. He castigated the judiciary for "working at cross purposes" with the executive, interfering in government policy, releasing terrorist suspects, and overstepping their authority. The real issue, though, was that Musharraf had just won reelection as army chief but was not sure the Supreme Court would rule the contest valid.

The regime used its new emergency powers to crack down on the lawyers' movement as well. Police in Lahore violently raided the High Court Bar Association and arrested more than eight hundred lawyers. Ahsan and other leaders were placed under house arrest for months. But, astonishingly, the protests kept going, with lawyers boycotting the courts and pressing for a restoration of the judiciary and democratic rule.

It was both a tense and exhilarating time, infused with the self-conscious bravado of ordinary people swept up in a revolution. In Rawalpindi, the bar association office had been transformed from a tearoom into a command post, and paunchy, middle-aged lawyers, who usually spent their days making grubby deals in tiny cubicles and shabby courtrooms, were donning armbands and marching out to face lines of police with riot shields and batons.

In Lahore, the high court bar association became unofficial head-quarters for the lawyers' movement, and its spacious brick plaza, shaded by a huge banyan tree, bustled with activity, punctuated by whiffs of tear gas and mad dashes indoors when clashes between police and protesters came close. Lawyers circulated petitions, assigned tasks, and gave interviews to TV crews. I remember vividly a young man, fresh out of law school and wearing a shiny black suit, who grabbed my arm excitedly and started quoting from historic American figures such as Tom Paine and Justice John Marshall about freedom and law and democracy. I could almost see Mohammed Ali Jinnah smiling from the grave.

The fight to restore Chaudhry and Pakistan's independent judiciary would not be over for another two years, and the lawyers' movement would eventually fracture and fizzle out. But by the end of November, Musharraf would be forced to resign as commander in chief and retire from the army, becoming a lame-duck civilian dictator. By August 2008, he would be gone from power in Pakistan's first-ever peaceful transition from military to civilian rule—a feat largely achieved by the hundreds of black-garbed men and women who marched out of their obscure and orderly microcosm and staged Pakistan's first-ever peaceful revolution.

A CASE OF EXPLODING MANGOES is a riveting tale, based on the imagined confession of an anonymous army officer who planted the bomb that brought down General Zia's plane in 1988, killing the Pakistani dictator and ending a decade of military rule. The novel, by Mohammed Hanif, was an instant bestseller in Pakistan when it appeared in 2008—and as good an explanation as any for a mysterious, high-level death in Pakistan, where such crimes are rarely solved and always used for political purposes, and where novels can be more truthful than nonfiction.

The book's nameless plotter, lost to history in the crash and never identified, provided a kind of public satisfaction that is not often available in a country with a wealth of conspiracy theories and a paucity of facts. The novel offered a kind of answer—however darkly tongue-in-cheek—to a question that otherwise would linger forever.

Pakistan has been described as a more subtle version of Haiti, the impoverished former slave colony where superstition and rumor reign and where illiterate people believe in spells, curses, and half-dead spirits whose hands reach out of the earth and pull innocent victims down forever. During decades of dictatorial rule in Haiti, voodoo was a preferable, more comforting explanation than the alternative, which was that the invisible hand of the national security state, the Tontons Macoutes, was pulling victims down into the murky abyss.

Just as there was never a satisfactory explanation for the death of Zia, there has been no credible account or official closure on the assassination of Benazir Bhutto, the two-time prime minister and the most charismatic Pakistani politician of her era. Bhutto, who had returned home to launch a political comeback after years in exile, was killed in Rawalpindi on December 27, 2007, shot by a young man at an outdoor political rally while she waved to fans from the sunroof of her vehicle.

Many groups and individuals stood to gain from Bhutto's murder.

These included Musharraf, who had agreed to permit her return under heavy American pressure, Bhutto's rivals from the Pakistan Muslim League, and the intelligence agencies that had plotted to sabotage her earlier stints in power. The behavior of Pakistani officials after the incident—from appallingly negligent to highly suspicious—spawned an array of conspiracy theories that continue to circulate today. The crime scene, which should have been taped off and preserved, was instead hastily hosed down. The body, which should have been autopsied, was instead buried on orders from Bhutto's widower, Asif Ali Zardari, who insisted that Muslim custom demanded a quick interment.

Zardari, a disreputable businessman who had spent years in prison on never-proven corruption charges, was in Dubai at the time of his wife's death. But there was continued speculation and rumor that Zardari, who went into full grieving-widower mode and won election as president less than two months later, had been behind the assassination. People whispered that he was watching the rally on TV and called her on a cell phone, urging her to rise out of the vehicle and wave to her adoring fans.

The truth will probably never be known. Official blame was immediately leveled at Baitullah Mehsud, and most Pakistanis found that explanation both plausible and easiest to swallow. But no official conclusion was ever reached, and the postmortem police investigation was compromised and delayed.

The Zardari administration, eager to dispel questions about its motives, requested an additional probe by the United Nations, but then stonewalled the investigators and repeatedly delayed making the results public. When the U.N. report finally appeared in April 2010—nearly two and a half years after Bhutto's death—many Pakistani commentators expressed disappointment and suspicion that it did not identify the culprits, and some dismissed it as a whitewash. But the document bears close reading because of what it revealed about the politicization of law enforcement in Pakistan, the omnipresent and intimidating role of the intelligence agencies, and their enduring, habitual efforts to manipulate every major event and controversy.

The UN team was headed by Heraldo Muñoz, a Chilean politician and academic who had once been a leading dissident under military rule in his own country. His report was scathing and frank, and its tone showed how shocked the authors were by what they found. They concluded that security for Bhutto at the rally was glaringly absent despite the attempt on her life two months earlier, that no serious investigation had been carried out afterward and no real attempt made to determine who was behind the crime, and that even police officials were hamstrung by fear of interference from the "Deep State."

"The investigation was severely hampered by intelligence agencies and other government officials, which impeded an unfettered search for the truth," the report stated. It said that the intelligence agencies had carried out their own probe but had only "selectively shared" their findings with the police. It said the police had hesitated to act vigorously, in part from fear of those agencies, and that the UN commissioners themselves were "mystified" by the efforts of some officials to prevent them from meeting with military and intelligence sources. The authors said it remained up to Pakistani authorities to find out "who conceived, ordered and executed" the historic crime. "No one," they added in disgust, "believes that this boy acted alone."

In short, the report was a formal international indictment of Pakistan's politico-military system and an awed double take at the reach and influence of its permanent military-intelligence establishment. The central message was that no one in authority really cared about the facts, only about how to spin them and avoid sharing the blame.

Although it did not spell out who had murdered Bhutto, the UN report reinforced the suspicions that had been whispered so many times in so many cases. It made all the conspiracy theories seem much more plausible, and it suggested that to many powerful state actors, it was far more useful to sow confusion, doubt, and fear about Bhutto's death than to bring clarity and closure to a shocking political crime. Given the historical ties between Islamic militants and intelligence agencies, it was possible that they had colluded to eliminate Bhutto. Since no one in authority sought to put this notion to rest, it remained lingering in the air like a warning whiff of poison.

"The present government is no more eager to get to the bottom of who killed her than its predecessor" or to "expose the deeper truths" behind the assassination, the editors of *The News International* suggested bluntly. "Why, we must ask, has an administration led by Benazir Bhutto's husband done so little to find out who killed his wife?" The UN report, the editorial added, leaves "an inescapable impression of purposeful and directed obstruction, which will raise questions in the minds of a suspicious and doubting public already inured to being lied to by successive governments."

JUST LIKE A NASTY land dispute or a score-settling murder case in any district court, high-level crimes in Pakistan have complex plots, large casts of characters with few clean hands, cross-charges of political manipulation, and multiple explanations that few people believe. Whether it is the murder of a former ISI officer in the tribal region, the execution-style killing of a Supreme Court official in Islamabad, or the kidnapping and reappearance of a wealthy businessman and presidential crony in Karachi, rumors swirl and fingers point, but clarification and closure—let alone confession or conviction—rarely come. A light shines briefly into a murky world, and then it switches off.

The role of the judicial system becomes even trickier and more opaque when matters of national security, intelligence, and Islamic militancy are involved. Often the courts perform a diplomatic cooling-off function, aimed at placating Pakistan's Western allies after a major suicide bombing or gaining credit for being tough on terrorists, rather than acting as a serious prosecutorial brake on militancy.

During the past decade, numerous leaders of radical and violent militant groups, including Hafiz Saeed of Lashkar-e-Taiba, Masood Azhar of Jaish-e-Mohammed, and Abdul Aziz of the Red Mosque, have been repeatedly arrested, jailed, or put under house arrest, but then released by the courts after several months for lack of evidence. This has been especially true in Lahore, where provincial authorities are sympathetic to local militant groups that have fought in Kashmir.

Arrests and releases are also used as a way to manipulate militant groups and keep them under control. In 2002, after Musharraf announced a ban on violent sectarian groups, hundreds of their members were rounded up in high-profile raids but then quietly freed after a few weeks. "It was clear that the ISI was not keen to offend its jihadi partners by keeping them in jail for too long," author Husain Haqqani wrote.

As the number of terrorist attacks multiplied, prosecutors complained they were understaffed and that police often sent them poorly investigated cases that judges would then throw out for lack of evidence. Analysts said other terrorist cases were tainted by false accusations or fell apart when nervous witnesses recanted.

Two men were charged with helping to plan the Marriott hotel truck bombing in 2008, but the key witnesses backed down in court, saying they had been threatened, and the case was dismissed. After a terrorist commando squad invaded a Lahore police academy in 2009, holding hundreds of recruits hostage and killing eight people, the sole attacker captured alive was convicted of possessing a grenade but acquitted on terrorism charges, again for lack of evidence.

Most violent crimes committed in Pakistan are far less spectacular or politically significant than the murder of Benazir Bhutto. They usually involve long-running feuds among neighbors or clans, property or labor disputes that turn violent, or so-called honor killings of flirtatious daughters or eloping couples. They revolve around jealousy or revenge, cultural or religious offense, accusations of deception or betrayal.

Yet just like a high-profile assassination, even the most paltry or pathetic local crimes are fodder for political manipulation, financial extortion, and official intervention. Every hand is out, from the lowliest policeman to the most minor court clerk. The facts matter far less than the status and connections of accused and accuser, and the impact on people's daily lives is far more direct and enduring.

Access to justice is especially difficult in rural areas. Relationships among police, judges, and local politicians are often close, even through blood. The majority of inhabitants are illiterate and economically dependent on landowners. Everyone is linked to private patrons and accustomed to having them solve disputes; no one has confidence that if they go to the police or the courts, they will be treated fairly or even given a hearing if their adversary has a stronger, better-connected patron.

"The system can only work if the state is strong. In our region it is weak. The police are a failure and the judicial system is in collapse. Everyone understands they are only after money," said Ghaus Bux Bhayo, a tribal chief in northern Sindh. Rural Sindh is notorious for its highway robbers and outlaw gangs, whose members are called dacoits, but Bhayo said people who fall afoul of the law can be forced into a life of crime, and that some police and landlords use dacoits as their own enforcers.

"It takes ten to fifteen years to decide a murder case. People do not get justice, so they become dacoits," Bhayo said. If a complaint of robbery or murder is filed with the police, he said, instead of hunting for the culprit, they may kidnap his relatives as collateral or pick up people at random, arrest them, and make deals for their release. "It is no different than buying something in a shop," he said.

Like many rural leaders, Bhayo insisted that the traditional system of tribal control worked better, although provincial governments have been doing more in the last few years to professionalize their law enforcement agencies. "Our way is better, fairer, and more result-oriented," he said. "If there is a problem in my tribe, even murder, I sit with everyone and get it solved in one month. If you leave it to the police, it will take ten years and ten more murders and cost a great deal of money."

AS A RULE, MOST Pakistani policemen do not carry guns. Instead, they carry long bamboo poles called *lathis,* which look quaint and flimsy, like something one would use to prop up a tent or poke around in the garbage. Pakistani cops also affect a languid, half-asleep demeanor in public; one often sees them sprawling on chairs or snoozing in trucks, looking utterly bored.

In the pecking order of the national security state, they occupy the lowest rung, below a panoply of military, intelligence, investigative, paramilitary, and antiterrorist agencies. This can complicate their jobs enormously, as in the case of the Bhutto assassination, when ordinary police functions were superseded by more powerful agencies whose role may have been to obfuscate rather than solve. Police departments may arrest a wanted militant leader, only to have him released by people over their heads.

To survive, the police must also be keenly attuned and subordinate to Pakistan's entrenched VIP culture, a combined legacy of militaristic and feudal habits. This can work at direct cross purposes with security, such as when a politician in his powerful SUV objects to being stopped and searched at a roadblock set up to keep terrorists from attacking people just like him. On the other hand, developing good relationships with politicians, especially in small communities dominated by a few powerful clans, is often key to being promoted, securing bribes, and keeping the peace.

According to a close Pakistani observer of the law enforcement world, police officers have long been routinely appointed, promoted, and transferred on "political, punitive, pecuniary, and personal grounds," mostly based on relations with politicians and other influential people. In 2009, the Zardari government instituted new merit-based policies of promoting police officials based on tests, training, knowledge of law, and service record, but old-school officers and their ways were resistant to change.

Just as they are subservient and accommodating to those above, Pakistani police wield absolute power over those below. Their methods are notoriously simple and brutal, and suspects or prisoners are routinely stripped and whipped with leather straps called *chhittars,* an institutionalized practice known as *chhitrol.* Sometimes this is done to force confessions, other times to punish impoverished miscreants or upstarts—teaching them a lesson that has as much to do with enforcing the established political and class order as it does with enforcing the law.

In the streets, police ordered to quell or disperse rioters can also inflict considerable bodily harm with their flimsy-looking bamboo *lathis.* Guns are redundant; unarmed protesters facing a *lathi* charge by an advancing line of men in uniform often panic and sprint for safety.

Occasionally an incident comes to light that reveals the customary cruelty inside police stations and lockups, known as *thana* culture after the Urdu word for "police station." Human rights groups protest, politicians claim to be shocked, and cynical observers accuse them of hypocrisy. In March 2010, two young men who had reportedly stolen rice from a truck were caught by the Punjabi police. They were dragged into a station house yard, their trousers and tunics were yanked off, and they were beaten with *chhittars.* The incident was captured on cell phone video and shown repeatedly on TV news channels, unleashing a public outcry. Authorities promised to investigate, and officers were transferred.

But several analysts pointed out that the practice was widely known and tacitly condoned by Pakistani society as a means of maintaining law and order—and that it was strikingly similar to the cruel punishments inflicted by the Taliban. Indeed, the videotape of the two prisoners being whipped in the yard of the Chiniot police station looked very much like the notorious videotape of the teenage girl being whipped on the ground by Taliban enforcers in Swat one year earlier, except that they had worn beards and turbans instead of uniforms.

Interestingly, although the televised beating of the girl also provoked revulsion and helped reinforce public support for the army invasion of Swat, opinion surveys across Pakistani society found that a large majority of people *approved* of harsh physical punishments being meted out in the name of enforcing sharia.

Violent punishment, in fact, was commonplace across the society. Religious seminaries were infamous for beating boys as a method of teaching them to memorize the Koran, public school teachers in poorer areas often hit unruly students, and killing or maiming wayward wives or eloping daughters in the name of family "honor" was an illegal but acceptable practice in much of the country. Thus, the moral confusion and resignation of the society—its expectation of cruelty in the name of law and order—carried over into its expectation and acceptance of religious repression in the name of Islam. The Taliban were treading on fertile ground.

AS SOON AS MUSHARRAF agreed to relinquish power and parliamentary elections were held in February 2008, the nation naturally expected the independent judiciary to soon be functioning again. Asif Ali Zardari and Nawaz Sharif, rival leaders of the two dominant parties, signed a pact to restore Chief Justice Chaudhry and the other dismissed justices within one month, and the new prime minister, Yousuf Raza Gilani, ordered all detained judges released.

But the deadline kept slipping, while the ruling coalition quickly collapsed and Zardari's early conciliatory tone gave way to suspicion and suppression. In August, after Musharraf resigned and Zardari was chosen as president, the legal community stepped up its agitation for Chaudhry's return, taking to the streets again in a reprise of the Black Revolution that had helped topple a dictator. But Zardari, like his military predecessor, was afraid of the independent courts and especially of the crusading chief justice, who the president worried would reopen old corruption cases against him and possibly even declare his election invalid.

By early 2009, the legal community had joined forces with political opposition groups, and public protests intensified. Leaders began calling for a "Long March" from Lahore to Islamabad to bring Chaudhry back to power. On March 12, thousands of lawyers and political activists began converging on the city and emboldened crowds poured into the streets, clashing repeatedly with police amid clouds of tear gas.

Zardari refused to budge, banning the march and invoking an old emergency law that prohibited public gatherings. Security forces were ordered to block the highway and move steel shipping containers into a protective circle around the federal district in Islamabad. Nawaz Sharif, Aitzaz Ahsan, and other opposition leaders were put under house arrest. For three days, the sense of crisis and confrontation grew more intense, with breathless TV news coverage of protests and arrests in far-flung cities adding to the fever.

"A year after the dawn of democracy, the long night of dictatorship stubbornly persists," Rubina Saigol, a social activist from the Punjabi elite, wrote in *The News International*. "In these conditions, the idea of rule of law has totally seized the popular imagination. The figure of Justice Iftikhar Chaudhry has become an object of desire for a large number of people travelling across barriers, barricades and blockades to actualize their dream of an independent judiciary that would release them from the clutches of tyranny."

On March 15, as a fresh outbreak of protests consumed Lahore, Sharif emerged from his home, drove through police barricades, and took command of the march. Thousands of people followed his convoy onto the motorway to Islamabad, 200 miles west, honking horns and chanting for the judges' return. As darkness fell, TV footage showed the highway packed with moving people and vehicles and groups heading from other cities to meet them. The prospect of a bloodbath loomed.

Zardari, huddled with aides in his office, remained silent and invisible. Calls started coming from leaders in Washington and London. Midnight passed, and throngs kept marching toward the capital. Sometime in the next several hours, General Kayani called on the president and made it clear that the army, focused on the fight against Islamic militants, would not countenance mass civil repression. Zardari finally relented, but he could not face the public. Just after 5:00 a.m., Prime Minister Gilani appeared on state television and calmly announced that all deposed judges would be reinstated within the week and the emergency ban immediately lifted.

By midmorning, thousands of jubilant people had converged on Chaudhry's official residence in Islamabad. The barbed wire and police posts had vanished, and the lawn was filling with raucous celebrants from every walk of life. They pounded drums, tootled on bagpipes, broke into impromptu dances, and filed into the house to shake his hand. "It's the end of feudal rule!" declared a middle-aged man, flushed from happy exertion. "Now the common people will be able to raise their voices and get justice."

The new chief justice did not disappoint his adoring public. He announced a series of judicial reforms and set strict deadlines for thousands of pending court cases to be heard and resolved. He delivered ringing sermons from the bench on issues from honor killings to corruption, and used his proactive powers, known as *suo moto* authority, to intervene in cases that had not come before the Supreme Court. Lawyers described feeling a brisk, fresh breeze wafting through the grubby courthouse precincts and a stirring of unaccustomed pride and urgency in their work.

Chaudhry also received a swelling stream of personal petitions from ordinary citizens who said they had been denied justice in a thousand petty ways, from a rigged job appointment process in the federal bureaucracy to a marital dispute with their more influential in-laws or a police department that demanded exorbitant bribes.

A sample of comments and messages posted on one Chaudhry-related website over the following year showed the extreme levels of despair felt by many Pakistanis, their profound shame and anger over the culture of official corruption and abuse, and the impossible hopes they placed in one man to help them as individuals and to bring justice, morality, and honor to their country. A few chided him for initially supporting Musharraf, but others compared him to the only Pakistani heroes they could think of—nuclear scientist A. Q. Khan and poet Allama Iqbal.

"God has given us a ray of hope in your self and you must do justice to this trust people have shown in you . . . history will remember that how bravely you stand up in front of a dictator . . . sir, plz do something for poor people . . . please save my family and families like mine all over Pakistan . . . please help me I am in big problem of my marriage . . . I want to inform you about my humiliation by Rawalpindi police . . . why Pakistani citizens have to wait for ten or twenty years to get justice in your courts . . . the man of dignity, the pride of Pakistan . . . Sir I am really a pore man but it doesn't metter I am happy in my life, but I am worried about Pakistan . . . this is the only institution that has given us hope . . . may Allah give you strength and power to take off the mud from face of Pakistan."

IN PAKISTAN, IT IS hard for even the worthiest cause or the newest hero to keep their luster. Inevitably they are poisoned by personal arrogance or temptation, discredited by cynical detractors, sabotaged by hidden hands from the Deep State, or bogged down in partisan politics.

Iftikhar Chaudhry's cult-figure image as the nation's moral conscience soon began to conflict with some of his actions. As the crusading jurist reached out more widely and aggressively from the bench, using his *suo moto* powers more and more often, critics began to question his motives. His growing personal and legal confrontation with Zardari began to smack of personal vendetta, and many Pakistan analysts feared it was building to the same kind of institutional clash that had derailed other governments and provided justification for military takeovers in the past.

The legal issue at the heart of the struggle was Zardari's immunity from prosecution on a variety of old corruption charges, based partly on his presidential status and partly on the 2007 amnesty law, known as the National Reconciliation Ordinance (NRO), that Musharraf had issued in 2007. The NRO had granted amnesty to Zardari and hundreds of other officials, politicians, and business leaders on charges ranging from graft to murder. It had enabled Benazir Bhutto to return home and run for Parliament—and Zardari to become president after her death.

Zardari tried hard to get the NRO extended in Parliament but failed. Shortly after that, in November 2009, the government published the entire list of accused individuals and their crimes, sensationally spelled out in columns of fine-print legalese. "The ugly truth of the abuse of power has a face—8,041 faces to be precise," crowed *The News*.

In addition to Zardari, the NRO list included the interior and defense ministers, a governor, two ambassadors, countless bureaucrats, and several leading legislators. The most common charges were financial offenses such as "assets beyond means" and "misuse of authority," but there were also thirty-one pending murder charges against an exiled political party leader, Altaf Hussain of the MQM.

Just over a month later, a seventeen-member Supreme Court panel headed by Chaudhry ruled that the NRO was unconstitutional and declared it null and void, effectively reviving all cases quashed under the original order. With legal cover stripped away from the unpopular president, and more than 248 officials barred from leaving the country, the government was thrown into chaos. The spectacle amused the public but alarmed the diplomatic and human rights communities. It looked to some as if Chaudhry, possibly in cahoots with the army, might be pulling off a judicial coup.

Asma Jehangir, chairman of the Human Rights Commission of Pakistan and no fan of Zardari, called the court's ruling a "witch hunt" and warned that it could prove counterproductive over time. "Perpetrators," she pointed out in a column, "are often viewed as victims if justice is not applied in an even-handed manner" or is "administered in undue haste with overwhelming zeal."

The contest of wills continued for months, with Zardari clinging to power but the government lurching from crisis to crisis. In February, another institutional meltdown was barely averted after the president promoted several judges to the appeals courts and Supreme Court against Chaudhry's recommendations—apparently on the advice of two senior aides who have been accused of trying to buy judges in private cases. Only a personal apology by the prime minister, who showed up unexpectedly at a dinner Chaudhry was hosting for a retiring colleague, smoothed things over.

In April, the attorney general resigned after less than four months on the job, telling the Supreme Court he had been obstructed by the minister of law and justice, a Zardari loyalist, from investigating and reopening old cases of money laundering and graft against the president, involving about $60 million, that had been languishing in Swiss courts for years. In his resignation letter, he wrote that he could not continue to function "due to the non-cooperation" of the minister, Babar Awan.

The people of Pakistan watched this spectacle with impotent disgust. They wondered if the promise of the lawyers' movement and the Long March had come to nothing, if the chief justice was a flawed mortal after all, and if the return to democracy meant nothing more than a change of uniform.

Down below, in the grubby alleys and cramped cubicles of the lower courts, there was some talk of change. Cases seemed to be moving faster; police salaries and training had been bolstered. But for most people caught up in the system—a bicycle thief beaten in a police station, a graduate cheated out of a government job by a bribe, a man languishing in prison because his brother eloped with a girl from another tribe, a truck driver accused of assault by a vengeful boss with political connections—truth remained a lie told by the person with more money, and justice remained an abstract idea meant for someone else.

CHAPTER 10

DRONES

EVEN NOW, YOU HEAR it. Even in plush parlors and air-conditioned offices in the capital, even from people who speak perfect English and who surely know better. Even after almost ten years, dozens of investigations, millions of words. You hear it from a brigadier in the army, a man selling sari cloth, a graduate student, a seminary director, a taxi driver, a politician who has visited the White House, a businessman who sent his sons to college in California.

You know it was the Jews, don't you? The Jews and the CIA and Mossad. Everybody knows that. They did it to put the blame on Muslims. People in Pakistan lean forward and whisper knowingly, confidentially, impervious to argument, utterly convinced. *They warned all the Jews the night before so they wouldn't come to work the next morning. It was a plot by the Americans and the Zionists. They destroyed the Twin Towers to discredit Islam.*

This stubbornly enduring canard says a great deal about the defensiveness, anger, and confusion that have turned millions of Pakistanis against the United States, even though their country receives millions of dollars in U.S. aid every year, their former prime minister went to Harvard, their army officials study at American military campuses, and their most ambitious and talented citizens incur life-long debts and concoct fabulous stories in hopes of obtaining an elusive U.S. visa.

It also says a great deal about the failure of decades of American financial assistance, educational opportunities, cultural appeal, and strategic alliances, through a dozen U.S. administrations from the 1950s to the present, to overcome the deep-seated suspicions—shared by a majority of Pakistanis—that the United States and its Western allies are out to destroy their religion, trample on their sovereignty, and seize their nuclear arsenal.

A generation ago, the United States and Pakistan forged a successful strategic alliance against Soviet communist aggression in next-door Afghanistan. Today they have formed a similar partnership in the war against Islamic terrorists, whose fanatical utopian crusade is taking a heavy toll on life and security in Pakistan, while posing an even more serious threat to Afghanistan. But this time, the relationship is plagued by hostility, deception, and conflicting agendas. Where Washington sees a global terrorist menace, Islamabad and Rawalpindi see a containable problem, a potentially reusable proxy, and a fount of military aid.

Pakistanis have had a complicated, love-hate relationship with the United States for years. Like people in other parts of the world, they envy and crave much of what America has to offer—fast food, high-tech innovation, and opportunities and freedoms many are denied at home. There are also more than half a million emigres from Pakistan living in the United States, from garage mechanics in Detroit to graduate students in Los Angeles and cardiologists in Baltimore.

Yet many Pakistanis harbor deep resentment and suspicion of their longtime Western patron and partner. They view the United States as a manipulative superpower that has used and discarded Pakistan in the past, often supporting corrupt or repressive rulers for its own ends, while it has built more enduring friendships with some of Pakistan's foreign antagonists. Despite billions of dollars in U.S. aid, the bulk of which has gone to its armed forces, they believe the

United States has a fundamental antipathy toward Muslim nations and is itching to get its hands on Pakistan's "Islamic bomb."

Year after year, opinion surveys continue to show that a large majority of Pakistanis see the United States not as a reliable friend or ally but as a potential threat to their existence. The most recent such study, conducted by the Pew Research Center in early 2010, found that the image of the United States "remains overwhelmingly negative in Pakistan," with only 17 percent of respondents saying they had a "favorable" view of the country.

The Pew survey also found that about six of every ten Pakistanis see the United States as an enemy of their country and fear it could present a military threat. This opinion was most pronounced in Punjab, the province that is most military-influenced and closest to India. But in all four provinces, a strong majority of people said they opposed U.S. efforts to fight terrorism in the region and wanted Western troops to leave Afghanistan as soon as possible. Nearly half believed U.S. policy favors their archrival, India, and nearly half believed—very inaccurately—that the United States gives little or no economic aid to Pakistan.

In the months after that survey was conducted, anti-American sentiment was further inflamed by incidents and issues that seemed to drive a deeper wedge between the perceptions and priorities on both sides. What officials in Washington viewed as progress in the war against Islamic terrorism, many Pakistanis—egged on by religious groups and the ultranationalist press—saw as further encroachments on their sovereignty or assaults on their fellow Muslims.

"Many people here feel Pakistan and the U.S. cannot be strategic partners, that this is only a marriage of convenience," Rifaat Hussain, a professor and defense analyst at Quaid-e-Azam University in Islamabad, told me in 2010, after a particularly noisy period of America-bashing in Pakistan and a particularly depressing stretch of mutual frustration and finger-pointing between Islamabad and Washington. "They are in the same bed, but they have different dreams."

ON THE EVENING OF May 1, 2010, an abandoned 1993 Nissan Pathfinder, with smoke curling out of its windows, was spotted near a curb in Manhattan's Times Square, one of the most famous intersections in the world. The fumes turned out to be from a homemade fertilizer-based bomb that had failed to detonate, and the vehicle turned out to have been recently purchased by a thirty-one-year-old Pakistani American named Faisal Shahzad, a financial analyst who lived in Connecticut. Shahzad was caught two days later while boarding a flight from New York to Dubai. He was arrested, tried, and eventually convicted on five terrorism-related charges, including attempting to use a weapon of mass destruction.

There was nothing in Shahzad's background to suggest he had jihadist leanings. He was neither poor, deprived, nor raised in a hardline religious environment. His military family was well-educated, and his father had retired as a vice air marshal, the second-highest rank in Pakistan's air force. Although an indifferent student, Shahzad was sent to the United States to attend college, where he earned degrees in computer studies and business administration. He became a U.S. citizen, returned home in 2005 to marry a Pakistani girl in an arranged match, and settled with his wife near Bridgeport to begin raising a family.

After Shahzad's arrest, relatives and friends in Pakistan seemed stunned that he would have turned into a violent fundamentalist. An uncle in his mother's village recalled watching him dance with girls at his wedding just five years earlier, something a conservative Muslim would never do. A longtime colleague of his father's in Islamabad recalled noticing during one of Shahzad's visits home that he had begun wearing a beard, but said he thought nothing was amiss.

"I was happy that even though he was living in America, he was staying close to almighty God and to our traditions," the retired air force officer, Iftikhar Ahmed, told me. He described Shahzad's father as an "enlightened" man who had raised his son to have "balanced" views. "We sent a clean and innocent boy to America," Ahmed said with evident bitterness. "If he went bad in America, why don't you blame America instead of his family and his country?"

But American and Pakistani investigators learned that the young man had begun changing in 2008. He prayed and visited mosques more often, pressured his wife to wear a veil, and asked his father for permission to go fight foreign forces in Afghanistan. Over the Internet, he began logging onto Islamic websites and sending messages to friends about saving "oppressed" Muslims from Western "humiliation."

What was especially disturbing about this transformation was that within a matter of months, Shahzad, who despite some recent financial reverses appeared to be immersed in middle-class American life, became rapidly consumed by an angry ideology of religious victimization that clearly contradicted his own experience.

Although Shahzad's latent radicalism was probably awakened through website sermons and social contacts while he was in the United States, it appeared to have been quickly recognized, molded, and sharpened by Pakistani militants he met during a series of visits home. In 2009, he told interrogators, he received training at an Islamic militant camp in Pakistan's northwest tribal region. He was also said to have recorded a suicide video in which he praised the leader of the Pakistani Taliban and warned of a "revenge" attack on the United States for waging war in Afghanistan.

During the months after the Times Square bombing attempt, Shahzad was mostly out of sight as a prisoner, but he made a series of appearances in Manhattan courtrooms for various legal hearings. His looks and demeanor changed markedly during that time. He grew a full beard, donned a skullcap, and declared himself to be a "soldier of Islam." In June he pleaded guilty to all charges.

Three months later, just before he was sentenced to life in prison by a Manhattan judge, Shahzad read out a long, handwritten statement in court. It is worth quoting at length, because it shows how quickly and easily this young man, offered opportunities in the West that most young Pakistanis could only dream of obtaining, was converted to a narrative and worldview that depicted an ongoing Manichaean struggle between Islam and the West that would inevitably lead to the triumph of Muslim forces. The courtroom statement was a fanatic's manifesto for the clash of civilizations, a Taliban sermon delivered in perfect English. Faisal Shahzad had become a drone.

"If I am given a thousand lives, I will sacrifice them all for the sake of Allah fighting this cause, defending our lands, making the word of Allah supreme," he began. "The sentence by the judge will not mean anything to me, for how can I be judged when the Court does not understand the suffering of my people?"

Addressing the Western powers who have "occupied the Muslim lands under the pretext of democracy and freedom," he declared that "we don't accept your democracy nor your freedom, because we already have sharia law and freedom." Shahzad said the war in Afghanistan had achieved nothing for the West but had awakened Muslims' fighting spirit. He vowed that "proud terrorists" would keep fighting until America's defeat and the coming of the "Muslim caliphate," a world dominated by Islam.

Turning to his own society, Shahzad said he felt "ashamed that I belong to a slave country like Pakistan, who has accepted the slavery of the West from the day it was born." Just as the Bush administration had asked Pakistan after the 9/11 attacks whether it was "with us or against us," he said, "it's very clear for us Muslims, either we are with the mujahideen or we are with crusading losing Christians . . . brace yourselves, because the war with Muslims has just begun," he warned. "Consider me only a first droplet of the flood that will follow me."

IN THE UNITED STATES, the Times Square bombing attempt was depicted mainly as an inexplicable outrage, a new terror attempt that, fortunately, had failed—but which added new evidence to alarmist narratives about Pakistani Muslims posing a potential terrorist threat to America's way of life. Shahzad joined the ranks of Khalid Sheikh Mohammed, Omar Sheikh, and other educated Pakistanis who had turned violently against the West. There were calls for tougher airport screening and more rigorous checks on immigrants from the Muslim world. If a U.S. citizen with children and two college degrees could not be trusted, who could?

In Pakistan, not surprisingly, the public and press response was completely different. Scrambling for an explanation, the foreign minister suggested Shahzad might have acted in "retaliation" for unnamed American offenses, presumably the unpopular cross-border strikes by drone planes against Islamic militants in the tribal northwest.

Most commentators, however, shifted quickly from the crime and its motives to the harm it could cause Pakistan's image and relationships abroad. From a Pakistani perspective, Shahzad had done more damage to his own country than to anyone else's.

Young Pakistanis with ambitions to study and work abroad were quick to condemn Shahzad's actions, in part because they worried the incident would undermine their own career prospects. Some said they already felt all Pakistani Muslims were being unfairly branded as terrorists in the United States, and that they would rather apply elsewhere for work or study than be grilled by consular officers or singled out for embarrassing scrutiny by airport security guards.

"All these U.S. policies have given a whole generation of Pakistanis the psyche that the United States doesn't want us," Arsalan Ishtiaq, a visa advisor, told me in his office in Rawalpindi. He said his industry had once been flooded with students applying to study in the United States but that the demand had slowed since the attacks of September 11, 2001, and stopped entirely since 2008.

Students at high-tech training courses in Islamabad and Rawalpindi, who once would have given anything to work in the United States, said they were now seeking jobs instead in Britain, Australia, Canada, or the United Arab Emirates. Several said they had heard about humiliating searches at U.S. airports and spoke angrily of Pakistanis being branded as Islamist radicals. The Times Square incident, they said, was the last straw.

"Now the Americans will think we are all terrorists," said Asalan Khan, twenty-one, a student I met who had recently completed a course in cell phone technology and said he planned to go work for a phone company in South Africa. "Why should we study so hard, take all those tests, and pay all those expenses if they are not going to respect us?"

The Times Square bombing attempt brought a stern warning to Pakistan from Secretary of State Hillary Clinton. She had already lectured Pakistan during a three-day visit the previous October, casting doubt on its willingness to hunt down al Qaeda leaders in their tribal sanctuaries and insisting that the bilateral alliance against terrorism had to be a "two-way street."

Now, even as she praised Pakistan for a "sea change" in its cooperation overall and for going after Taliban militants in particular, Clinton told CBS News, "We want more. We expect more. We've made it very clear that if, heaven forbid, an attack like this that we can trace back to Pakistan were to have been successful, there would be very severe consequences."

Pakistani commentators took predictable umbrage at this latest scolding from Washington, which some dismissed as the latest round in a long history of "Pakistan-bashing." Only a few voices from the small liberal intelligentsia suggested that Shahzad's act called for more introspective concern on Pakistan's part.

"Tragically, anti-Americanism plays squarely into the hands of Islamic militants," Pervez Hoodbhoy, the physicist and outspoken secular crusader in Islamabad, wrote the week after the Times Square attempt. He suggested that newly minted jihadis such as Shahzad had been goaded by a flood of "anti-US lava from the fiery volcanoes" of Pakistan's media and were acting out of misplaced anger against the West.

The true enemy of Pakistan, Hoodbhoy argued, was its homegrown violent extremists, who he described as vigorously promoting the abstract notion of a war between Islam and the West while they are actually waging a ruthless armed struggle to remake Pakistan into a primitive religious utopia. "They will keep waging this war," he added, "even if America were to miraculously evaporate."

FAISAL SHAHZAD'S TRANSFORMATION FROM middle-class American immigrant to rage-filled Islamic warrior was neither an isolated anomaly nor the product of a deranged mind. It was an extreme but far from unique response to a range of cues from both Pakistani society and the virtual Muslim world, all depicting the United States as an aggressive, powerful hegemon that sought to roll back Islamic influence worldwide and that was politically united with Jewish Israel and Hindu-led India against the interests of Pakistan.

What was astonishing, given the barrage of anti-American rhetoric pouring out of Pakistani mosques, think tanks, and TV screens, was that Washington and Islamabad were cooperating at all. In fact, they had always been necessary allies rather than natural friends, and their mutual resentment, suspicion, and annoyance had festered in the wake of the 9/11 attacks and the rise of a global struggle that pitted violent Islamic movements against the West and some of its closest allies.

During the two years that Shahzad was becoming radicalized, U.S.-Pakistan relations had been most publicly defined by a series of impatient American demands that Pakistan "do more" to curb domestic-based terrorism and militancy, and by a series of testy and indignant responses by Pakistan that it was doing all it could to rein in the violent extremists, but within the unavoidable limits of national sovereignty and sensitivity to public emotions. Some of the official Pakistani rhetoric was posturing, but the public resentment that fueled it was real.

Although the two governments had been formal partners in the war against terror since 2001 and the United States continued to pour large amounts of economic and military aid into Pakistan's coffers, a fundamental "trust deficit" persisted. It was reinforced by a series of incidents and contretemps, both large and small, that were magnified inside Pakistan by the ultranationalist press and the small but highly vocal religious parties, and which were filtered inside the United States through the prism of post-9/11 suspicions and security concerns.

The U.S. and Pakistani military establishments shared a general agreement on the need to curtail international terrorism in the region, and they cooperated closely in hunting down al Qaeda suspects on the ground. The Pakistani army also tacitly supported CIA cross-border drone strikes on militant targets in the tribal region, and its intelligence services provided information that helped guide U.S. missiles to compounds or last-seen locations of certain al Qaeda and Taliban leaders.

The picture was murkier, however, when it came to other Pakistani militant groups based in the tribal region. Even after the Pakistan army launched its high-profile operation against Taliban militias in Swat and South Waziristan, American officials believed ISI was maintaining selective and strategic ties with friendly tribal militants in a covert "good Taliban, bad Taliban" policy. Pakistan always denied this, but a trove of military cables and other documents published by the controversial group Wikileaks in 2010 supported the allegations in extensive detail.

On the civilian side of things, there had been an expectation that the departure of General Musharraf in 2008 and his replacement by an elected administration under the liberal Pakistan People's Party—which coincided with a change in Washington leadership from Republican George W. Bush to Democrat Barack Obama—would offer a fresh start to the U.S.-Pakistan friendship.

Benazir Bhutto, although tainted by the long-standing allegations of corruption against her and her husband, had been a popular figure and frequent visitor in Washington as prime minister in the 1990s. Her assassination in 2007 had sabotaged a quiet, U.S.-brokered deal to ease Musharraf out of power and Bhutto in. Now her widower—a man with virtually no credentials to lead the nation—had been elected president on a wave of grief for the slain icon of Pakistani democracy.

The mood in both countries, however, was more religiously conservative and xenophobic than it had been during the Bhutto era, and Zardari was as deeply disliked by the Pakistani public as his wife had been revered. His initial overtures to Washington were pounced on by his opponents in the domestic establishment as signs of unseemly kowtowing, and he was hounded relentlessly in the Pakistani press as an American stooge.

In a similar vein, gestures by the Obama administration aimed at persuading Pakistanis that Washington was not going to abandon them again—as it had after the Soviet withdrawal from Afghanistan in 1989—were greeted in Pakistan with suspicion and mistrust instead of thanks.

The United States had already provided Pakistan with more than $10 billion in aid since the 9/11 attacks, most of which had gone to the military. In September 2009, the U.S. Congress passed an unprecedented package of economic assistance, worth $7.5 billion over five years. The act tripled U.S. nonmilitary aid to Pakistan in one stroke. The bipartisan bill, entitled the Enhanced Partnership with Pakistan Act, was cosponsored in the Senate by Democrat John Kerry and Republican Richard Lugar. A companion measure passed the House of Representatives, where its sponsors stressed that the money would be used to bolster Pakistan's democratic political and judicial systems, as well as education and rural development.

But instead of welcoming the overall gift, Pakistani officials and opinion makers focused on the fine print. Sponsors in both houses of Congress, wary of Pakistan's legendary corruption and the black hole into which much previous military aid had vanished, required close American oversight of how the money would be spent, especially for military purposes. "We fully appreciate the urgency of the situation . . . and the need for appropriate flexibility," said Representative Howard Berman, a major backer. He added, however, that Congress would "no longer provide a blank check."

The restrictions set off a wave of angry protests among student and religious groups, who denounced the aid as part of an American plot to take control of Pakistan. The army chief, General Kayani, called the conditions an "unacceptable" insult to his institution.

Members of Parliament, debating the bill, used similar expressions. Mushahid Hussain, a veteran politician and government opponent, said it "borders on the humiliation of Pakistan."

During this same period, further anti-American sentiment was being stirred up by a drumbeat of reports in the Pakistani press that the U.S. government was sending spies and security agents to wage a secret war on Pakistan, and that it was planning to vastly expand its civilian and military operations in the country.

Pakistanis are extremely sensitive to issues of national sovereignty and suspicious of Western designs on the country's nuclear arsenal, in part because of congressional sanctions imposed in 1990 after Pakistan began developing nuclear weapons. The reports of a growing American presence, which coincided with a buildup of American troops in next-door Afghanistan, played to the nation's paranoia.

Some of the problems stemmed from plans to expand the U.S. embassy in Islamabad. Because of terrorist threats, the official American presence in Pakistan had retreated from a once-welcoming stance. The U.S. embassy was now isolated inside a high-security zone, off-limits to all Pakistanis except VIPs. Visa seekers were no longer allowed to park and wait in line outside the consular office, and most transactions were conducted through a courier service. The American Center, which once offered free library services and a cultural gateway to a generation of Pakistanis, had shut its doors after 9/11.

The "secret" embassy expansion generated a wave of suspicion, and even a series of diplomatic briefings and tours for the Pakistani press during the summer of 2009—as well as an ambitious embassy initiative to foster local goodwill and interaction—did not stop the commentaries about an "imperial" American agenda to weaken and destabilize Pakistan as a Muslim nuclear power. There were multiple press reports that as many as a thousand U.S. Marines—a universal symbol of American occupation—were going to be stationed there, although U.S. officials insisted that no more than twenty Marines would be assigned to the compound as guards.

The conspiracy theories were bolstered by a parallel set of rumors and reports that American spies, assassins, and security teams were living in secret houses, roaming the country, and making trouble. Some of these reports were prompted by actual incidents, including street altercations between police or other Pakistanis and U.S. security contractors or their local employees. Rumors began circulating that the U.S. government had hired Blackwater, a controversial security firm accused of abuses in Iraq, to work in Pakistan under its new name, Xe Services.

"People worry that Pakistan's nuclear assets aren't safe. They have never forgotten American opposition to them, and now they hear these stories about a thousand Marines coming to the heart of Islamabad, and they wonder why," said Rifaat Hussain, a scholar and friend with whom I had held countless discussions over the years.

Hussain mentioned that on the most recent celebration of National Defense Day, August 14, Pakistani cell phones everywhere popped up with messages saying the country had to be defended from the Marines. "There are four mobile phones in my family, and we all got those messages," he said.

Alarmist warnings like these put some Pakistanis over the edge. One blogger, a U.S.-educated engineer, warned that the American "war on terror" had now reached the streets of Pakistan, where "hired killers" from Blackwater and legions of Marines at the monstrous new embassy were "terrorizing this nation" and could soon unleash "slaughter and destruction" as they had in Afghanistan and Iraq.

American diplomats repeatedly denied that Blackwater was operating in Pakistan, but the accusations took on a deadlier significance when a national newspaper and the top-rated Geo TV channel published photos and addresses of houses where CIA or Blackwater agents were said to be living. The implication was that they were fair game, and the embassy reported that some bloggers were urging people to attack the occupants. Local press reports also wrongly identified a U.S. aid contractor in Peshawar as a secret agent, just months after another U.S. aid contractor had been assassinated on a Peshawar street.

The U.S. ambassador, Anne Patterson, sent an angry letter to officials of the Jang Group, owner of both media outlets that had fingered the alleged U.S. spy houses, accusing them of spreading "wildly incorrect" information and endangering American lives. She also expressed bewilderment and frustration that the rumors about the U.S. embassy metastasizing into an imperial fortress had been so difficult to fend off. "I can't really understand it, because what we're doing is actually quite straightforward," she told an American journalist. "We've tried to explain it carefully to the press, but it just seems to be taken over by conspiracy theories."

It was clear that most Pakistanis had two distinct and contradictory feelings about the United States. They wanted access to its knowledge and culture, and they had nothing in particular against its people, but they abhorred its foreign policies and mistrusted its religious motivations. In peaceful times, these contradictions could coexist. In wartime, suspicion and hostility prevailed.

During a decade of repeated visits to Pakistan, I often found myself in debates with people about the United States, from angry seminary students at anti-America rallies to polite Westernized professionals, from sidewalk vendors to strangers on planes. Generally people were friendly and curious, though the seminarians were often reticent and uncomfortable in the presence of a Western woman.

But except for the most sophisticated and worldly of my interlocutors—and sometimes even including them—we always ended up at the same impasse. I would try to convince people that there was no great Western plot against their country or their religion, and they would tick off a list of items—the U.S. alliances with Israel and India, the U.S. invasion of Iraq, Jewish control of American business, prisoners in Guantánamo, airport searches of Muslims— to prove I was wrong. Often they would add one more item: the World Trade Center attacks of 9/11. *We all know who was behind that,* people would tell me, utterly convinced. *They did it to defame Islam.*

In a 2008 survey conducted by the U.S. Institute for Peace, 84 percent of respondents said the U.S. military presence in Asia and especially in next-door Afghanistan, was a "critical" or "important"

threat to Pakistan's vital interests. Two-thirds said they did not trust
the United States to act responsibly in the world, and 86 percent
said one goal of the United States was "to weaken and divide the
Islamic world." Only one-quarter believed that security cooperation
with the United States had brought Pakistan any benefit.

One year later, the Pew Research Center survey found that 64
percent of Pakistanis viewed the United States as an enemy, and only
9 percent saw it as a partner. Looking back at polls taken during the
previous decade, it found that the proportion of Pakistanis with a
favorable view of the United States never reached more than 25
percent—except after a major U.S. relief effort to help Pakistani
earthquake victims, when it inched up to 27 percent.

Nearly three-quarters said the United States should remove its
troops from Afghanistan as soon as possible, and more than half opposed U.S.-led efforts to fight terrorism, even during a year when
Pakistan had suffered a record-breaking number of terrorist attacks
and resulting civilian casualties.

One of the most relentless purveyors of anti-American thinking
was Shireen Mazari, Pakistan's best-known intellectual hawk. Although she had received her doctorate from Columbia University,
Mazari was such a harsh critic of U.S. policy that she was sometimes
referred to as "Lady Taliban." She was an unwavering proponent of
the view that the United States was an unreliable ally, fundamentally
hostile to the Muslim world, which had abandoned Pakistan once
and would surely do it again.

Through this prism, which epitomized the cynical and conspira-
torial tendencies of Pakistani thinking, every American gift was seen
as a Trojan horse and any bilateral partnership as temporary and self-
interested. The Western war against Islamic terrorism was equated
with a threat to Pakistan's stability, while America's cozy relations
with India and Israel made it imperative for Pakistan to ensure its
own regional influence by any means it could.

In 2009, after the Zardari administration came to power, Mazari
was asked to leave her longtime post as director of a government-
backed think tank in Islamabad, but she then became editor of an

English-language newspaper and continued her crusade, writing columns that bristled with references to "the Ugly American" and the "diktat from Washington." She was an expert at weaving bits of fact, rumor, insinuation, and speculation into arch questions about American perfidy and plotting that hung in the air like poison.

Mazari's agenda might have been cynical and provocative, but she had her finger on the pulse of the Pakistani street, a place American diplomats no longer dared venture. In one column she wrote something that was partly a shot at her own class but also rang true.

"Americans do not understand the ordinary Pakistani," she wrote in September 2009. "Their interaction with the ruling elites," who have a "tendency towards subservience" and a "constant gaze toward Washington," had led American policy makers to assume this attitude was reflective of Pakistani opinion at large. "To their dismay," she noted with a smirk, "they are finding out otherwise."

Even after a number of high-profile international terror attacks were traced to groups or individuals of Pakistani origin, including the Mumbai siege, Pakistanis were affronted the next year when their country was included in a U.S. government list of fourteen Muslim nations whose visitors would require extra screening at U.S. airports.

In March 2010, a group of Pakistani legislators were invited to Washington in a fence-mending trip, and they met with a variety of top officials in Washington. But when they were asked to undergo full-body scanner searches before boarding a domestic flight, they refused and did not take the flight. When the legislators reached home, they were feted as national heroes by the media. One of the lawmakers, appearing on the country's most popular TV news show, said that going through the scanner would have made him—and the whole Pakistani nation—naked.

FAISAL SHAHZAD WAS MOSTLY an accidental jihadi, a confused and angry middle-class Muslim who logged onto the Net, started getting ideas, and fell into the wrong hands. Dr. Aaafia Siddiqui was an entirely different creature—a scientist who apparently spent years plotting to do violence against the United States, even as she studied in some of its most renowned institutes. In Pakistan, however, she was seen by many people as a martyr, heroine, and victim of American abuse.

Siddiqui, a Pakistan-born neuroscientist and longtime U.S. resident with degrees from MIT and Brandeis University, vanished with her three children in 2003. She reappeared five years later in Afghanistan, where she was arrested carrying bomb-making plans and toxic chemicals.

When American army officers arrived to question her, she allegedly grabbed an assault rifle and tried to shoot one of them but was shot and wounded in return. She was taken to the United States, hospitalized for treatment, and then tried and convicted on assault charges. On September 22, 2010, just a few weeks before Shahzad was sentenced to life, Siddiqui was sentenced to eighty-six years in prison.

Siddiqui, who was thirty-eight at the time of her sentencing, had led a life full of secrets and contradictions. She was a highly trained and Western-educated scientist drawn to violent religious extremes; a recipient of scholarships and prizes from American academia who came to hate and revile the United States as a fount of evil.

But whereas the bumbling Shahzad had conducted only a single amateur bomb attempt, Siddiqui allegedly spent years as a sophisticated financial and planning operative for al Qaeda. U.S. and other intelligence agencies reported her making purchases of diamonds in Africa and military equipment on the Internet. After being divorced by her arranged husband, a Pakistani-born anesthesiologist, she married an alleged al Qaeda member and nephew of Khalid Sheikh Mohammed.

There are two starkly contrasting versions of what happened to Siddiqui during her five unaccounted-for years. According to one version, Siddiqui went into hiding in 2003 and lived underground until 2008. During that period, U.S. officials listed her as one of the seven most-wanted al Qaeda fugitives. However, she and her supporters have insisted that she was kidnapped in Karachi by U.S. and Pakistani intelligence agents, then held secretly for years in U.S.-run and Pakistani prisons.

American officials have said she was never in U.S. custody before 2008. It was not clear what happened to her children during that time, but a twelve-year-old girl believed to be her daughter mysteriously appeared outside her family's home in Pakistan in the spring of 2010, and her older son, Ahmed, was found with her in Afghanistan.

The facts of Siddiqui's attack on the U.S. officials in Afghanistan are also contested; she repeatedly denied having tried to harm anyone and said she was shot for no reason, while witnesses gave several confusing accounts. In court, she behaved erratically and defiantly, which raised questions about her mental health. After a jury found her guilty, she blamed the verdict on Israel. At her sentencing, the judge found no evidence that she had been detained or held prisoner by U.S. agencies, and he noted that she had called out "Death to America" in court.

In Pakistan, the public image of Siddiqui could not have been further from the U.S. government version. Rather than a dangerous terrorist, she was seen as an innocent victim of American lies, injustice, and anti-Muslim conspiracy. Her conviction touched off angry anti-American protests by groups across the country, from female seminarians in Islamabad to the secular MQM party in Karachi.

The ordeals faced by her children added drama and sympathy, as did posters of a distraught Siddiqui behind bars and rumors that she had been raped and abused in American custody. Her sister spoke at packed public rallies, calling for her release and repatriation.

Despite the considerable evidence that Siddiqui was a dedicated terrorist and the numerous unanswered questions about her life, almost no attention was paid to that side of her story by the Pakistani press or public. Instead, virtually the entire society rallied to her cause. The nationalist media and religious groups turned her into a martyr and folk hero, an Islamic female rebel similar to the black-robed girls from the Jamia Hafsa seminary in Islamabad who had formed religious vigilante squads in 2007.

Nawa-e-Waqt, a popular Urdu-language newspaper, called Siddiqui's prison sentence "a challenge to the honor of the Muslim *umma,*" or faithful masses. Shireen Mazari blamed it on the "vindictive mind-set" of Americans since the 9/11 attacks. The government had little choice but to support her, paying for three defense attorneys in New York. After she was convicted, Prime Minister Gilani called her a "daughter of the nation," President Zardari formally asked U.S. officials to repatriate her, and the Pakistani senate passed a resolution asking for her immediate release.

"In a country that has been ravaged by bomb blasts, kidnappings, beheadings and public lashings at the hands of extremists, nothing has elicited as strong a response as the strange case of Dr. Afiaa Siddiqui," observed columnist Saba Imtiaz in the *Express Tribune* newspaper, one of the few voices of caution in the torrent of hyperbole about Siddiqui's suffering at American hands. Noting that supporters had proposed a "Dr. Afiaa Pride of Performance Award," Imiaz added, "the 'pride' of this country lies in the hands of a woman who, for all we know, was working to destabilize the region."

IT WAS THE DRONES, beyond any other real or imagined provocation, that most inflamed Pakistani emotions against the United States. Few people outside the remote tribal regions ever saw or heard these pilotless planes, which looked like snub-nosed gliders. They appeared silently in the skies, launched Hellfire missiles on mud-walled village compounds, and returned to mysterious bases. But their psychological impact on society was so disproportionate that the CIA might as well have dropped an atom bomb on Karachi's Fatima Jinnah Avenue during rush hour.

The drones were a major U.S. weapon in the war against Islamic terrorists based in Pakistan. Their intended targets were all violent militants, especially members of al Qaeda and Taliban fighters who were sworn enemies of the Pakistani state. But the invisible air attacks, which evolved from an occasional foray into a relentless siege against suspected militants and their sanctuaries, captured the nation's fervid imagination and personified its worst suspicions of a stealth invasion by U.S. forces.

Just as the high-flying B-52 bomber had become an iconic object of both fear and derision among Afghans during the U.S.-led war against the Taliban regime, the word "drone," with its spooky connotation of soulless robotic action, became a sharp, symbolic focus of Pakistani anger over America's military role in the regional war against terror.

From a military standpoint, the drones were highly effective assets. They sidestepped the ardent Pakistani opposition to American "boots on the ground," and they did far less damage than the clumsy carpet-bombing tactics used by the Pakistani army that decimated villages in Swat and South Waziristan. Guided by satellite imaging and local intelligence, the drones zeroed in on known militant locations and fired missiles that often hit their targets, although usually with some loss of civilian life.

When the U.S. military began using drones on occasional raids between 2004 and 2006, most Pakistanis were not aware of it. The Pakistani army was kept informed in advance of specific aerial strikes, and it tacitly accepted the operations, in part because they reduced the need to involve troops in a dangerous and unpopular conflict at home, and in part because they were an acceptable substitute for foreign troops, whose presence in Pakistani territory would have been strongly opposed by the military establishment as well.

Through 2007, there were relatively few drone attacks and relatively few signs of public opposition. Several important Taliban and al Qaeda militants were either killed or nearly killed, building a track record of success. In the summer of 2008, the CIA decided to increase the pace of its unmanned strikes, launching twenty-seven between August and December at houses, villages, mosques, and rural compounds in the tribal areas of North and South Waziristan and towns just outside them. According to official figures and news reports, a total of 296 people were killed in thirty-three drone attacks that year. Most of the dead were described as Taliban forces, al Qaeda members, or militants.

In 2009, under orders from the new U.S. president, Barack Obama, the pace of attacks intensified further and the scope of targets broadened. Between January and December there were fifty-three missile strikes in North and South Waziristan and the nearby areas, causing 709 confirmed deaths. The locations were still remote, but the escalating pace and death toll created a huge public backlash. Religious groups began staging anti-drone protests, and security hawks fired volleys of criticism. They charged that the strikes were killing hundreds of innocent civilians and suggested that the surge in Islamic terror attacks in Pakistan was a form of retaliation for America's cross-border drone war.

"Mothers run with their babies as soon as they hear the drones," wrote Mazari in early 2009. Rejecting the argument that some civilian deaths were unavoidable in the war against violent militants, she wrote, "It is not collateral damage, it is the wanton and illegal murder of human beings—a war crime." She called on the Pakistani army to stop fighting "America's war," and even suggested that its air force should shoot down the planes, "rather than helplessly waiting for US goodwill."

Officials of the Zardari government, desperate to avoid the appearance of bowing to American aggression, voiced repeated public objections to the drone campaign. Every time a new strike was reported, the foreign ministry denounced it as a violation of national sovereignty, and Pakistani officials suggested that the United States could solve its public relations problem simply by handing over its drone technology to Pakistan.

"If we want a success in this fight against extremism and terrorism, we have to carry the people along," Foreign Minister Shah Mahmood Qureshi said in March 2009, the day after a drone strike killed twenty-four people. He praised the "superior technology" of the strikes but said their "collateral damage" was leading to public alienation, and that the U.S. government should consider whether the advantages outweighed the disadvantages. What he clearly meant to suggest was that killing a few militants was hardly worth turning nearly 180 million people against the United States.

A short-lived reprieve for the much-maligned drone came that August, when a CIA-ordered missile strike killed Baitullah Mehsud. Mehsud, whom the CIA had been tracking closely for weeks, was finally isolated in a village compound in South Waziristan, where he was visiting his new wife and her parents. The drone attack killed them all.

Mehsud's death was an enormous triumph for the U.S.-Pakistan antiterror alliance and an indicator that the drone strikes were becoming more accurate. Pakistan's "Public Enemy No. 1" had been blamed by officials for masterminding a string of high-profile terror attacks, and his demise was greeted with relief nationwide. "Good Riddance!" read a banner headline in *The News International,* summing up Pakistani opinion.

Yet the brief glow of success brought little letup in public opposition, and it was overshadowed by growing concerns that the tactic was taking too high a toll on the civilian populace, all for the sake of eliminating a few militants. It was impossible to know how many civilians were actually being killed by the strikes. American military officials never released those figures, there was no way to independently verify local claims, and the strikes were often aimed at compounds where armed fighters mingled with their local tribal supporters and relatives.

The war zone along the Pakistani-Afghan border was essentially off-limits to the press, except for limited tours arranged by the armed forces. Local journalists, even those with tribal backgrounds, faced threats from both the militants and government security agencies, and several Pakistani reporters died in mysterious circumstances trying to cover the conflict. Foreigners were permanently banned from the tribal region except under official escort, and when a reporter from the *Wall Street Journal* traveled to the area alone and tried to question local authorities, he was accused of being a foreign spy by the nationalist press and had to leave the country for fear of being killed.

The absence of facts made it easier for opponents to exaggerate both the death tolls and the local reaction to them. After several early reports of angry armed villagers protesting missile strikes, it became a common saying in Pakistan that a drone attack that killed one militant only created a hundred more, a notion that suggested the bombing campaign was a tactical success but a strategic failure.

Were the missile strikes in fact producing more drones, the kind who could be brainwashed, set on automatic pilot, and launched to blow themselves up in a market full of shoppers or a mosque full of worshippers? Was the United States destroying villages to save them, creating more enemies than it killed, using terrorist methods in the name of fighting terrorism?

American officials, responding to such criticism, insisted that the drone attacks were legal. Harold Koh, a legal advisor to the State Department, asserted that under the laws of war, the cross-border aerial attacks fell under the doctrine of "self-defense" against terrorists who might be planning to attack the United States. He said the missile strikes also passed the wartime legal test of "proportionality," meaning they did not cause excessive loss of life in relation to their goals.

Human rights activists and legal critics from Pakistan disagreed on both grounds, arguing that even a few civilian casualties robbed the attackers of moral credibility, and noting that there had been no proportional decrease in terrorist attacks as a result of months of intense drone strikes in the heart of militant sanctuaries.

"If democracy and the rule of law are to be defended, then the tactics used against terrorists must not undermine them," wrote Rafia Zakaria, a Pakistani American lawyer and official of Amnesty International, in a column for *Dawn*. "If US leaders continue to believe that sacrificing ten civilians for the possibility of eliminating a handful of al Qaeda or Taliban leaders is a fair bargain," he wrote, "then little hope remains for the partnership."

During 2009, a series of senior U.S. officials visited Pakistan in a concerted campaign to win over public support. Defense Secretary Robert Gates, speaking at the national defense university, admitted that the United States had made a "grave mistake" in abandoning Pakistan in 1989 and said U.S. military leaders were keen to forge a "new relationship" with Pakistan's armed forces. But one student, obviously unimpressed, asked him flatly, "Are you with us or against us?" Local press coverage of Gates' visit focused obsessively on a brief comment in which he inadvertently suggested that Blackwater employees were working in Pakistan, a charge U.S. officials had repeatedly denied.

Secretary of State Hillary Clinton tried too, with a goodwill trip in October that included open meetings and freewheeling exchanges with students and media. But as the newspaper *Dawn* observed, her "charm offensive rolled into a wall of suspicion." News anchors outdid each other in asking tendentious questions, and students angrily challenged her about the drone attacks, the Kerry-Lugar bill, and America's friendship with India. "What guarantees can Americans give Pakistanis that we can now trust you?" demanded another student. How could they be sure the United States wouldn't "betray us like you did in the past"?

Pakistani concerns about the human damage caused by drone attacks were reinforced by several international reports, including one from the Brookings Institution in the summer of 2009, which found that ten civilians had died for every militant killed. Separately, a report from the UN Human Rights Council sharply criticized the U.S. failure to collect and share information about civilian casualties in Pakistan, especially after drone attacks.

Unless it could show otherwise, the council's chief investigator said later, it seemed that "the Central Intelligence Agency is running a program that is killing significant numbers of people, and there is absolutely no accountability in terms of the relevant international laws."

The first-ever comprehensive opinion survey to be conducted in the tribal zones, conducted in 2010 for the New America Foundation in Washington, confirmed that an overwhelming majority of residents condemned the American drone attacks; three-quarters said they opposed them and 70 percent "strongly" opposed them. Asked who was being killed by the strikes, nearly half said they killed mostly civilians, and only 10 percent said they killed mostly al Qaeda and Taliban members.

Nearly 80 percent of inhabitants said they opposed the U.S.-led war on terror and that its real purpose was to weaken the Islamic world and ensure American global domination. Nearly six in ten agreed that suicide attacks against American military targets were sometimes or often justified. Forty percent named America as being "most responsible" for the violence in their region, far ahead of all other choices. Only 11 percent chose al Qaeda, the Pakistani Taliban, or the Afghan insurgents.

And yet the survey also showed that even in traditional and remote tribal areas, most people had no deep-seated hostility toward the United States, no "intractably held anti-American beliefs." Asked what would improve their opinion of the United States, the top choice was a U.S. military withdrawal from Afghanistan (77 percent), followed closely by more U.S. visas, educational scholarships, and a U.S. role in brokering peace in the Middle East.

The poll also made clear that opposition to U.S. military actions among the tribal population did not translate into broad support for the Islamic militants, nor did it carry over to Pakistani military operations against them. Over half said they did not support the presence of Taliban or al Qaeda fighters in their area, and nearly 70 percent said they supported the Pakistani army pursuing the militants. Remarkably, one-third said they would even support drone strikes if they were conducted by Pakistani rather than American forces. Asked to rank major Pakistani leaders by popularity, 70 percent chose General Kayani first.

The entire time, of course, the Pakistani army was quietly supporting the American drone strikes, allowing civilian officials to take the heat from the public while the armed forces kept its reputation high. Always hungry for U.S. money and weapons despite their bluster about aid conditions and national sovereignty, military officials worked quietly to keep the U.S. military happy by cooperating with the drone campaign against al Qaeda and certain Pakistani and

Afghan militant groups, while continuing to maintain covert links with others as a hedge against the future.

As the barrage of documents published by Wikileaks in the summer of 2010 revealed, there was an ongoing practice of what the *New York Times* called "cynical collusion" between Pakistan's military intelligence and at least some of the Taliban militants. The documents, the paper said, "confirm a picture of Pakistani double-dealing that has been building for years." At the same time, Pakistan drew the line against drone attacks in Balochistan, a far more volatile tribal area where the real Taliban leadership was believed to be living.

This adroit balancing act reinforced a narrative of extreme cynicism and self-interest in Pakistan's high-level attitudes and agenda toward the United States. In this version of bilateral relations, spelled out in compelling detail by Pakistani experts such as Ahmed Rashid and Amir Mir, the tail always wagged the dog and generally managed to get the bone. Pakistan's security establishment had used the United States for its own ends before, taking advantage of its strategic location in the Cold War. Now, as critics charged and as the leaked U.S. documents seemed to confirm, it was doing the same in the war on terror.

American officials stated repeatedly that the United States could not defeat the Afghan Taliban or curb regional terrorism without Pakistan's help. Pakistan's security establishment responded by doing only as much as was needed to keep the faucet turned on, manipulating public opinion while protesting that it faced domestic constraints, and keeping its western border on the boil to make sure it had a strong hand in Afghanistan when the Americans finally pulled out.

"Fixing Pakistani anti-Americanism is a fool's errand," a Pakistani American blogger wrote in a frank online discussion of America's image problem and the drone strikes. "For all the money that's been spent, the ISI and the army still want to protect the Taliban and encourage them to wear us out in Afghanistan so they can rule in our absence. The Pakistani generals," the blogger added, "keep playing us for the fools we are," dangling an engagement ring while the

United States keeps dreaming of marriage "like some love struck teenager."

If this analysis was accurate, then the fuss kicked up about the drones—as well as the Blackwater spies, the Marine invasions, and all the rest—was part of a calculated ploy by Pakistan's Deep State, a frenzy whipped up among the gullible Muslim masses by its accomplices on the religious and nationalistic right. Its purpose was essentially to keep up the pressure on Washington so that those in power could demand more for their apparent cooperation in the latest version of the Great Game.

ON DECEMBER 30, 2009, a man crossed the border from Pakistan into southern Afghanistan and was driven to a secretive U.S. base, a facility at which many drone attacks were planned. A group of CIA agents and officials was waiting there to meet him, expecting to debrief a reliable spy with a trove of information about the Pakistani militant world. Lightly searched and eagerly welcomed, the man stepped inside the meeting facility and blew himself up, instantly killing seven CIA officers and one other American.

It was the deadliest attack on the American intelligence establishment in a quarter century, a crime of shocking boldness and sophistication. It was also carried out with the cooperation and support of the Pakistani Taliban, suggesting a new nexus between the tribal militants and international terrorist networks.

The bomber, Khalil Abu Mulal al-Balawi, was a radical Jordanian doctor who had been recruited from prison in Jordan and recommended to the CIA. But after being sent into Pakistan, he apparently switched sides again and became close to Baitullah Mehsud. After Mehsud's death, al-Balawi made a video statement calling Mehsud a hero of Islam and saying he planned to avenge his death.

Despite the blow to the CIA as an institution and the setback in its efforts to infiltrate the tribal areas, the Americans struck back immediately by ramping up the drone campaign even further. In the first three weeks of January, a rain of missiles fell on North Waziristan, aimed chiefly at the Haqqani insurgent network and killing ninety people. January 1, Ghundikala village, three dead. January 3, Mosakki village, five dead. January 6, Sanzali village, thirty-five dead. More waves of aerial strikes followed in March and April, pounding some of the same militant hideouts and villages over and over: Data Khel, Miram Shah, Mir Ali, Data Khel again, Miram Shah again, Haider Khel, Wana.

The drone strikes became more accurate, hitting more insurgent targets and killing fewer civilians. Militant fighters interviewed in the tribal areas described the missile attacks as ferocious and frequent, forcing them to lead a "jungle existence" and keep moving to avoid being detected or endangering civilians. However, the escalating drone campaign also provoked a fresh and more forceful wave of anti-American protests, and relations between the United States and Pakistan became increasingly strained.

In late summer, when heavy monsoon rains and flooding inundated vast areas of Pakistani cropland and sent more than a million people fleeing for safety, the U.S. government quickly pledged a generous amount of relief aid and rushed military helicopters from Afghanistan to help rescue stranded villagers. But the goodwill gesture was barely noticed by most Pakistanis, and any salutary effect was quickly overshadowed by a new drone offensive in North Waziristan, a major militant stronghold where the Pakistani army had refused to send its own troops and planes.

All during September, the aerial attacks continued at an unprecedented pace, hitting the same constellation of tribal villages in at least twenty strikes. American officials reported they were hitting more and more important targets: a cousin of a Haqqani network leader, an al Qaeda militant who was allegedly plotting an attack in Europe, a man wanted by the FBI for the bombing of a U.S. warship in Yemen.

Once more, however, the battlefield success was met by a new eruption of public anger in Pakistan, exacerbated further by a series of armed clashes on the Pakistani-Afghan border in which two squadrons of NATO attack helicopters chased a group of insurgent fighters back into Pakistan. The multiple assaults killed more than fifty people, including three identified as Pakistani border forces.

American officials insisted they had acted in self-defense, and there were suspicions that the dead Pakistani troops had been aiding the militants to cross into Afghanistan and back. But officials in Islamabad protested strongly, calling the attacks a "clear violation" of UN rules governing international forces in Afghanistan.

Amid escalating anger, confusion, and suspicion on all sides of a messy guerrilla war that showed no signs of abating, both the Pakistani government and the insurgents took retaliatory aim at a vulnerable and vital source of support for American troops in Afghanistan. More than 75 percent of their nonlethal supplies came by road from Pakistan, and they had to enter Afghanistan at one of two major border stations. That week, in quick succession, Pakistan shut down one border station to all U.S. supply trucks, and militants besieged the waiting NATO convoys in a spree of torching and shooting, burning more than twenty fuel tankers.

Back in Islamabad, officials regarded the conflagration with strategic coolness, and they kept the border shut to U.S. military suppliers for a few more days. "We will have to see whether we are allies or enemies," said Interior Minister Rehman Malik.

CHAPTER II

THE MURDER
OF DEMOCRACY

SHE CAME RIDING HOME through a sea of frenzied and adoring crowds, plunging eagerly back into politics after a long and frustrated exile, hoping to become the next head of state even though she knew an array of enemies lurked in her path.

Benazir Bhutto had been a flawed and compromised leader in two truncated turns as prime minister during the 1990s. But her political homecoming, in the fall of 2007, was a bold move that might well have ushered in a new era of hope in a country where, for more than half a century, the early promise of democracy had been dashed by coups, corruption, conflict, and the curse of feckless leadership.

Bhutto's death cost Pakistan its most charismatic and liberal figure and its best chance for redemption after a decade of corrosive military rule. Instead it got her husband, Ali Asif Zardari, an indifferent and poorly qualified leader with a shady past, who was elected president on a wave of public sympathy just over eight months after Bhutto's death.

Zardari, then fifty-three, was a fabulously wealthy businessman, but he had little talent for politics or interest in his country's fortunes. He had spent nearly a decade in prison on various corruption charges, although he had never been convicted, and he was widely rumored to have had a hand in the death of his brother-in-law.

It was an inauspicious rebirth of civilian rule, and the unseemly scramble that followed did little to improve things. During the next two years, after a short-lived attempt at power sharing between Zardari and perennial opposition leader Nawaz Sharif, Pakistan's political life was to be dominated by pitched battles between the accidental president and his adversaries in the press, the political establishment, and the judiciary.

There were constant rumors of likely army takeovers or "creeping" civilian coups, fresh allegations of corruption in high places and desperate efforts to fend off old ones, and the permanent specter of a government that always seemed to teeter on the brink of collapse.

This entertaining but depressing spectacle played out under national circumstances that demanded urgent attention, wise planning, and strong leadership at the top. The economy was spiraling downward, with investment and capital fleeing as insecurity spread. Power shortages and consumer price hikes were punishing the urban poor, while persistent illiteracy, poverty, and soaring population growth stymied rural development. The monsoon of 2010 both highlighted and worsened this bleak picture.

Pakistan's weak civilian institutions were also in dire need of strong leadership to tackle a daunting array of problems, from bureaucratic corruption to tax evasion, abuses against women, and the proliferation of unregulated seminaries. Civilian authority and legal powers needed to be strengthened after the abuses and impunity of lengthy military rule, including antidemocratic changes to the constitution and the unfettered, intrusive growth of domestic intelligence agencies.

But although Zardari did not suffer from the lack of electoral legitimacy that haunted his predecessor, General Musharraf, he lacked both political and moral legitimacy because of the trail of unresolved corruption charges and other allegations from his past. And although legally immune to prosecution as long as he remained in office, Zardari was widely viewed as corrupt and permanently preoccupied with safeguarding his protected status as head of state. Wary of both the public and the law, he tended to make decisions by closeting himself with a few aides, rather than encouraging other democratic institutions to function.

Zardari had international leanings, and he took advantage of his stature as a newly installed democratic leader to reach out to both New Delhi and Washington. He achieved notable success on the economic front, winning U.S. congressional support for the massive Kerry-Lugar aid bill. He also proposed exchanges with India's democratic leaders and attempted to ease tensions between the two nuclear-armed states, suggesting that Pakistan might be willing to change its long-standing policy and agree to no first nuclear strike.

But his efforts at rapprochement toward both countries were viewed with suspicion by many of his countrymen, and especially by army leaders, who publicly bristled at provisions for military expense monitoring written into the Kerry-Lugar bill and were quick to refute the civilian leader's hint of a less belligerent nuclear policy. At a time of rising anti-American sentiment, Zardari was ridiculed as Washington's puppet and accused of being too willing to do the Pentagon's bidding, even though he repeatedly asked U.S. officials to stop the politically poisonous drone strikes. Similarly, Zardari's early offer of an olive branch to India was overtaken by events, lost in the torrent of angry recriminations that followed the terrorist rampage in Mumbai.

Zardari seemed genuinely alarmed by Islamic terrorism, and he often spoke of the need to unite the nation against the scourge of religious extremism and violence. Yet he did little to follow through on that theme, essentially ceding control of antiterrorist and foreign policy to the security establishment. He also seemed personally indifferent to the human toll of the war on terror, never bothering to visit troops in the field and sending other officials to the funerals of prominent victims.

He often mentioned that his wife had been a victim of terrorism, but his actions after her slaying, such as refusing to allow an autopsy and instantly pardoning an intelligence official accused of hampering police procedures, reinforced public suspicions that Zardari too was involved in her death. The case was never officially solved despite lengthy investigations by several Pakistani agencies, Scotland Yard, and the United Nations.

Zardari's real power derived mainly from his replacement of Benazir as chairman of the Pakistan People's Party and from his influence in the party's stronghold in his native Sindh, which has long competed with the Punjabi-dominated political establishment. He repeatedly invoked the Bhutto name and attempted to conflate his political fortunes with the survival of Pakistani democracy. His aides unabashedly used Benazir's memory to promote its policies and projects, especially those that had a populist or social theme.

Some, like the Benazir Income Support Program, were widely praised for helping hundreds of thousands of poor families through periods of economic emergency. But in Pakistan, where no cause was too noble to subvert, no beneficiary too humble to cheat, and no martyr too sacred to exploit, even the Bhutto magic could not protect every project in her name from corruption and abuse.

A case in point was the Benazir Tractor Scheme (South Asians use the word "scheme" in a neutral sense, meaning "project"). This was an innovative program to assist poor farmers, in which thousands of tractors were to be given away based on a random, computerized lottery. Only people who owned less than 25 acres of land were supposed to be eligible. When the lottery results were announced, however, a substantial number of winners turned out to be large landowners, including forty-eight relatives of one member of Parliament.

Zardari also alienated many of the best and brightest PPP activists, especially those who had been close to his late wife, revealing the depth of his insecurities and the bitterness of the strains within the party's top membership. Shunning their counsel and talent, he instead surrounded himself with a coterie of loyal and malleable aides, who critics said were often of lower caliber.

"Benazir Bhutto would not recognize her party if she were to see it today," wrote one commentator, indignant at Zardari's public snubbing of her closest aides. "Hers must be a tortured soul."

Zardari was often his own worst enemy, and he skipped many opportunities to sow goodwill where he needed it most. During the terrible summer of 2010, when the nightly news was showing farm families and their animals struggling against the tide of monsoon floods, he committed the irreparable blunder of remaining on vacation in his French château.

By November of 2009, the barrage of criticism from the media and other establishment voices rose to a fever pitch. The army was annoyed at Zardari's conciliatory relations with Washington, the public was struggling with rising food and energy costs, and terrorists were bombing markets and mosques. There were calls for the president to step down, and thinly veiled hints that he should be forced out.

The issue that stalked Zardari relentlessly was the trail of corruption charges, especially a clutch of money-laundering cases in Switzerland, where a tangle of bank accounts containing more than $60 million linked to Zardari had been frozen for years. The president's efforts to keep these charges bottled up often eclipsed the business of governance, especially his running battle with the Supreme Court over the legality of President Musharraf's 2007 National Reconciliation Order, which had granted amnesty to Zardari along with hundreds of politicians and officials on a variety of charges.

On December 16, when the Supreme Court finally declared the NRO unconstitutional, pandemonium ensued. A total of 248 officials were barred from leaving the country, and an arrest warrant was issued for Interior Minister Rehman Malik. The defense minister, Chaudhry Ahmed Mukhtar, was stopped at the airport while boarding a plane for China. It was no longer clear who was running the country, and the government was forced to deny rumors of an imminent military coup.

Zardari quickly pardoned all his aides, deepening the image of recklessness and rot at the top. There were rumors of his involvement in new corrupt dealings and land-grabbing schemes, and periodic incidents that gave off a suspicious smell. One was the mysterious disappearance of a wealthy globe-trotting businessman and close friend of Zardari, who suddenly reappeared alive and well under a highway overpass in Karachi after the president dropped everything to intervene in the case.

As the government lurched from crisis to crisis, pressure mounted on Zardari to step down, relinquish some powers, or face the perennial remedy of a coup. Yet despite his evident distaste and patent unsuitability for the office, Zardari refused to give up his job, in part because it protected him from prosecution and in part because of the many advantages even an unpopular official in his position enjoyed. To keep the wolves at bay, though, he began to relinquish some of his powers.

First the president agreed to hand over nuclear command authority to Prime Minister Gillani, who possessed little real power but exuded a much more sympathetic and reassuring public image. In the spring of 2010, Parliament revoked key presidential powers to dissolve the National Assembly and appoint army chiefs, effectively reducing Zardari to a ceremonial role. Finally in July, the prime minister announced that General Kayani's term had been extended for three more years, all but guaranteeing a stable power arrangement with which Pakistanis were very familiar—and with which its Western partners could easily live.

A few voices continued to insist that Zardari should be sacked, but others warned that the crusading media and courts were engaging in a personalized "witch hunt" against the president. If such a creeping civilian coup actually ended up toppling Zardari, most members of the establishment agreed it would be much worse for Pakistan than any of his continuing shenanigans in office.

What mattered most, in the end, was to allow the president to serve out his term, rather than repeat the counterproductive cycle of political or military intervention that so often aborted Pakistan's still-nascent democratic experiment. Tolerating Zardari until the 2013 election was the only way to break the cycle that had bedeviled Pakistan for so long.

So it came down to this: ensuring that an unpopular, corrupt, and indifferent leader stayed in office for his full term was likely to be the single greatest political achievement in Pakistan's entire sixty-six-year existence.

MOHAMMED ALI JINNAH GAZES out from thousands of office and classroom walls across Pakistan, elegant yet spectrally thin, with piercing eyes and sharply creased suits, the cool embodiment of reason and purpose and law. His speeches are quoted constantly, and his life story is memorized by schoolchildren. His birthday, December 25, 1876, is one of Pakistan's major holidays. So is his death day, September 11, 1948, when Pakistan's founding father succumbed to tuberculosis and overwork, just over a year after realizing his dream for an independent Muslim nation.

Every Pakistani knows what Jinnah stood for: the rule of law, the equality of all citizens, the tolerance of all beliefs, and the commitment to full constitutional democracy. The Jinnah Society, which periodically releases anthologies of his sayings and of others' writings about him, has kept his ideals alive, even as scholars and pundits continue to debate his decisions, motives, and legacy as Pakistan's founder. To the ordinary citizen, Jinnah remains the nation's single towering hero, its Washington, Jefferson, Lincoln, and Kennedy rolled into one.

Yet when people invoke Jinnah's name, it is with either rueful nostalgia or hollow emulation. Jinnah's Pakistan ceased to exist long ago, and many people yearn for a return to the principles he embodied, yet no one seems to know how to get them back. The country's political system is morally bankrupt and many of its civilian leaders seem too compromised or indifferent to set an example. Its pundits and educated voters are reduced to sarcastic finger-pointing and self-deprecating cynicism, the glib but unsatisfying refuge of those who know better.

After Jinnah, it is hard to find anyone in Pakistan's political history whom people regard as a national hero. Asked to name Pakistanis they admire most, people come up with the same few icons, including Allama Iqbal, the late national poet; A. Q. Khan, the scientist who developed Pakistan's nuclear bomb; and Abdul Sattar Edhi, and the elderly founder of a free ambulance service. If they mention any former head of state, it is usually Ayub Khan, a benign military ruler from the 1950s. If they mention any current political leader, it is usually Imran Khan, the handsome former cricket champion who heads a tiny conservative party.

The disenfranchised Muslim masses identify democracy with corruption and view party politics as a brawl among egocentric gods, not a source of ideas or mission. They know that military rule freezes progress and stifles freedom rather than solving the problems of poverty and justice. More and more, they are listening to clerics with a different agenda altogether, who would toss out the constitution and Parliament and usher in a theocratic system—not so very different from what the Taliban sought to violently impose in Swat—in which Islamic law would trump modern rationality in the name of justice and piety.

"Today's Pakistan has drifted far away from Quaid-i-Azam Mohammed Ali Jinnah's vision" of a Muslim homeland and a "modern democratic state that derived its ethical inspirations from the teachings and principles of Islam," wrote political scientist Hasan Askari Rizvi in an essay for Jinnah's annual birthday celebration in 2009. "Pakistan's failure to evolve democratic institutions violated the principles Jinnah stood for," he wrote. "Now, the Islamic extremist groups, especially the Taliban, constitute an additional challenge to those who want Pakistan to return to Jinnah's vision."

There are few people still alive who knew Jinnah, who heard his call and felt the heady atmosphere and promise of a new nation, formed as a Muslim democracy. One of them is Roedad Khan, who retired in Islamabad after a long career in the federal civil service. Well into his eighties now, he remains a passionate public advocate for Pakistan's democratic ideals—and one of its sharpest critics for having failed to live up to them.

On the day Pakistan was born, Khan wrote in his political memoir, "I was a free man, a proud citizen of a free, independent and sovereign country which I could call my own." At age twenty-four, he recalled, "I was full of *joie de vivre,* hope, idealism and ambition. For me [and] for all those who belonged to my generation, Pakistan symbolized all our wishes and expectations. We all shared a seemingly unassailable certainty. We believed in Pakistan."

Today, those words sound both sad and quaint. Khan, who served in government posts all over Pakistan and saw the inside of power for nearly half a century, grew increasingly disillusioned with the behavior of its leaders. He watched civilian authority being squandered or thwarted and money prevailing over merit, corrupting the nation's spirit. He saw the bureaucracy, which Jinnah had exhorted to set an example of honor and integrity, become a politicized sinecure of gatekeepers who opened doors for a price.

Khan's book, *Pakistan: A Dream Gone Sour,* written in 1997 and revised in 2008, summed up the country's political history as one of "fake democracy." He describes it as a system covered by a façade of civilian institutions, political parties, and checks and balances, but ruled by hidden forces, which Khan calls the "coercive power," and which others have referred to as the "permanent establishment" or "Deep State."

"Political sovereignty in Pakistan," Khan wrote, resides "where the coercive power resides." It is this power—a core of economic, bureaucratic, and military elites—that decides when to follow or ignore the constitution, make or break governments, let democracy breathe or strangle. "We have an elected government today, but nobody knows when the ax will fall on it," Khan wrote elsewhere in 2009. "When it does fall, no tears will be shed . . . the people are sick and tired of fake democracy."

I tracked down Khan after reading his book, and after that we often met for lunch to discuss the lessons of Pakistani history and the prospects for its future. His personal library contained heavily underlined volumes of Tocqueville, the Federalist Papers, and studies of American history, and he confessed a lifelong awe of its founding fathers.

Khan's interest in democracy was far from academic, though. The irreverent and determined octogenarian filed a lawsuit against the National Reconciliation Order, often appeared as a combative liberal guest on TV talk shows, and delighted at recounting how he had been tear-gassed at a pro-democracy rally. But when he recited a favorite quote from Jefferson or Adams, it was with a kind of distant yearning for an ideal he knew he would never live to experience.

"We have had a string of victories, and it raised people's morale," Khan told me, ticking off the peaceful protest movements that forced Musharraf to remove his uniform as president, then forced Zardari to reinstate the chief justice. He described the excitement he and others in the courtroom felt when the NRO was overturned. "There was such jubilation in the room. Total strangers stood and embraced," Khan recalled with glee. "We realized that something unprecedented had happened, something that could change the future of Pakistan."

But he also acknowledged that the movement faced enormous obstacles in Pakistan, especially among the educated but complacent upper class. The major obstacle to democracy in Pakistan, he said, was not the anger, frustration, and religious activism of the poor, but the passivity, silence, and cynicism of the elite.

"We have a cultured elite that owes everything to Pakistan but is not prepared to lift a finger to help. Why? One, they think it is not their responsibility. Two, they are afraid. Three, they think it is unwise to antagonize whoever is in power and that if you stay on their good side, you may get something out of it," Khan told me. "Even if they want change, they think it is not respectable to get out on the street with the riff-raff. There are a hundred excuses for inaction. But Pakistan is sinking, and there is absolutely no excuse for people like us to sit back and do nothing."

PAKISTAN HAS FAMOUSLY BEEN called a failed state, suggesting a society that cannot function, a government that cannot govern, and a system that has proven incapable of serving its citizens, improving their lives, or protecting them from harm.

As Khan suggests, however, it might be more accurate to call Pakistan a fake state—one that possesses all the necessary institutions to manage, develop, and protect society, but which has failed to nurture the moral values or political will to use them for public good. The problem, he and others point out, is not that Islam is incompatible with a functioning democracy, but that none of Pakistan's leaders since Jinnah has fully adhered to the democratic message of Islam.

"The trains run, the planes fly, the sea-ports operate, the highways hum," Javed Jabbar, a former senator and federal minister under three Pakistani governments, wrote in another essay for Jinnah's 2009 birthday commemoration. The Pakistani state has all the tools it needs to face the nation's myriad problems, he asserted, "yet this is also a state unable to enforce the law equitably and efficiently." It is a state in which corruption has been allowed to poison society, self-examination and reason are often replaced by emotion and blame casting, and leaders have "only belatedly woken up to the threats from religious extremism and terrorism."

A search for the Pakistani state leads first through the labyrinth of its vast official bureaucracy, an administrative system set up by British colonial rulers a century ago. It is a world of endless corridors with identical doors, each stenciled with elaborate titles such as "Additional Joint Secretary for Water and Power" or "Sub-Director of Regional Management, Division of Revenue Services." Smaller parallel administrative universes exist at the four provincial levels, and again at the lower district levels.

Each office is a tiny fiefdom, and each titleholder possesses a small piece of power he (and occasionally she) can use to advance or hold up the progress of a small piece of official business, to serve or disserve the public, to benefit friends or harm enemies. The members of this vast and sinecured class are universally known, with a mixture of affection and disdain, as *babus,* a South Asian term of respect meaning "boss" or "dad."

Many bureaucrats are honest and hardworking civil servants who take their duties seriously and perform them with efficiency and pride. Khan is far from the only career government professional who laments the demise of Jinnah's Pakistan, and I have met several who kept a framed copy of Jinnah's famous 1948 speech to the country's new mandarins, in which he reminded them that "service is the backbone of the state" and that they must "not fall victim to any pressure, but do your duty as servants to the people and the state, fearlessly and honestly."

But the bureaucracy is also a rarefied and privileged environment. Fighting one's way up the federal administrative ladder is a finely honed art form, and the social status of an officer's family takes a giant leap with every grade he advances. A job in Pakistan's bloated bureaucracy is the aspiration of every middle-class family for its sons, but it is almost impossible for them to access without the right connections, and it is literally impossible to penetrate for those with none.

The advantage of joining the bureaucracy often boils down to the potential for graft and perquisites, whether it is the 1,000-rupee note a clerk demands to renew a taxi license or the government Land Cruiser a minister uses for his family vacations. Policemen, essentially bureaucrats with weapons, are in an especially good position to line their pockets.

"Everywhere you go, in every office, you have to pay bribes. I am sorry to say this as a Pakistani, but it's true," an off-duty police officer told me one day. "I have a house and a job, but what about everyone else? The people on top are all thieves, and nobody cares about those below. Nothing is done on merit; everything is corrupt. Even in my own department, 95 percent of the people are taking bribes. It is not right."

The very size and complexity of Pakistan's bureaucracy offers thousands of opportunities for graft, cheating, private deals, and plunder. In addition to the major federal and provincial ministries, there are hundreds of development authorities, municipal corporations, cantonment boards, and other agencies with large budgets and potentially lucrative powers, such as allotting plots of land and dispensing local licenses for everything from sidewalk vendors to construction plans.

As dozens of Pakistanis have told me and hundreds of news reports have documented, government employees regularly demand excessive "fees" for processing paperwork and permits that should be free or available at a nominal cost. By the late 1990s, Rahman reported, there were nearly a thousand public entities employing some 2.7 million people—a state apparatus that has only become more bloated and labyrinthine today.

A similar conundrum exists in the tax system, which exacts revenue for a vast array of services, enterprises, and activities from property sales to hotel rooms, telephone calls to taxi licenses, cargo export to old-age benefits. The problem is that such a complex and onerous system inevitably creates what one observer called the conundrum of "proliferation and pilferage," in which having too many rules makes them easier to break. The widely documented problems of corruption have added to a nationwide culture of tax avoidance. Since people expect officials to pocket revenues, they don't feel the need to pay them, depleting government coffers on both ends.

As I traveled around Pakistan, asking people about their problems and concerns, the issue of corruption came up all the time. Usually the amounts involved were small, or there was no money involved at all, just a question of having to know someone to obtain a service or a piece of paper that should have been provided at no cost, or a favorable decision that should have been judged on merit. The phenomenon of asking for personal favors from anyone with a little influence is so common that it has a name: *safardish,* which roughly translates as "touching."

Corruption is also the subject of a thousand cynical jokes, several of which I liked especially. "Corruption is so bad these days that if you try to commit suicide, you'll probably fail because the poison is diluted." Or "Corruption is so bad these days that even suicide bombers can't be sure the explosives will really go off."

President Zardari became the butt of so many corruption jokes that he finally ordered a legal ban on making fun of him in public. One that stuck in my mind was this: "A robber points a gun at Zardari and says, 'Give me all your money.' Zardari says he has none. 'Then give me all *my* money,' the robber retorts."

PAKISTAN IS REGULARLY LISTED by monitoring groups such as Transparency International as being among the world's most corrupt countries, but what they mostly measure is public perception—the vicious circle in which cheating is so universally assumed that everyone, including the victim, becomes part of the problem.

Even after a decade in which four successive elected governments—two headed by Benazir Bhutto and two by Nawaz Sharif—were thrown out amid charges of corruption or power abuse, Transparency International said in its 2008 report, there is an "unchanging" public perception in Pakistan that corruption is "widespread, systemic and deeply entrenched at all levels of society and government."

Sohail Ahmed, former chairman of the Federal Board of Revenue, said the aversion to paying taxes has become so entrenched that the government collects less than one-third of potential revenues. He confessed that he could not even trust many of his own auditors to resist the blandishments of influential businessmen, and that even the installation of a new electronic tax-filing system had not improved revenue collection. "The problem is people's attitudes," he said.

Usually the corrupt relations among Pakistan's business and political elite remain open secrets, widely rumored and assumed but never investigated or proven. Occasionally, though, all the dirty laundry comes spilling out, confirming the public's worst suspicions and darkest conspiracy theories: the systematic collusion among bankers, businessmen, and officials; the crude partisan politics that influence state loans and financial policies; the breathtaking levels of profiteering and bribery that grease this system at the public's expense.

The scandal involving the Bank of Punjab and Haris Steel Mills featured every one of these practices, plus an eye-opening cast of characters at the top of Pakistan's business and political echelons. The basic plot involved a 9-billion-rupee scheme in which a leading bank made a series of fraudulent loans in 2007 to a Pakistani steel magnate, who later claimed he had protected himself by bribing bank officers, a federal minister, and the attorney general.

Largely due to aggressive intervention by the Supreme Court, the whole sordid tale came out in public. It is worth relating in detail because of its ambitious scope, its creative criminality, and the astonishing ease with which a variety of senior officials and other prominent individuals were apparently willing to protect the scheme or its protagonists in exchange for money.

According to government investigators, the Bank of Punjab, headed by forty-three-year-old Hamesh Khan, made a series of loans in 2007 to Sheikh Afzal, the owner of three steel mills, through an elaborate scheme in which Afzal's associates "allegedly opened 23 fictitious accounts" and obtained 9 billion rupees worth of bad business loans "with the help of fake documentation, bogus collaterals, fictitious guarantees and mortgage deals executed by fake persons."

Afzal, who soon defaulted on the loans, was sued by the bank but fled to Malaysia. The NAB confiscated 130 homes and twenty-two vehicles he owned in Pakistan, and it traced real estate and bank accounts worth 3.25 billion rupees to him in Malaysia and Dubai. Such official diligence contrasted sharply with Afzal's claims that he had paid huge bribes to a number of "worthy" people, including bank officers, lawyers, and government officials, to help him obtain the loans, flee the country, and then win his legal case.

Testifying before the Supreme Court in 2009, Afzal pointed fingers in many directions. He said that two years before, he had paid Attorney General Malik Qayuum 15 million rupees to help suppress the government's case, and that Babar Awan, a close Zardari crony and the cabinet minister for law and parliamentary affairs, had demanded 30 million rupees in a similar deal and accepted 5 million. Both officials denied the accusations.

Hamesh Khan also claimed he was innocent, but he soon moved to the United States, where he holds citizenship, to avoid prosecution and then spent months fighting extradition. The once-rising banker and former chairman of the Lahore Stock Exchange said he had been "on vacation" when the loans were finally approved and that he had been framed for political reasons after refusing to make other business loans to the Sharif family, which he feared would default on the debt. "'No' is not taken very nicely by powerful people like them," he told an American interviewer.

Cynical observers assumed Khan would never set foot in a courtroom, but on May 14, 2010, national TV audiences awoke to the unprecedented sight of a former Pakistani bank president, disheveled and in shirtsleeves, tightly surrounded by dozens of security officers as he was escorted off a plane in Islamabad. After nearly three years, Khan had finally been extradited to face charges in the loan scheme. By Pakistani standards, it was a giant stride for the rule of law.

THE OTHER PILLAR PROPPING up Pakistan's democratic facade is the Parliament. There are two legislative houses: the 342-member National Assembly, which forms governing alliances and duly produces a prime minister from the party that wins the most votes, and the 100-seat Senate, based on regional populations, which has fewer powers but provides political balance among the provinces. Both houses hold sessions in a spacious, majestic building in Islamabad's guarded federal district. The members are provided attractive apartments nearby and reimbursed for all travel to and from their home districts.

Yet although the legislature is ostensibly the people's link to power, critics complain that it remains dominated by landed aristocrats, wealthy industrialists, tribal chiefs, and other members of the traditional power elite. Few outsiders bother, or dare, to run for office. There are no public sources of campaign funds, and few civic or grassroots groups to rally people around a candidate who has not received the imprimatur of party bosses.

Most MNAs, as members of the National Assembly are universally known, come from a few powerful families in their home districts that are closely linked with local agricultural, business, or tribal interests. These clans often run candidates for provincial legislatures and district council leadership offices, or *nazims,* as well. In many rural districts, members of the same family also show up as police chiefs or local administrators.

The constitution sets aside seventy seats for women and religious minorities, but many are filled by the spouses of political barons or other substitutes for the intended occupants. Still, a handful of female lawmakers, including Sherry Rehman and Marvi Memon, have become outspoken advocates for human and women's rights. Although both come from wealthy families, they express frustration and disgust with the indifference of their colleagues to the plight of poor and vulnerable Pakistanis.

When the National Assembly was discussing the proposed Swat peace accord with the Taliban, Rehman was the only legislator who questioned what its impact would be on conditions for women in Swat. When most legislators ducked the volatile issue of blasphemy law reform, Rehman introduced a private bill calling for a series of modest changes—such as the requirement that accusers produce evidence—and was hounded by death threats from religious groups as a result.

The economic privilege of Pakistan's political leadership cuts across party lines, or is at least shared between the two dominant parties, the Pakistan Muslim League and the Pakistan People's Party. In 2009, when escalating sugar prices led to public protests and accusations of hoarding, speculation, and collusion among the so-called sugar barons, the list of mill owners published in the Pakistani press included a who's who of lawmakers from both parties.

Political elitism has spawned a class-conscious VIP culture that insulates Pakistani leaders from the real world in which most of their compatriots must survive. When MNAs visit their constituencies, they are invariably driven between meetings and receptions in convoys of Land Cruisers. While sycophants shower them with welcoming rose petals, humble citizens in shabby clothes wait for hours outside with their petitions or problems, hoping for a glance or a word.

Politics is very much a family business in Pakistan, and despite a series of internal splits, both parties remain dominated by a single dynasty: the Sharifs of Punjab and the Bhuttos of Sindh. Candidacies are ritually parceled out among family members and friends, especially in safe districts. The parties offer individual "tickets" to the nephews, brothers, and younger cousins of longtime officeholders, and campaign posters appear featuring small portraits of the younger newcomers next to the larger, familiar visages of Nawaz Sharif or Benazir Bhutto.

There is a similar verticality in party offices, especially in the PPP. Bhutto ruled the organization with an iron hand for years, and now her older son, Bilawal, is already being groomed at age twenty-one to become its next chairman. This continuation of dynastic control can only discourage other potential young leaders from rising in the party that has traditionally been the only national political magnet for liberals and reformists.

The image of Parliament as a sinecure for privileged fat cats was reinforced in September 2010 when a group called the Pakistani Institute of Legislative Development and Transparency, or PILDAT, issued a report listing the declared incomes of all Pakistani legislators. The group found that on average, members of Parliament had tripled their wealth in the last five years, and that most were very wealthy by Pakistani standards.

Yet the real problem is not the wealth of the lawmakers but the attitude that comes with it. Many MNAs are intelligent, articulate individuals, accessible to the press and familiar with the issues that matter to their districts. They cringe at the suggestion that they are part of a feudal elite, and they explain that because of land reforms, inheritance laws, and changing economic patterns, the stereotypical feudal lord no longer exists.

But though hereditary land ownership patterns have gradually been diluted since Partition, the patronizing feudal mind-set still lives. Lawmaker-landlords tend to think of longtime tenant farmers and local laborers as "their" voters, whose loyalty at the ballot box they are obliged to reward with protection from rival clans, abusive police, or corrupt government agencies. But this political relationship—often reinforced by tribal or clan hierarchies—can also be a form of dependent thrall, which prevents the rural poor from becoming educated, skilled, and able to think for themselves.

"My family and my tribe have owned huge amounts of land here for generations. The villagers are my clansmen, my voters, my supporters. They depend on me, and I protect them," a rural legislator from the Muslim League explained to me during a visit to his district. He spoke proudly of the relationship, in a way that made perfect sense, yet he seemed not at all bothered by the high levels of poverty and illiteracy in his constituency and the sharp contrast with his own enormous wealth.

Abida Hussain, the veteran legislator and landowner from Punjab, pointed out that the problem of landlordism in Pakistan is no longer necessarily related to land. It is, rather, the persistence of a privileged attitude among the wealthy that goes hand in hand with the dominance of militarism. In recent decades, the focus of wealth in Pakistan has shifted from agriculture to manufacturing and services, yet this has only sporadically translated into more enlightened politics.

"Feudalism is a state of mind. It is the total absence of democratic culture in our country, which is not easy to develop," Hussain told me. "We still spend too much on national security and not enough on people and services. It is a fifty-year-old story. But if we keep going through the motions, but by bit, democracy can slowly emerge."

IN THEORY, THERE ARE enough political parties in Pakistan to represent every region, ideology, class, ethnic group, and comfort zone on the spectrum of secular and religious leanings. Yet with few exceptions, most Pakistanis feel excluded from organized party politics and view it as a spectator sport, a dirty game played among self-interested elites and competing personality cults, rather than as an open exercise in which they can participate and work for political change.

"Ever since Jinnah, our leaders have behaved in a way that denies the nation self-respect," a government administrator in Lahore told me during a discussion in a graduate class in public policy. "The people of Pakistan will work eighteen hours a day if you give them self respect, but they have no say in decisions at all, so they do not believe in democracy."

Membership in political parties is extremely low, and most people who join them do so out of personal loyalty to leaders rather than affinity for an idea. Young Pakistanis show almost no interest in joining the major parties.

Benazir Bhutto drew huge, frenzied crowds of supporters and commanded the loyalty of thousands of party "workers," as they called themselves, including women from the working class as well as those from elite backgrounds. People adored her because they believed she cared, but their support for the party was thin. When the far less popular Zardari came to power, the PPP lost its soul.

Yet even the PPP, which has promoted the cause of political and social justice since it was created in the 1960s, relies on small cadres of loyal party "workers" to get out the vote and is governed by a remarkable internal hierarchy. Benazir Bhutto, who championed democracy for the people of Pakistan, ran her party like an autocrat, even during her years in exile.

One exception is the MQM. It is the most participatory and modern of Pakistan's parties, and it has large numbers of activists, but its base is confined to the city of Karachi, its leader is in permanent exile because of criminal charges, and its appeal is marred by a history of thuggish violence. The other exception is Jamaat-e-Islami, the

Sunni-based religious party, which has a tightly organized member-ship and an aggressive youth wing but has never won more than a handful of elected offices.

The main role of these smaller parties in national politics has been to play kingmaker and form coalitions with either of the two warring elephants, the PPP and the Muslim League, who have dominated electoral politics in Pakistan for the past two decades. Because the major parties are led from the top down, idealistic young profession-als with ideas for change tend to seek other outlets, and poorer people outside the traditional political elite are discouraged from seeking public office. When they do, the establishment tends to quash or dis-credit them for fear of upsetting the classist order of things.

When Mai Jori Jamali ran for the Balochistan provincial assembly in 2010, it made dramatic political news and raised a firestorm in the local establishment. Jamali, a peasant woman whose candidacy threatened the cozy power structure of landlord-politicians, received many threats to her life and lost badly at the polls, but her candidacy nonetheless marked an important step for democratic rights.

A more successful upstart is Jamshed Dasti, a rough-hewn grass-roots leader from southern Punjab, who has been challenging the old political order and tapping into a thirst for change among the disen-franchised and rural poor. Dasti is a member of Parliament from Muzzafarghar, an agricultural district that was devastated by the floods in 2010. He became a local hero by championing the plight of his poor constituents and denouncing the feudal landlords who long held power there.

To the political elite, Dasti was little more than an ambitious thug. His record was unsavory, including an old murder charge. His credentials were questionable; he spoke no English and was found to have faked his college decree, a requirement for membership in the National Assembly. In March 2010, the Supreme Court disqualified him from office, but two months later Muzzafarghar's voters elected Dasti again, rejecting a prominent landowner whose social pedigree and influence would once have made him a shoo-in.

Dasti's political resurrection was not entirely pure—he reportedly got help from Zardari's sister to run for office a second time, humiliating the party's chosen candidate. But supporters mocked the pious indignation of upper-crust politicians over Dasti's dubious educational pedigree. And some observers suggested that Pakistan needs to encourage more Dastis to enter politics if it wants the alienated masses to start identifying with democratic institutions rather than turning to radical Islam for inspiration and guidance.

"The truth is that we have not had real democracy for a single day in our history," said Athar Minallah, a lawyer and political activist in Islamabad. "There is a very antidemocratic mind-set among the ruling elite; there is enormous hypocrisy and snobbery. The establishment ridicules Dasti because he has no degree. They don't realize that for people in places like Muzzafurghar, the state doesn't exist, and human beings live like animals. But they have the right to choose, and they chose to give him another chance. This is the beginning of democracy."

Occasionally there are signs of change at the top too. One of them occurred in the spring of 2010, when the National Assembly overcame its penchant for passivity and hyperpartisanship—much to the astonished delight of the nation—to pass the historic Eighteenth Amendment to Pakistan's constitution.

The sweeping measure removed the right of the president to dissolve the National Assembly and transferred essential powers to the prime minister, turning Pakistan from a semipresidential democracy into a full parliamentary democracy. It also reversed many of the legal infringements on the constitution that had been made by two former military rulers, granted more autonomy to the provinces, and made some reforms to the judicial appointment system.

The amendment occupied weeks of wrangling and horse-trading among lawmakers from half a dozen major parties, including a complicated fight over the renaming of Northwest Frontier Province that required satisfying various ethnic groups and resulted in its cumbersome new designation as Khyber Pakhtunkhwa. At one point Nawaz Sharif staged a political melodrama and threatened to pull Muslim League support.

When it was all over, though, Pakistan's much-maligned politicians had pulled off a major feat of legislative compromise and institution building that seemed to bode well for the nation. Much of the Charter of Democracy, the original agreement between Sharif and Zardari, was included in the bill. Although critics soon found numerous weaknesses and loopholes in the amendment, supporters called it a giant step that gave Pakistan's democratic system more insulation against military or executive autocracy.

Still, nobody harbored any illusions that Pakistan's political culture had changed overnight, or that its democracy was any less vulnerable to violent mischief. The judiciary and legislature were showing new promise, and the Zardari government had made peace with the army and the establishment, but it was the assassination of Benazir Bhutto that remained the dominant political event of the post-Musharraf era and a permanent setback to prospects for reclaiming Jinnah's lost Pakistan.

There were many, in fact, who believed Pakistan's nascent democracy had already died with Jinnah in 1948. Whether the murder of Benazir Bhutto was the product of a brainwashed Islamic militant or a cynical deal among her many political enemies, it was also, in some ways, the product of a long, slow death that had begun six decades before, when the man who dreamed of building the world's first modern Muslim democracy gave up the ghost.

EPILOGUE

THE OFFICE IS OLD and shabby, with files jumbled on desks and phone numbers scribbled on walls. There is a hum of activity and a battle-scarred van parked in the alley outside. It feels like a place where appearances don't matter but everyone has a purpose. There is an air of glee and gravitas, mayhem and mission, like the campaign office of a young firebrand running his first political race.

But the firebrand is in his eighties now, and the office is headquarters for a revolutionary charitable movement he has built over the past four decades. His mission has been to serve troubled and poor individuals who are shunned by society, while trying to shame the affluent establishment that ignores them and to change the traditions that condemn them to suffer.

His name is Abdul Sattar Edhi. He is a legend in Pakistan, where he has been hailed as a Mahatma Gandhi and Mother Teresa—yet also denounced as an infidel, communist, and madman. In a patronage-based society where wealth and bluster often pass for leadership and cruelty is more common than mercy, he may be Pakistan's only true living hero.

I found my way to Edhi's office in Mithadar, a run-down section of Karachi, in the summer of 2010. Until then I had known little about him except as the founder of a private, nationwide ambulance service that provided free emergency transport to anyone in need, from heart attack patients to earthquake victims. At every disaster scene, every bombing or train crash, there were always Edhi Foundation ambulances rushing about. I knew people admired him greatly, and I had seen photos of an old man with the flowing white beard of a wise elder or Muslim cleric.

I was not expecting to encounter the unrepentantly subversive, slightly cranky octogenarian who sat at his cluttered desk under a portrait of Jinnah. He didn't say much at first, but he handed me photographs of a tiny girl with deep wounds in her face. She had been found in a garbage dump, half eaten by dogs. Rescued by Edhi's volunteers, she had been sent abroad for multiple surgeries and eventually adopted by a family in Canada.

"Some people strangle them, the illegitimate children. Others just dump them to die. We believe there is no such thing as an illegitimate person," Edhi said. Indeed, he had spent forty years seeking society's outcasts and offering them what he could, from nursing abandoned infants to washing and burying the unclaimed dead. He had opened boarding schools for unwanted teenagers, built programs for drug addicts and AIDS patients, and helped senile shut-ins left to rot. Far more than an ambulance service, it was a philosophy of life.

I asked Edhi if he was a religious man, and he shook his head. "My religion is humanity. It is the only religion that matters," he said. Later, I learned that conservative Pakistani clerics had issued fatwas against him and banned mosques from helping him, but that humble people often greeted him as *maulana sahib,* a term of religious respect.

A few moments later, he shifted into a diatribe against the greed and selfishness of Pakistan's wealthy elites. Here was another contradiction: Edhi himself was a product of the prominent Memon business clan in Karachi, but he had been drawn to a humbler calling. As a young man he had served in Parliament briefly but grew disillusioned with politics. He has rejected organized charity as placating rather than empowering the poor. In the 1960s, he turned full-time to his fledgling mission in the slums.

"When we started out, I decided not to knock on the door of the industrialists and the landlords, because they are the root cause of all our social problems," he told me. "The rich have deprived the people of their rights, and the state does not take responsibility for their welfare. It is my dream to build a welfare state in Pakistan, but I have not seen it come in my lifetime. What keeps me going is working for the masses."

It was a speech with a dogmatic, socialist tinge, and it made me realize that Edhi was much more complex than a saintly do-gooder. He was a self-appointed conscience of the nation, an eccentric crusader who sought to shock the comfortable and galvanize the afflicted. The reason he got away with it, year after year, was not only because he received awards and honorary degrees from foundations and governments all over the world, but also because he lived what he preached.

Here is a passage from Edhi's 1995 autobiography, *A Mirror to the Blind,* about the primitive essence of human indifference to suffering, and about the ordeals Edhi embraced as a young man to challenge his own biases and set an example to others: "I began at Mithadar and I brought back bloated, drowned bodies from the sea . . . I picked them up from rivers, from inside wells, from roadsides . . . bodies infested with maggots . . . I bathed and cared for each and every victim of circumstance." But he found that "even those compassionate enough to help me grimaced . . . they complained vigorously of the stench . . . then they rushed home to bathe . . . only I was not disgusted." The experience, Edhi wrote, made him realize that "we could not reduce suffering unless we rose above our own senses . . . cringing was the first and greatest hindrance that blocked our way." The world of poverty and squalor was a "frightening world. Nobody wanted to stroll through it, let alone live in it. For me there was no other."

In my travels through Pakistan, I had glimpsed many pockets of

Edhi's adopted world and cringed a little too, but felt I needed to look. I had seen charitable and relief programs at work, some well-intentioned but others tarred by charges of aid siphoning, political favoritism, and corruption. I had met various apparently idealistic reformists, but they often denounced each other as frauds or egotists. Edhi seemed to be an exception, but he was also famously brusque and had little patience for foreign visitors like me.

It was his wife, Bilquis, who took the time to introduce me to the work of the Edhi Foundation. I had already seen how cruelly people in Pakistan suffered because of social convention and conservative traditions, but observing the Edhis' philosophy put into practice made me understand what a subversive act it was to shelter and defend people who had been trapped or cast off by stifling mores, and what a daunting mission to try to change them.

"People say we are crazy, but our main goal is to respect everyone and to create respect for everyone," Bilquis told me as we arrived at Sarabkot, a boarding school for 250 unwanted girls between the ages of five and eighteen. It was a welcoming cocoon with stuffed animals and books and bright colors, but there was a rigorous schedule of classes, prayer, meals, and homework. The girls wore tan uniforms and slept in eighteen-bed dorms. Twice a month they went on supervised outings to the beach or a park.

Two sixth-graders named Saira and Saima agreed to talk to me after their math class. They were shy, and the conversation was painful. Both girls had been dumped there by their families as small children, and neither had heard from them since. "I don't know why they brought me here. I miss them, but I think they forgot about me," ventured Saima, her eyes filling with tears. "Maybe if I study hard and get a good position, one day they will take me back."

Bilquis said many girls end up at Sarabkot because their mothers remarry, and the new husband either does not want to be responsible for the girls or tries to molest them. Sometimes, after years of no contact or support, the family suddenly reappears and claims the daughter. "If a mother comes and wants the girl back, I cannot legally stop her," Bilquis said. "But if she wants to marry her off to an old man for a lot of money, I try to find a better alternative."

Sarabkot is housed in an old seaside mansion, donated by a wealthy businessman. It has a labyrinth of high-ceilinged rooms, now filled with bunk beds and mountains of donated clothing. One musty parlor wall is hung with plaques and awards honoring Edhi's work, from governments and organizations all over the world. But it is the basement that showcases the foundation's real mission: to bring dignity, self-esteem, and a chance for happiness to those whom society has forgotten or deemed unworthy.

We descended the stairs and Bilquis snapped on the lights. We were in an elaborately decorated salon, with satin pillows and drapes and a red carpeted stage in the middle. The one jarring note was a painting of a small boy, probably a servant, who Bilquis said had died of burns after someone threw scalding water on him. Everything else made the room seem like a parlor for a fairy-tale princess.

"We give our girls birthday parties and engagement celebrations here. It makes them feel special. And we have had 210 weddings," she said proudly. "I work hard to find the girls good husbands, from progressive families who don't care about money and don't want *maulvis* involved. They have to finish high school first, and they have to meet the boy and be happy with the match. We even arrange their honeymoons."

The Edhis' work with girls has been particularly controversial. Bilquis said some neighbors had sued to shut down Sarabkot, charging that it was being used as a brothel, but the courts sided with the foundation. Edhi has spoken out strongly against forced marriages, domestic abuse, and the Hudood laws, under which raped women are often charged with adultery while their attackers go free.

But his overarching crusade is against the social attitudes and customs that keep millions of people submissive and trapped. In his autobiography, he bluntly condemns the "medieval" tribal practice of selling girls and dismisses the government as "merely an exclusive VIP service." He often displays a crusader's single-minded arrogance, saying he has tried to "goad many learned men."

Yet Edhi has always preached from an unassailable perch on the lowest rung of the ladder. Even as he has become a much-traveled, often-interviewed, and honored celebrity, he has continued to practice personal poverty as a way of reinforcing his message, and he clearly revels in the contradiction. In one anecdote in his autobiography, he recounts how he horrified his hosts on a first-class foreign tour by washing his socks and underwear and hanging them out to dry.

He is not an easy man to be around, demanding that his associates and acolytes give up even small luxuries to stay true to their mission. Bilquis had a hard time when they were first married, wishing for a bride's moment of pampering, but Edhi was too busy saving the world, and she had to adjust fast to a life of simplicity and sacrifice.

Now, after forty years, she is his indefatigable partner and ally. Edhi still preaches to the rich and powerful, crusading to build a modern welfare state that will be at least another generation in the making, but his wife's greatest joy is in saving one child at a time, and in fussing over brides no one in Pakistani society would once have thought fit to marry.

acknowledgments

I WOULD LIKE TO thank the following people—friends and colleagues, sources of insight or inspiration—who helped me navigate a vast, complex society and explain it to distant readers in a way that I hope will be constructive and concerned rather than polemical or pedantic.

In Pakistan, I appreciated those who made time for many frank and thoughtful conversations, including Salman Abbasy, Sen. Khursheid Ahmad, Aitzaz Ahsan, Ayaz Amir, Abdul Sattar Edhi and Bilquis Edhi, the late Nahida Mehbooba Elahi, Imtiaz Gul, Tami Haq, Pervez Hoodbhoy, Abida Hussain, Mushahid Hussain, Prof. Rifaat Hussain, Ahmed Khan, Afrasiab Khattak, Anwar Kamal Marwat, Athar Minallah, Talat Masood, Hamid Mir, Ahmed Rashid, Sherry Rehman, Hassan Azkari Rizvi, and Saeed Shafqat. I am particularly grateful for my stimulating encounters with Roedad Khan, an iconoclastic octogenarian who still believes.

I also want to thank the friends and colleagues in Pakistan who often made grim events easier to bear or helped me understand them better: Akhtar Abbas, Veronique Ahmed, Dr. Hamid Akbar and Jackie, Haroon Akbar and his staff, Noshe Forrest, Carlotta Gall,

Atle Hetland, Sarfraz Hussain, Tahir and Samra Ikram, Shabbir Hussain Imam, Anwar Iqbal, Babur Kamal, Behroz Khan, Haq Nawaz Khan, Nisar Mehdi, Sidra Omer, Ali Paracha and his staff, Fareed Qureshi and his family, Aoun Sahi, Fayyaz Shah, Hussain Shaiq, and Zulqernain Tahir, who gamely accompanied me on meandering missions to rescue stray dogs and visit Sufi shrines.

In Washington, I am indebted to Bob Hathaway, Sanaz Talaifar, and the staff of the Woodrow Wilson International Center for Scholars, where I was able to hide away and think for an entire summer. Thanks also to Huma Yusuf, Steve Cohen, Griff Witte, Bill Milam, Shuja Nawaz, Rashid and Bano Makhdoom, Ray and Shaista Mahmood, and several other friends who offered their thoughts or read chapters with a sharp and helpful eye.

Finally, I am eternally grateful to Don Graham, David Hoffman, Doug Jehl, and my other editors at the *Washington Post* over the past seventeen years, who have given me rein to roam and write and learn something new every day.

notes

CHAPTER 1: *The Flood*

4 **Between June and September** The UN Office for the Coordination of Humanitarian Affairs in Islamabad issued weekly "Pakistan Flood Response Fact Sheets" with detailed updates and images of damage, losses, costs, and assistance. For a haunting glimpse of the tragedy, read Daniyal Mueenundin's essay "A Lifetime, Washed Away," *New York Times,* August 18, 2010.

8 **The Indus first reaches,** For a detailed overview, see *Running on Empty: Pakistan's Water Crisis,* an edited collection of essays from the Woodrow Wilson International Center for Scholars, Washington, DC, 2009.

9 **The situation is even worse,** "Public Opinion in Pakistan's Tribal Regions," September 2010, New America Foundation, Washington, DC. This was the first comprehensive opinion survey in the tribal region, and its findings are cited throughout this book.

11 **"This is how it works"** From extensive interviews with the author, villages in rural Punjab, June 2009.

16 **The most volatile problem,** See "Population, Labor Force and Employment," *Pakistan Economic Survey, 2009–2010,* Ministry of Finance, Government of Pakistan.

18 **In this fast, gritty,** See "Manufacturing," *Pakistan Economic Survey, 2009–2010.*

22 **The growing "Talibanization"** "The Social Dimensions of Food Insecurity in Pakistan," by Abid Qaiyum Suleri, in *Hunger Pains: Pakistan's Food Insecurity,* Woodrow Wilson International Center for Scholars, Washington, DC, 2010.

CHAPTER 2: *Sahibs*

29 **"From the beginning"** Interview with author, Lahore, May, 2010. One of many conversations I had with Ahsan about politics, law, and Pakistani history during more than a decade.

30 **Since the mid-2000s** See "Growth and Investment," *Pakistan Economic Survey, 2009–2010.*

31 **The high concentration** *Who Owns Pakistan,* published in 1999, and later updated, by Pakistani journalist Shahid-ur Rehman, remains the most detailed and comprehensive history of Pakistan's wealthiest families and businesses, including their relations with successive governments.

34 **By the time Musharraf** See the National Accountability Bureau website, www.nab.gov.pk, for a detailed description of its mandate and activities.

36 **"There is probably no multinational"** Country Study Report, National Integrity Systems, Pakistan, 2003, published by Transparency International, Berlin.

37 **Even after a decade,** see "Overview of Corruption in Pakistan, 2008," Transparency International. www.transparency.org.

37 **A few Pakistani officials** Interview with the author, Islamabad, April 2010.

40 **"People love to hate the rich"** Interview with the author, Lahore, November 2009.

42 **"I still get up at four"** Interview with the author, Islamabad, April 2010.

44 **"My drawing room"** Interview with the author, Islamabad, June 2010. This was one of many conversations I had with Hussain, mostly about Pakistani politics, between 1999 and 2010.

45 **"You have to have standards"** Interview with the author, Karachi, January 2010.

46 **Shahid Javed Burk** Essay in *Dawn*, April 28, 2009.

48 **"My father was an officer"** Interview with the author, Faisalabad, February 2010.

CHAPTER 3: *Honor*

51 **"Back home, the entire establishment"** Interview with the author, undisclosed location, spring 2010. This was one of several lengthy conversations I had with the couple while they were living in a government-sponsored shelter.

52 **According to two women's rights groups** Statistics of violence against women in Pakistan in 2009, Press Statement, Aurat Foundation and Members of Violence Against Women, Islamabad, February 1, 2010.

53 **The case that drew** Mukhtaran Mai's story was covered extensively in the Pakistani and international press between 2002 and 2007. Nicholas Kristof of the *New York Times* drew early and repeated attention to her plight in numerous columns.

57 **Violent domestic abuse** *My Feudal Lord,* an autobiography by Tehmina Durrani first published in 1994, was extremely controversial in Pakistan but became an international bestseller.

58 **Occasionally, a news story** The case of Shazia Masih was extensively covered in the Pakistani press. This account was drawn from numerous news articles and commentaries.

62 **Jamali, who campaigned against** Quoted in "Pakistani Lawmaker Defends Honor Killings of Burying Women Alive," In the Media, Digital Journal, August 30, 2008.

63 **These laws, known as the Hudood Ordinances** There have

been numerous articles, commentaries, and reports on efforts to reform the Hudood Ordinances. One example is "Despite Sound and Fury, Hudood Laws Still Stay," ipsnews.net, September 26, 2003.

65 **The elders offered** Interviews with the author, villages in northern Sindh, spring 2010.

67 **"My position came from my grandfather"** Interview with author, northern Sindh, spring 2010.

69 **"Pakistan's dirty little secret"** Interview with author, Islamabad, May 2010.

71 **"Things are changing"** Interview with author, Islamabad, April, 2010.

CHAPTER 4: *Hate*

74 **Pakistan's founding father,** This speech has been cited in dozens of books and articles. One of the best references is Ian Talbot's *Pakistan: A Modern History,* published in London in 1998. He cites the speech on p. 136, nothing that Jinnah's pronouncement would prove "so uncomfortable for those seeking to transform Pakistan into a theocracy."

78 **The editors of the newspaper *Dawn,*** Editorial in *Dawn,* May 30, 2010.

78 **Columnist Huma Yusuf** Common Ground News Service, June 15, 2010.

82 **"We never saw such hatred"** Interview with the author, Gojra, April 2010.

84 **What came next was even more stunning,** The assassination of Governor Taseer, and the outpouring of public support for his killer, aroused a flood of anguished commentary in Pakistan and abroad, as well as thousands of impassioned blogs. Less than two months later, Shabbaz Bhatti, the federal minister for religious minority affairs and a Christian rights activist, was gunned down outside his family home. A radical Islamist group claimed responsibility, saying it had targeted him because of his opposition to the blasphemy law.

87 **But the formal ban had little impact,** See chapter 22 of Amir Mir's book, *Talibanisation of Pakistan,* published in 2009 by Pentagon Security International in New Delhi. This is the best and most comprehensive study of Islamic militant organizations in Pakistan, including the anti-Shiite groups described here.

89 **"We are peaceful"** Interview with the author, Jhang, May 2010.

CHAPTER 5: *Khaki*

93 **"The paradox that hobbled Pakistan's"** From *Crossed Swords: Pakistan, Its Army and the Wars Within,* by Shuja Nawaz, Oxford University Press, 2008, p. xxviii. This is a minutely detailed insider's history of the Pakistan army, written by a Pakistani American scholar and son of a former Pakistani army chief.

95 **In 2009, a survey,** See "Concern About Extremist Threat Slips in Pakistan," a report from the Global Attitudes Project of the Pew Research Center, Washington, DC, July 29, 2010.

97 **"The military's hegemony in Pakistan"** From *Military, Inc.: Inside Pakistan's Military Economy,* by Ayesha Siddiqa, Pluto Press, 2007. This is a groundbreaking study of how Pakistan's military establishment has gained economic, political, and social sway over Pakistani society, becoming very wealthy in the process.

99 **"Unrelenting misery"** *Dawn,* January 27, 2010.

99 **"In the military, eight o'clock means eight o'clock"** Interview with the author, National University of Science and Technology, Islamabad, February 2010.

101 **"Whenever the army has come in"** Interview with the author, Rawalpindi, April 2010. This perception was echoed by a variety of military and civilian observers.

102 **The official motto of the Pakistani army** See the army's official website, www.ajmalbeig.addr.com/pak_army.htm.

104 **"Zia's iron-fisted rule"** Hussain Haqqani's book, *Pakistan: Between Mosque and Military,* published in 2005 by the Carnegie

Endowment for International Peace, is a knowledgeable, frank, and damning portrait of political and religious manipulation by Pakistan's military establishment over the past several decades.

107 **Musharraf defended his decision** In addition to his numerous public comments on these issues, Musharraf published an English-language memoir in 2006 called *In the Line of Fire,* in which he sought to justify his military takeover, his longevity in power, his role in the Kargil invasion of India, and his support for the U.S. war on terror as decisions made for the good of Pakistan.

110 **As ISI grew in size and ambition** Haqqani's book describes this process in detail, especially the agency's deepening role in domestic politics. Both Ahmed Rashid's *Descent into Chaos,* published by Viking in 2008, and Amir Mir's *Talibanisation* describe the ISI's more recent role as a covert liaison to militant groups officially disavowed by the government.

112 **Yet Pakistan's military and intelligence officials** *News International,* September 21, 2010.

112 **Shocked and mortified** *Crossed Swords,* p. 578.

117 **"Many secrets died with Khalid Khwaja"** *The News International,* May 6, 2010. Other intriguing accounts of Khwaja's murky role were published in the same newspaper by Hamid Mir, the TV journalist who was also a key actor in the drama.

121 **Nevertheless, Pakistan sees India** From "Concern About Extremist Threat Slips in Pakistan," a report from the Global Attitudes Project of the Pew Research Center, Washington, DC, July 29, 2010.

122 **Yet the core of his argument** Author's notes from lecture at Center for Strategic and International Studies. Washington, DC, November 22, 2010.

124 **A wealth of detail** A comprehensive public report on the background of the Mumbai attack was researched by the nonprofit group Pro Publica and published in the *Washington Post,*

October 16, 2010. The *New York Times* published a similar account.

125 **"The military is still spending"** "The Road to Kabul Runs through Kashmir," *Foreign Policy*, November 10, 2010.

128 **The morning after Zardari relented** Editorial in *The News International*, March 16, 2009.

128 **Columnist Cyril Almeida** From opinion column in *Dawn*, September 10, 2010.

CHAPTER 6: *Talibanization*

134 **"I was afraid"** Interview with author, Peshawar, September 2009.

136 **"Zia used official coercion"** Interview with author, Lahore, May 2010.

136 **The largest and most successful** Jamaat-e-Islami also has its own think tank, the Institute for Policy Studies in Islamabad, whose leading scholar, national senator Khurshid Ahmad, I interviewed numerous times on religious issues.

139 **"An entire generation has been brought up"** Interview with the author, Islamabad, May 2010.

141 **Pakistanis were confused** From "Concern About Extremist Threat Slips in Pakistan," a report from the Global Attitudes Project of the Pew Research Center, Washington, DC, July 29, 2010.

143 **The doyenne of Pakistan's hawks** Mazari, the former longtime director of a state-sponsored research institute in Islamabad, is now editor of the *Nation* newspaper. Her opinion columns also appear regularly in the Pakistani press.

144 **Some of these changes were reflections** Cited in "The Conservatively Hip," a blog archive from *Newsline* magazine, September 3, 2010.

145 **"We are good Muslims"** Interview with the author, Lahore, April 2010.

148 **"I am certain the Taliban would never"** Interview with author, Peshawar, October 29, 2009.

150 **Several years before** The cartoons of the Prophet Mohammed were originally published in the Danish newspaper *Jyllands-Posten* in September 2005, provoking protests throughout the Muslim world and death threats against the cartoonist. They were reprinted in 2008, triggering further protests. The issue flared again in April 2010 when a Seattle artist, Molly Norris, posted a tongue-in-cheek item online proposing "Everybody Draw Mohammed Day."

152 **Then the conversation took** Interview with the author, Lahore, May 2010.

153 **"The public schools do not teach"** Interviews with the author, School of Islam and Modern Sciences, Barakho, April 2010.

156 **For those two hours, I felt** From author's notes of student debate, Islamic International University, Islamabad, October 2009.

158 **"We have no fear of martyrdom"** Interviews with the author, Jamia Naeemia, Lahore, June 2010.

CHAPTER 7: *The Siege*

162 **The battle of the Red Mosque** Amir Mir's *Talibanisation of Pakistan* includes a lengthy section on the siege of the Red Mosque, the events that led to the confrontation, and the violent retaliation by militant groups.

162 **The history of this netherworld** The profiles of these groups are drawn in part from Mir's book, which includes individual chapters on the history, formation, and activities of the major militant factions. Several are also partly based on the author's interviews with Islamic clerics and militant spokesmen.

164 **"The walls were filled with anti-Western slogans,"** Bilal's account was published in *The News International*, June 23, 2008.

167 **"How much slavery will you accept"** From author's notes of a Friday sermon by Hafiz Saeed, Lahore, April 2010.

169 **"Notwithstanding any ramification"** Quotation from the

Lahore High Court ruling issued shortly after the petition of *Hafiz Muhammad Saeed v. Province of Punjab* and other official respondents was heard in court on October 12, 2009.

170 **"The Indians and the Americans"** Interview with the author, Lahore, April 2010.

173 **The attack had been planned meticulously** The siege of Mumbai was covered exhaustively in the Indian media, including dramatic live TV coverage. A documentary aired on HBO called *Terror in Mumbai* featured chilling phone conversations between the attackers and their handlers as the siege unfolded; the calls were taped by foreign intelligence agencies. See also the note for page 124 regarding detailed reports by the nonprofit group Pro Publica.

176 **Since the 1980s, the number of madrassas** The International Crisis Group has published several important studies of Pakistani madrassas, especially its March 2007 report, "Pakistan: Karachi's Madrassas and Violent Extremism."

179 **"Everyone knows that suicide bombing"** Interview with the author, Karachi, January 2010.

CHAPTER 8: *The Girl from Swat*

183 **"There was something in the soil"** Interview with the author, Peshawar, April 2009.

184 **It was hard to know** Associated Press report, December 30, 2008.

185 **"When the militants first came"** Interview with the author, Islamabad, April 2009.

186 **A night watchman said** Interview with journalist Haq Nawaz Khan, Mardan, April 2009.

188 **A rogue's gallery of these warlords** Author Amir Mir describes many of these militant leaders, including Baitullah Mehsud, in *Talibanisation of Pakistan.* Mehsud was also described and filmed by several Pakistani journalists who visited his tribal hideout.

190 **"What is happening in South Waziristan"** Interview with

the author, Peshawar, July 2008. Khattak, a longtime human rights leader and Pashtun political activist, shared many insights with me about tribal and militant issues over the years. He is now a member of the National Assembly.

193 **"We were the first to challenge them"** Interview with the author, Peshawar, May 2010. Marwat and I met several times in Islamabad, Peshawar, and Lakki Marwat, where he introduced me to elders from the decimated village of Shah Hassan Khel.

198 **On February 15, the government capitulated** The complete text of the Nizam-e-Adl order was published by the Associated Press of Pakistan, April 14, 2009.

198 **In Peshawar** *USA Today,* February 16, 2009.

199 **"We are not sure what is going to come"** Telephone interview with the author, April 2009.

199 **"The problem wasn't Nizam-e-Adl,"** Interview with the author, Islamabad, April 2009.

200 **On April 19, the true nature** For a report on this event and its political and religious significance, see "Extremist Tide Rises in Pakistan," *Washington Post,* April 20, 2009.

201 **"It is now clear"** *Dawn,* April 23, 2009.

202 **Even after a Taliban spokesman had stated** Interview with the author, Islamabad, June 2009.

206 **"It doesn't really feel like Eid"** Interview with the author, Batkhela, September 2009.

208 **"This place was a fountainhead of terrorism"** From author's notes during army-arranged tour of Sararogha, November 2009.

209 **"The myth had to be broken"** From briefing at army's general headquarters, Rawalpindi, February 1, 2010.

CHAPTER 9: *Justice*

212 **"The ordinary perception in Pakistan"** From opinion piece in *The News International,* February 14, 2009.

218 **I had always admired Elahi,** These interviews were con-

ducted at the Rawalpindi District Court complex during several weeks in April 2010. I wrote a lengthy article in 2000 on the case of Zahida Perveen, the woman disfigured by her husband. See "In Pakistan, Women Pay the Price of Honor," *Washington Post,* May 8, 2000.

218 **"In the beginning, Pakistan was created"** Interview with the author, Lahore, October 2009.

221 **All spring the protests continued** It was extraordinary to witness the transformation of Pakistan's staid and bookish legal fraternity into a movement of street protesters defying the law. Ahsan, the veteran barrister who led many of the protests, is a politician and writer whom I had often interviewed in his book-lined home and office in Lahore. During the state of emergency, he was confined there under house arrest.

223 *A Case of Exploding Mangoes,* The comic novel by Mohammed Hanif was published by Alfred A. Knopf, May 2008.

225 **"The investigation was severely hampered"** The report of the United Nations Commission of Inquiry into the assassination of Benazir Bhutto was reprinted in full in *The News International* edition of April 17, 2010.

227 **Arrests and releases** Husain Haqqani, *Pakistan: Between Mosque and Military,* p. 303.

228 **"The system can only work"** Interview with the author, Islamabad, May 2010.

232 **"A year after the dawn"** *The News International,* March 16, 2009.

233 **The new chief justice did not disappoint** The complex legal and political battle between President Musharraf and Chief Justice Chaudhry, and the lawyers' movement that drove the campaign to restore him, was covered extensively in the Pakistani press. A detailed and useful document is "A Chronology of the Lawyers' Movement," published in the *Daily Times,* March 11, 2008.

234 **"God has given us a ray of hope"** These comments were taken from a long list of online postings in the *Pakistan Herald* between August 2008 and October 2010.

234 **The legal issue at the heart** The National Reconciliation Ordinance was promulgated by President Musharraf on October 5, 2007, and the full text was published the same day by the Associated Press of Pakistan. The edict was declared null and void by the Supreme Court on December 16, 2009. The long list of individuals who lost immunity from prosecution, and the charges against them, were published the following day in *The News International.*

235 **Asma Jehangir** *Dawn,* December 19, 2009.

CHAPTER 10: *Drones*

239 **Year after year, opinion surveys show** See "Concern About Extremist Threat Slips in Pakistan," a report from the Global Attitudes Project of the Pew Research Center, Washington, DC, July 29, 2010.

242 **"If I am given a thousand lives"** Taken from statement of Faisal Shahzad in Federal District Court, Manhattan, October 5, 2010. The entire statement can be found online in "Times Square Bomber's Message of Hate," October 7, 2010, at www.familysecuritymatters.org/publications/id.7588/pub _detail.asp.

244 **Now, even as she praised** Comment by Secretary of State Hillary Clinton, made to CBS News, May 8, 2010.

244 **"Tragically, anti-americanism"** *Dawn* newspaper, May 8, 2010.

246 **The picture was murkier, however** The Wikileaks group released more than ninety thousand cables and other classified U.S. government documents on Afghanistan and Pakistan. The most significant documents were compiled and cited in the *New York Times* in a series of reports beginning on July 24, 2010.

247 **But instead of welcoming** Rediff India Abroad, June, 12, 2009.

249 **The U.S. ambassador** Saeed Shah, "Anti-Americanism Rises in Pakistan's Media Rumor Mill," McClatchy Newspa-

pers, September 8, 2009. In early 2011, Pakistanis' worst suspicions about American spying activities suddenly came true. Raymond Allen Davis, a burly CIA contractor, was arrested in Lahaz after shooting and killing two young Pakistani men who had been following him on motorbikes. The explosive incident led to months of public recriminations, diplomatic wrangling, and ultimately a controversial secret deal in which Davis was allowed to leave Pakistan and avoid trial after the families of his victims were paid huge sums in blood money under Islamic law.

250 **In a 2008 survey conducted** "Pakistani Public Opinion on Democracy, Islamist Militancy and Relations with the US," published by the United States Institute of Peace, January 7, 2008, Washington, DC. The Pew Research Center survey has been cited in previous notes.

252 **"Americans do not understand"** Mazari, Pakistan's most hawkish public intellectual and newspaper columnist, became editor of the *Nation* newspaper in 2010, but abruptly left after less than a year.

253 **Siddiqui, a Pakistan-born neuroscientist** The coverage of Siddiqui's case in the Pakistani media was often highly emotional and nationalistic, especially in the vernacular language press. The Imtiaz column in the *Express Tribune* of April 7, 2010, was an exception.

257 **"Mothers run"** *Pakistan Patriot,* January 28, 2009.

259 **"If democracy and the rule of law"** *Dawn,* January 11, 2011.

260 **Pakistani concerns about the human damage** The U.S. government did not release detailed information about drone strikes or resulting casualties, but the Pakistani press kept track of many. The Brookings Institution essay, by scholar Daniel Byman, was published in July 2009. The UN Human Rights Council report, by investigator Philip Alston, was cited in the *New York Times,* October 28, 2009. Wikipedia also compiled an extremely detailed but disputed list of drone strike

dates, targets, and estimated casualties between 2004 and early 2011. See Wikipedia.org/wiki/Drone_attacks_in_Pakistan.

261 **Nearly 80 percent of the inhabitants** See "Public Opinion in Pakistan's Tribal Regions," New America Foundation, published September 2010.

262 **This adroit balancing act** Ahmed Rashid's *Descent into Chaos,* published by Viking in 2008 and subsequently updated, explores this issue in depth.

263 **It was the deadliest attack** See "Bomber Took in CIA," *New York Times,* January 5, 2010.

CHAPTER 11: *The Murder of Democracy*

270 **The issue that stalked Zardari** Criticism of Zardari and his policies was especially vituperative in *The News International,* usually a more balanced publication. Accounts of his personal wealth and corruption cases can be found in *Who Owns Pakistan,* by Shahid-ur-Rehman, and in a special report by the *New York Times,* "House of Graft—Tracing the Bhutto Millions," published January 9, 1998.

273 **"Today's Pakistan has drifted far"** Essay in *Dawn,* December 25, 2009. Dozens of books have been written about Jinnah's life and career. He left a voluminous public legacy of speeches and writings, but his motives and vision for founding Pakistan remain a source of heated academic and political debate. The standard biography is *Jinnah of Pakistan,* by Stanley Wolpert, Oxford University Press, 2002.

274 **On the day Pakistan was born** From *Pakistan: A Dream Gone Sour,* published by Oxford University Press, 1997. I cite several passages from the book, as well as from Khan's newspaper columns and from lengthy conversations with me at his home in Islamabad during 2009 and 2010.

276 **"The trains run,"** *Dawn,* December 25, 2009.

277 **Many bureaucrats are honest** This speech has been reproduced in many books and studies. Khan cites large portions of it on pages 182–83 of *Pakistan: A Dream Gone Sour.*

279 **Even after a decade** See "Overview of Corruption in Pakistan," Transparency International, The Anti-Corruption Resource Centre, www.transparency.org/pk/policy_research /surveys_indices/cpi/2007.

280 **The scandal involving the Bank of Punjab** This case received sensational attention in the Pakistani press. For example, see "Stunning Disclosures as Haris Steel Scam Probe Continues," *Nation,* October 23, 2008.

283 **The image of Parliament as a sinecure** The full report, entitled "How Rich are Pakistani MNAs?" can be found at www .pildat.org.

284 **"Feudalism is a state of mind"** Interview with the author, Islamabad, May 2010.

286 **A more successful upstart** Dasti's saga was widely seen as beginning to crack open the privileged sanctuary of Pakistani politics. See "Upstarts Chip Away at Power of Pakistani Elite," *New York Times,* August 28, 2010.

Epilogue

289 **I found my way to Edhi's office** From *Abdul Sattar Edhi: A Mirror to the Blind,* published by the Edhi Foundation, Karachi, 1996. All other comments and observations here come from interviews with the author in Karachi, June 2010.

index

Abbas, Athar, 119, 205, 208

Abbasy, Sofia, 61

Abu Zubayda, 22

Adamjee family, 31

adultery laws, 63

Afghanistan, xiv

   migration to Pakistan, 45, 143

   Soviet war, 29, 45, 86, 98, 103–5,
     135, 238

   Taliban rule, 113–17, 197

   U.S./NATO war, xv, 113, 196, 239,
     251, 264–65

Afzal, Sheikh, 280–81

agriculture. See land ownership; rural
   culture

Ahmad, Mirza Ghulam, 74

Ahmad, Mushtaq, 194

Ahmad, Sohail, 37

Ahmadi Muslims, 74–80, 89

Ahmed, Iftikhar, 240

Ahmed, Qazi Hussain, 60, 136–37

Ahmed, Sohail, 279

Ahsan, Aitzaz, 29–30, 221, 232

Akhtar, Qari Saifullah, 165

alcohol use, 81

Almeida, Cyril, 128–29

al Qaeda

   leadership, xvi, xviii, 113, 187

   public opinion of, 261

   Siddiqui's work for, 252–55

   U.S.'s war on, 107, 113, 119, 187, 244

American Center, 248

Amin family, 31

anti-American sentiment, 143, 147–48,
   152, 237–39, 242–65

Arafat, Yasir, 155

army. See military establishment

Army Welfare Trust, 97

Asghar, Ali, 99–100

Ashar, Masood, 227

Ashura, 89–91

Asian Tigers, 115

Aurat Foundation, 52

Awami National Party (ANP), 196–200,
   202

Awan, Babar, 236, 280–81

Ayub Khan, Muhammad, 21, 39, 273

Azam, Moavia, 88–89

Azhar, Maulana Masood, 87, 163–64
Aziz, Abdul, 88, 227

Bahadur, Hafiz Gul, 188
Bahria Foundation, 97
Baksh, Imam, 24
al-Balawi, Khalil Abu Mulal, 263
Baloch, Liaqat, 110
Balochistan, 138, 262, 286
Bangladesh, 32, 94, 121–22
Bank of Punjab, 280–81
baraderi (kinship groups), 10, 216
Barakaho suburb, 20, 152
Basir, Mohammed, 105–6, 120
Benazir Income Support Program, 269
Benazir Tractor Scheme, 269
Benedict XVI, pope, 83–84
Berelvi sect, 84, 156–57
Berman, Howard, 247
Bhatti, Shabbaz, xvi–xvii
Bhayo, Ghaus Bux, 228
Bhayo, Wahid Bux, 67
Bhutto, Benazir
    assassination and investigation, 140,
        173–74, 191, 223–26, 229, 266,
        268–69, 288
    corruption charges, 33–34, 41, 279
    family background, 46, 86
    homecoming and campaign, 234–35,
        266
    ISI opposition, 110
    PPP chairmanship, 283, 284
    progressive reform agenda, 59, 77,
        138, 144
    on Qari Saifullah Akhtar, 165
    rivalry with Sharif, 33, 110
    Western ties, 246
Bhutto, Zulfiqar Ali, 13–14
    imprisonment and death, 32, 86, 94,
        101, 140, 219
    nationalization program, 32, 33
    Sufi rivals, 132–33
Bhutto family, 33, 35–36, 39, 86, 283
Bibi, Asia, 83–84

Bibi, Chand, 201–3
Bilal, Ahmed, 164
bin Laden, Osama, xvi, xviii, 187
Binoori Town madrassa, 177–79
"black" economy, 16
Black Revolution, 221–22, 231
Black Thunderstorm, 204–6
Blackwater, 148, 249, 260
blasphemy law, xvi, 79, 83–85, 150
brick kilns, 23–24
Brookings Institution, 260
Buner district, 204
Burki, Shavid Javed, 46–47
Bush, George W., 107, 242, 246

Café Leopold, 171
cantonments, 92–93, 96
A Case of Exploding Mangoes (Hanif),
    223
celebrity marriages, 55
chappatis, 9
Charter of Democracy, 288
Chaudhry, Mohammed Iftikhar
    as Chief Justice, 51, 68–69, 234–36
    conflict with Zardari, 231–34, 275
    judicial independence movement,
        219–22
    popularity, 155, 233
Cheema, Umar, 111–12
chhitrol, 230
child labor, 57
child marriage, 61
Chinioti trader clan, 31
Christians, xvii, 58, 78, 81–85
CIA. *See* United States
civil society, xix–xx, 14, 60, 70–71, 235
class, 46–49
    gap between rich and poor, 26–30
    Islamic movements, 21–22
    middle classes, 29–30, 44–49, 60,
        142
    military class, 96–98
    See also poverty; ruling elite
Clinton, Hillary, 244, 260

Cold War. *See* Soviet war in Afghanistan
communications technology industry, 37
cotton, 8, 18–19, 48
Crossed Swords (Nawaz), 93, 112

dal, 9
Dasti, Jamshed, 286–87
Data Ganj Bakshs shrine, 131, 134–35
Davis, Raymond, xvii
Dawood family, 31, 35
demographics. *See* population
    demographics
Deobandi sect, 86, 89, 90, 135
Dewan family, 35
diet, 9, 20
divorce, 56
domestic violence, 23–24, 57–59
"Draw Mohammed Day" event, 150
drone attacks, xvii–xviii, 190, 206–7,
    243, 246, 255–65
Durrani, Mahmud, 101
Durrani, Tehmina, 57

East Pakistan, 31–32, 94, 102, 121–22
the economy, xii
    communications technology industry,
        37
    controlling families, 8–9, 25–26,
        31–38
    corruption, xx, 26, 36–38
    gap between rich and poor, 26–30
    inflation, 20–21
    informal economy, 16
    middle classes, 29–30, 44–49
    military expenditures, 30
    nationalization programs, 32, 33
    privatization programs, 32–34
    stagnation, 29–38
    terrorism, 174–75
    See also employment
Edhi, Abdul Sattar, 273, 289–94
Edhi, Bilquis, 292–94
Edhi Foundation, 290, 292–93
Edison, Thomas, 156

education
    access challenges, xx, 7, 11, 65
    affluent women, 54, 59–62
    Edhi's Sarabkot school, 292–93
    fundamentalist girls, 180–81
    higher education, 30
    house servants, 57–58
    Islamic schools, xv, xx, 21, 135,
        139–40, 152–53, 167–68, 176–81
    jobs for educated workers, 48–49
    literacy rates, 6, 9–10, 60
    poverty, 9, 176–77
    rural settings, 9–10, 11, 60, 65–66
    urban settings, 17
Eighteenth Amendment to Pakistan's
    Constitution, 187–90
Elahi, Nahida Mahbooba, 216–17
Elahi family, 35
elopement, 63, 64–66
employment
    agricultural labor, 9, 11, 60–61
    brick kilns, 24
    child labor, 57
    government regulations, 26
    labor unions, 14
    middle-class jobs, 48–49
    servants, 26–27, 29, 30, 57–59
    textile industry, 18–19, 48
    urban settings, 16–18
    women, 54, 57–62
Enhanced Partnership with Pakistan Act,
    247–48, 260, 268

Facebook, 79–80, 149–51
Faisalabad, 16, 18–19, 22
Faisal Mosque, 136
Fashion Week, 20, 55
Fauji Foundation, 97
Mullah Fazlullah, 184–85, 195
Federal Board of Revenue, 37
Federal Investigative Police, 127
Federally Administered Tribal Areas
    (FATA), 186–95, 196
feudal system. *See* ruling elite

Fieldcrest, 18
floods of 2010, xx, 3–24, 270
   diversions of water, 42–43
   exposure of rural poverty, 4–7
   media coverage, 14
   relief efforts, 4, 12–15, 21–22, 29, 93,
     129, 264
   urban migration, 14
foreign relations, xiv, 170
   anti-U.S. rhetoric, 143, 147–48, 152,
     237–45, 264–65
   trust deficit with U.S., 244–65
   Zardari's policies, 268
   See also Afghanistan; India; United
     States
founding of Pakistan. *See* origin of
   Pakistan

gap between rich and poor, 26–30
Gates, Robert, 259–60
gender. *See* honor system; women
the generals. *See* military establishment
Ghazi, Abdul Aziz, 161
Ghazi, Abdul Rashid, 161
GHQ/Parade Lane attacks, 125–28
Gilani, Yousuf, 109, 128, 167, 231, 233,
   255, 270
Gojra attacks, 82–83
government. *See* political institutions
Gul, Hamid, 116

al-Habib, Akbar, 91
Habib family, 33
Hadayat, Shafiq, 82–83
Hamid, Zaid, 142
Hanif, Mohammed, 115, 223
ul-Haq, Anwar, 219
ul-Haq, Ehsan, 95, 122–23
Haqqani, Husain, 104, 114, 227
Haqqani, Jalaluddin, 188
Haqqani, Sirajuddin, 188
Haqqani network, 263–64
haris (landless peasants), 10
Haris Steel Mills, 280–81

Harkat-ul-Jehad-ul-Islami, 165
Hashwani family, 33
Headley, David Coleman, 124, 173
High Court Bar Association, 222
honor system, 67–72, 215
   assault convictions, 216
   elopement, 64–66
   honor killings, 50–54, 62
   kidnapping and rape, 63, 70
   legislation on, 63, 70–71
   Rukshana case, 50–52, 67–68, 71–72
   upper classes, 56
Hoodbhoy, Pervez, 139–40, 244
Hoti, Haider Khan, 198
al-Huda, 137
Hudood Ordinances, 63
Human Rights Commission of Pakistan,
   235
Hurs of Sindh, 132–33
Imam Hussain, 89–90, 155
Hussain, Abida, 43–44, 284
Hussain, Altaf, 235
Hussain, Malik Riaz, 14
Hussain, Mohammed, 90
Hussain, Mushahid, 248
Hussain, Rifaat, 239, 249
Hyat, Kamila, 60, 117, 142

Imam, Colonel, 116
Imtiaz, Saba, 255
India
   Indus River, 8
   middle classes, 29–30
   Mumbai siege, xiv, xvi, 22–23,
     120–21, 171–73
   nuclear weapons, 120, 122
   Pakistan's preoccupations with, xx, 87,
     94, 98, 102–4, 120–25, 127
   Partition, 4, 45, 121, 213
   peace negotiations, 125
   war of 1965, 102, 121
Indus River, 3, 8
informal economy, 16
Intelligence Bureau, 109

interethnic conflict, 73–91
  against Ahmadi Muslims, 74–80
  blasphemy accusations, xvi, 79–80,
    83–85
  against Christians, 81–85, 87
  against foreigners, 87
  Iranian and Saudi roles, 85, 86, 89,
    135, 176
  against Sufis, 133–35
  Sunni-Shiite conflict, 85–91
  See also Islamization of society
International Crisis Group, 177
international donors
  flood and earthquake relief, 5, 251,
    264
  religious extremism, 85–86, 89,
    135–36, 176
  U.S. military aid, 98–99, 238–39,
    247–48
Inter-Service Intelligence (ISI), xvi, 94,
    109–17
  headquarters, 160
  Kashmir training camps, 110, 123–25
  politics and power, 103–4, 110–11,
    116, 226–28
  terrorist attacks on, 127
  tolerance of Sunni violence, 87–88
  two-pronged approach to terrorism,
    107, 110, 113–17, 119, 122,
    187–91, 246, 262–65
Iqbal, Allama, 155, 233, 273
Iqbal, Javid, 218
Iqbal, Major, 124
Iqbal, Sabar, 19
Iran, 85, 86, 89, 176
Iraq War, xv, 141
irrigation systems, 8
Ishtiaq, Arsalan, 243
ISI. *See* Inter-Service Intelligence
Islam
  Ahmadis, 74–80, 89
  fundamentalism. *See* Islamization of
    society
  Islamization. *See* Islamization of society

  moderate practices, 26–27, 29, 135,
    142, 157–58
  moral guidance, 152–54
  Shiites. *See* Shiite Muslims
  Sufis. *See* Sufism
  Sunnis. *See* Sunni Muslims
  terrorist activities. *See* terrorism
Islamabad, 20
  Faisal Mosque, 136
  Long March of 2009, 93, 128, 231–34
  Marriott attack, 27, 30, 147, 174–75,
    227
  Red Mosque siege, 107–8, 115–16,
    118, 159–63, 180–81
  Serena hotel, 28
  U.S. embassy, 18, 19
  VIP enclaves, 27–28, 46
Islamic International University, 154–56
Islamization of society, xii–xvi, xx,
    21–23, 135–58
  anti-Western rhetoric, 143, 147–48,
    151–52, 237–39, 242–65
  blasphemy accusations, xvi, 79, 83–85,
    150
  clerics, 137–38
  conflation of religion and state, xii–xvi,
    23, 143–47
  conflict with modernity, 148–51
  Faisalabad, 22
  floods of 2010, 4–5, 15
  Islamic ethics, 152–54
  Islamic schools, xv, xx, 21, 135,
    139–40, 152–53, 167–68, 176–81
  jihadist agenda, 87–91
  middle classes, 46
  military establishment, 102–8,
    126–27
  moral guidance, 152–54
  political parties, 136–40
  public opinion, 141, 151–52
  social groups, 137
  social services, 4–5, 136–37
  student groups, 137, 144–45
  urban poverty, 21–23

Islamization of society (*cont'd*):
  Zia's policies, 63, 79, 105–6, 135–36,
    140, 196
  See also interethnic conflict; terrorism

Jabbar, Javed, 276
Jacobabad, 6
Jaish-e-Mohammed, 86–87, 177
Jamaat-e-Islami, 22, 60, 105, 136–37,
    143, 168
  electoral politics, 110
  floods of 2010, 15
  membership, 285–86
  peace rallies, 148
  sharia law, 197–98
Jamaat-ud-Dawa, 15, 22, 166–71
Jamali, Mai Jori, 62, 286
Jamia Binooria, 178–79
Jamia Hafsa seminary, 160, 180–81
Jamia Mohammedia, 179–80
Jamia Naeemia seminary, 156–57
Jamiat-e-Tulaba, 137, 144–45
Jamiat-e-Ulema-e-Islam, 137, 177,
    197–98
Jamshed, Junaid, 143
Jatoi, Ashraf, 3–4
Jatoi, Ghulam Mustafa, 41
Jatois family, 41–42
Jawan, Pura and Bannu, 7
Jehangir, Asma, 60, 203, 235
Jinnah, Mohammed Ali, xiv, 155–56,
    272–74
  death, 99, 288
  democratic secular vision, xv, xvi,
    74–75, 86, 218, 276
  founding of Pakistan, 148
Jinnah Society, 272
judicial independence movement, xix–xx,
    30, 58–59, 218–22, 231–36
Junoon, 133
justice system. *See* legal system

Karachi, 16
  Ashura attacks of 2009, 90–91

Clifton neighborhood, 25, 46
  economic status, 44–49
  madrassas, 177–79
  middle classes, 44–46
  Pashtuns, 143
  ruling families, 31
  terrorism, 44
Kargil border clash of 2000, 122
Karim, Hajji Abdul, 185–86
Karzai, Hamid, 122
Kasab, Ajmal, xvi, 22–23, 172
Kashmir, xiv, 103, 104, 122–25, 127
  ISI training camps, 110, 123–25
  Lashkar-e-Taiba, 123–25
  Line of Control, 110, 122
  terrorist missions, 163–64, 166,
    168–69
  uprisings of 1990s, 122
Kayani, Ashfaq, 108, 117–19
  anti-terrorism policies, 126–29, 191,
    204, 208–9
  as ISI chief, 114, 118
  Long March of 2009, 232
  popularity, 261
  term extension, 271
  on U.S. aid, 247–48
Kayani, Muhammed Rustam, 217–18
Kerry, John, 98, 247, 260, 268
Khalid, Omar, 188
Khan, A. Q., 73–74, 155, 233, 273
Khan, Akbar, 213
Khan, Asad, 183, 184
Khan, Asalan, 243–44
Khan, Hamesh, 280–81
Khan, Humayun Akhtar, 38–40
Khan, Imran, 143–44, 273
Khan, Ismael, 18
Khan, Mohammed, 47–48
Khan, Roedad, 273–76
Khan, Sadiq, 206
Khattak, Afrasaib, 190, 196
Khwaja, Khalid, 115–17
Khyber Pakhtunkhwa, 287
kidney sales, 24

King, Martin Luther, Jr., 155
kinship structures, 10, 216
Koh, Harold, 259
Kohinoor Textile Mills, 34
Kurianwala Road, 18–19

labor unions, 14
"Lady Taliban." *See* Mazari, Shireen
Lahore, 16, 143
　Data Ganj Bakshs shrine, 131, 134–35
　Gulberg neighborhood, 25
　terrorist bombings, 22
Lahori, Akram, 165
Lakhvi, Laki ul-Rehman, 123, 172
Lala, Afzal Khan, 198–99
Lal Shahbaz Qaladar shrine, 131
land ownership
　feudal system, 8–9, 25–26, 31, 284
　reform programs, 41, 42, 43–44
　rural poverty, 8–12
Lashkar-e-Jhangvi, 86–87, 164–65
Lashkar-e-Taiba (LET), 121, 123–25,
　　127, 143, 162, 166–73
　floods of 2010, 15
　government ties, 163, 167–68
　media coverage, 168–69
　Mumbai siege, xiv, xvi, 22–23,
　　109–10, 120–21, 124–25, 171–73
　public opinion, 168
　suicide forces, 169
lathis, 230
lawyers' movement, xix–xx, 30, 58–59,
　　218–22, 231–36
legal system, xvi, 210–36
　blasphemy law, xvi, 79–80, 83–85,
　　150
　Chaudhry's reforms, 233–34
　conflict with sharia law, 196–203, 231
　conflict with tribal rule, 51–54, 67
　district courts, 210–11
　independent judiciary movement,
　　xix–xx, 30, 58–59, 218–22, 231–36
　influence and corruption, 211–17,
　　228, 235–36

Mai rape case, xviii–xix, 53–54
　Musharraf's intervention, 106, 108,
　　219–22
　Nawaz's Islamization attempts, 138,
　　219
　police, 229–31
　political manipulation of, 226–28
　Supreme Court, 217–22
literacy rates, 6, 9–10
Lodhi, Maleeha, 200
Long March of 2009, 93, 128, 231–34
lower classes. *See* poverty
Lugar, Richard, 247, 260, 268

Maher, Ghaus Bux, 42, 71
Maher family, 11, 18
Mai, Mukhtar, xviii–xix, 53–54
Malakand, 204
Malik, Rehman, 265, 270
Malik, Shoaib, 55
Mandela, Nelson, 156
Mansha, Mian Muhammad, 35
Mansha family, 33
marriage, 60
　adultery laws, 63
　arranged marriages, 9, 50–51
　celebrity marriages, 55
　divorce, 56
　domestic violence, 23–24, 57–59
　dowries, 56
　elopement, 63–66
　family and clan alliances, 35, 54,
　　63–64
　teenaged girls, 9, 60–61, 66
　upper-class customs, 55–56
　weddings, 56
　See also honor system
Marripura (village), 15
Marwat, Anwar Kamal, 192–95
Masih, Shazia, 58–59
Mazari, Shireen, 60, 143, 251–52, 255,
　　257
media, xix–xx
　English-language press, 142

media (*cont'd*):
  flood of 2010, 14
  honor killings, 51
  private TV channels, 142
  social media, 79–80, 142, 150–51
  women journalists, 60
Mehsud, Baitullah, 188–90, 193, 206–7,
    224, 258, 263
Mehsud, Qari Hussain, 188–92
Memon, Marvi, 70, 282
Memon trader clan, 31
middle classes, 29–30, 44–49, 60, 142
migrant labor, 9, 24
Military, Inc. (Siddiqa), 97
military establishment, xii, xvi, 14,
    92–129
  anti-terrorism offensives, 102, 105–8,
    113–17, 119–20, 147–48, 156–57,
    203–9
  cantonments, 92–93, 96
  conflicting terrorism policies, 102,
    105–8, 113–17, 122, 127–28,
    187–91
  discipline and merit, 99–100
  East Pakistan war, 31–32, 94, 102,
    121–22
  educational institutions, 99–100
  expenditures, 30, 94, 98–99, 125
  flood relief, 4, 93, 129
  GHQ/Parade Lane attacks, 125–27,
    128
  Indian preoccupations, xx, 87, 94, 98,
    102–4, 120–25, 127
  India war of 1965, 102, 121
  Islamization, 102–6, 126–27
  Kashmir, xiv, 103, 104, 122–25, 127
  Musharraf's moderating policies, 63,
    94, 106–8
  Muslim-style uniforms, 104, 136
  political role, 29, 30, 34, 48, 100–102
  public opinion of, 95, 118–19
  size, structure, and lifestyle, 95–98
  sphere of influence, 93–94
  U.S. aid, 98–99, 238–39, 247–48

  U.S. covert activities, xvii–xviii, 113
  See also Inter-Service Intelligence;
    Kayani, Ashfaq; nuclear weapons
Minallah, Athar, 287
Minallah, Samar, 202
Mir, Amir, 162, 168, 262
Mir, Hamid, 116–17
Mir, Sajid, 124
A Mirror to the Blind (Edhi), 291
Mirza, Sania, 55
modernity
  Facebook, 79–80, 148–51
  vs. traditional cultural, xviii–xx, 51–52
  See also Islamization of society; urban
    culture
Mohammed, Khalid Sheikh, 113, 242
Moharram festival, 89–91
Mohmand, Shandana, 95
monsoon rains, 3
Movement to Defend the Finality of the
    Prophet, 75–76
Mufti, Maulvi Naeem, 178–79
Mujahid, Yahya, 170–71
Mukhtar, Chaudhry Ahmed, 270
Mumbai siege, xiv, xvi, 22–23, 109–10,
    120–21, 124–25, 164, 171–73
Muñoz, Heraldo, 225
Musharraf, Pervez
  alliance with MMA, 138
  assassination attempts, 161, 164, 165
  banning of religious militias, 86–89,
    138, 163–66
  on blasphemy laws, 79
  coup against Sharif, 33–34, 101
  dictatorial use of power, 94, 104,
    106–8
  on honor killings, 62
  intervention in the judiciary, 106, 108,
    219–22
  ISI scandal, 112–13
  Kashmir policies, 123, 124
  madrassa policies, 177
  on Mai rape case, 53–54
  military policies, 48, 106–8

National Reconciliation Ordinance,
    34, 234, 270, 275
political positions, 63, 101, 106
Red Mosque siege, 107–8, 115–16,
    118, 159–63
removal from office, 108, 117–18,
    195–96, 222, 231
U.S. war on terror, 113
Muttahida-Majlis-e-Amal (MMA), 138
Muttahida Qaumi Movement (MQM),
    44, 254, 285
My Feudal Lord (Durrani), 57

Naeem, Chaudhry Mohammed, 58–59
Naeemi, Munib, 157
Naeemi, Sarfraz, 156–57
Napoleon, 136
National Accountability Bureau (NAB),
    34, 39
National Assembly, 281–84, 286–87
National Integrity Systems, 36–37
nationalization programs, 32
National Reconciliation Ordinance
    (NRO), 34, 234–35, 270, 275
Nawaz, Maulana Haq, 88
Nawaz, Shuja, 93, 96, 112
Nazir, Maulvi, 188
New America Foundation, 260–61
Nishat Group, 35
Nobel Prize in Physics, 73
North Waziristan, 188–92, 256–57,
    263–64
Northwest Frontier Province, 138,
    196–200, 202, 287
    See also Swat Valley
nuclear weapons, xi, 29, 239, 248
    command authority for, 270
    in India, 120, 122
    Khan's peddling, 73–74, 155

Obama, Barack, xviii, 246–47, 257
Omar, Mullah Mohammed, 188
Omar Saeed Sheikh, 87, 242
organ sales, 24

origin of Pakistan, xiv
    Jinnah's secular ideals, xv, xvi, 74–75,
        86, 148
    Kashmir dispute, 122–23
    Pakistani gold rush, 31, 44–45
    Partition, 4, 45, 121, 213
    ruling families, 8, 28–29

Pakistan: A Dream Gone Sour (Khan),
    274–75
Pakistan: Between Mosque and Military
    (Haqqani), 105
Pakistan Economic Survey, 30
Pakistani Christian Association, 58
Pakistani Institute for Legislative
    Development and Transparency
    (PILDAT), 283
Pakistani Taliban. *See* Taliban
Pakistan Muslim League, 110, 224, 282,
    286
Pakistan People's Party (PPP), 84, 195
    chairmen, 269, 283, 284
    founding, 13
    membership, 284–85
    reform goals, 140
    ruling elite, 41, 282–83
    See also Bhutto, Benazir; Zardari, Asif Ali
Pakistan Sugar Mills Workers Federation,
    39–40
Parliament, 281–84, 287
Partition, 4, 45, 121, 213
    See also origin of Pakistan
Pasha, Ahmed Shuja, 109
Pashtuns
    Deobandi sect, 177
    migration to Pakistan, 45, 143
    militias, 162
    in the Tribal Areas, 186–95
    See also Swat Valley
Patterson, Anne, 249–50
Pearl, Daniel, 87, 163
Peshawar
    Meena Bazaar attack, 148, 175–76
    Pashtuns, 143

Peshawar (cont'd):
   Pearl Continental attack, 27, 30
   Rahman Baba shrine, 131, 133–34
   Talibanization, 138–39
Pew Research Center, 95, 121, 251
Pir Pagaro, 132–33
pirs, 132–33
Pir Samiullah, 133
police, 229–31
political institutions
   bureaucracy, 276–78
   as coercive power, 274–76
   Constitution's Eighteenth
      Amendment, 287–88
   corruption, xx, 26, 36–38, 99, 141,
      277–81
   emergency powers, 221–22
   employment regulation, 26
   failures, 272–76
   floods of 2010, 12–13
   ISI and military intervention, 14, 29,
      30, 34, 48, 100–102, 110–11, 116
   in Karachi, 44
   minority groups, 78–80, 86
   Parliament, 281–84, 287
   presidential power, 270, 287–88
   renunciation of Zia ul-Haq, 140
   ruling elite, 28–29, 40–44, 229,
      281–84
   tax system, 37, 278, 279
   unpopularity, 98–99, 127–28
   See also legal system; representative
      democracy
political parties, 136–40, 282–88
   See also names of specific parties, e.g.,
      Jamaat-e-Islami
population demographics
   Ahmadi Muslims, 75
   Christians, 81
   military establishment, 96
   urban growth, 15–17
poverty
   diet, 9
   domestic violence, 23–24

education, 9, 176–77
organ sales, 24
rural areas, xx, 4–7, 9
terrorism, 46–47, 185
in the Tribal Areas, 187
in urban areas, 16–21
See also tribal society; upper classes
Punjab
   anti-American views, 239
   military recruitment, 96, 124
   political assassinations, xvi–xvii,
      84–85, 146–47, 157
   religious extremism, xvi–xvii, 116–17,
      124
   Sharif family, 33, 35–36, 39, 281, 283

Qadri, Mumtaz, 84–85
Qayuum, Malik, 280
qazis, 197
Qureshi, Abdul, 216
Qureshi, Shah Mahmood, 257

Rafi, Mohammad, 11–12
Rah-i-Rast, 205
Rahman Baba shrine, 131, 133–34
rape, xviii–xix, 53–54, 63, 70
Rashid, Ahmed, 114, 125, 262
Rawalpindi bombing, 22
Red Mosque siege, 107–8, 115–16, 118,
     159–63, 180–81
Rehman, Shahid-ur, 31, 41
Rehman, Sherry, 60, 146, 199, 282
religious extremism. See Islamization of
    society
religious minorities, xiv–xvi
   Ahmadi Muslims, 74–80, 89
   Christians, xvii, 58, 78, 81–85, 87
   in government, 282
   Jinnah's secular ideals, xv, xvi, 74–75
   Shiite Muslims, 78, 85–91
   See also interethnic conflict
religious moderation, 26–27, 29
representative democracy, 5, 273–88
   building of, 10, 141

conflation of state with religion,
  xii–xvi, 23, 143–47
Jinnah's vision, xv, xvi, 74–75,
  272–75, 277
See also political institutions
Riaz, Bilal, 126
Riaz, Nazim, 126
rice, 8
Rizvi, Hasan Askari, 136, 273
Robin-Hood strategies, 22
Rukshana case, 50–52, 67–68, 71–72
ruling elite, 42–43, 275
  corruption, 36–38, 141
  economic control, 31–38
  land ownership, 8–9, 25–26, 31, 41,
    42, 284
  political involvement, 40–44, 229,
    281–84
  Shiites, 86
  sugar industry, 38–40
  See also upper classes
rural culture, 7–15
  agriculture, 7–9, 11, 60–61
  education, 9–10, 11
  kinship and leadership structures, 10,
    50–52, 64, 66–68, 216
  land ownership, 8–12, 31, 41, 42,
    43–44
  poverty, xx, 4–7, 9
  See also tribal society

Saeed, Hafiz, 166–67, 168–70, 172, 227
Saigol, Asim, 35
Saigol, Nasim, 34, 35
Saigol, Rubina, 232
Saigol, Yousuf, 31, 35
Saigol family, 31, 33, 34, 35
Salam, Abdus, 73–74
Sarabkot school, 292–93
sardars (tribal leaders), 10, 66–68
Sarwar, Samia, 56
Sattar, Babar, 213
Saudi Arabia, 85, 135, 154, 176
Senate, 281

September 11, 2001, attacks, xv, 113,
  141, 250
servants, 26–27, 29, 30, 57–59
sexual violence, 52–54, 57–59, 61–63
  See also honor system
Shabana (dancer), 185
Shafi, Kamran, 112
Shaheen Foundation, 97
Shah Hassan Khel village, 193–95
Shahzad, Faisal, xv–xvi, 240–45
sharia law, 197–203, 231
Sharif, Nawaz
  Islamization of the courts, 138, 219
  Long March of 2009, 231–32
  political opposition role, 267, 287–88
  popularity, 144
  privatization policies, 32–33
  removal from office and exile, 26,
    33–34, 101, 279
  rivalry with Benazir Bhutto, 33, 110
  wealth, 26, 32, 36
Sharif, Shabbaz, 36
Sharif family, 33, 35–36, 39, 281, 283
Sheikh Bahaddudin Zakria shrine, 131
Shiite Muslims, 78
  Iranian support, 85, 86, 89, 176
  Moharram festival, 89–91
  Sunni conflicts, 85–91
Sialkot, 16, 19
Siddiqa, Ayesha, 31, 97, 144
Siddiqi, Kamal, 146
Siddiqui, Afiaa, 252–55
Sindh River, 3, 6
Sipah-e-Sahaba Pakistan (SSP), 86–91,
  177
social media, 79–80, 142, 150–51
South Waziristan, 206–9, 256–57
Soviet war in Afghanistan, 29, 45, 86,
  98, 103–5, 135, 238
Sufi Mohammed, 184, 195–96, 200
Sufism, xx, 21, 130–35, 178
sugar, 8, 38–40
sugar crisis of 2009, 40
Suleri, Abid Qaiyum, 22

Sunni Muslims
  Berelvi sect, 84, 156–57
  blasphemy law, xvi, 79–80
  Deobandi sect, 86, 89, 90, 135, 177
  religious schools, 135, 176–81
  Sunni-on-Sunni violence, 154–58
  Wahhabi sect, 86, 135
  Zia's Islamization program, 63, 79, 86,
    135–36
  See also interethnic conflict;
    Islamization of society
Supreme Court, 217–22
  Bank of Punjab decision, 280–81
  Dasti decision, 286–87
  judicial independence movement,
    xix–xx, 30, 58–59, 218–22, 231–36
  See also Chaudhry, Mohammed Iftikhar
Sustainable Development Policy
    Institute, 22
Swat Valley
  flogging of Chand Bibi, 201–3
  military offensive, 119–20, 156–57,
    183, 203–6
  refugees, 183, 186, 204–5
  Taliban and sharia law, 182–86,
    196–203

Tableeghi Jamaat, 137, 144
Tandlianwala Sugar Mills, Ltd, 38–40
Taj Mahal Palace, 124, 171
Taliban, xiii, xvii, 119, 135, 162
  assassination of Bhatti, xvii
  attacks on moderate Sunni institutions,
    156–57
  attacks on religious minorities, 78, 89,
    133–34
  CIA bomber, 263
  ISI support, 107, 110, 113–17, 119,
    122, 246, 262–65
  Islamabad Marriott attack, 27, 30,
    147, 174–75, 227
  Marwat opposition, 192–95
  military missions against, 102, 203–9
  public opinion, 147–48, 157–58, 261

in Punjab, 116–17
social policies, 56, 145
in Swat, 119–20, 156–57, 182–86,
    196–206
in the Tribal Areas (FATA), 186–92
Talibanisation of Pakistan (Mir), 162
Talibanization. *See* Islamization of society
Tanzim Nifaz Shariat-e-Muhammadi
    (TNSM), 184
Tariq, Azam, 88–89
Taseer, Salman, xvi–xvii, 84–85, 146–47,
    157
taxation, 37, 278–79
Tehrik-e-Taliban Pakistan (TTP), 191–92
Telli, Siraj, 45
terrorism, xii, xvi, 5, 118–20, 173–76
  affluent targets, 27–28, 30
  Ahmadi Muslim targets, 77–80
  Ashura attacks, 89–91
  CIA bomber, 263
  death rate, 173
  GHQ/Parade Lane attacks, 125–27,
    128
  government connections, 163, 167–68
  Islamic International University
    attack, 154–56
  Jamia Naeemia seminary attack,
    156–57
  jihadist agenda, 87–91
  Karachi bombings, 44
  Kashmir missions, 163–64, 166,
    168–69
  military missions against, 102, 105–8,
    113–17, 119–20, 147–48, 156–57,
    203–9
  military's double standard toward,
    107, 110, 113–17, 119, 122,
    187–91, 246, 262–65
  Mumbai siege, xiv, 22–23, 109–10,
    120–21, 124–25, 164, 171–73
  Peshawar's Meena Bazaar, 148, 175–76
  public's double-standard re blame,
    147–48, 151–52, 157–58, 162,
    168, 176, 179–80, 237–38, 261

Punjab assassinations, xvi–xvii, 84–85, 146–47, 157

Punjabi groups, 120–25, 143, 163–81

Red Mosque siege, 107–8, 115–16, 118, 159–63, 180–81

roots, 46–47, 176–81, 185

September 11, 2001, attacks, xv, 113, 141, 250

Sufi targets, 133–35

suicide forces, 169

Sunni-on-Sunni violence, 154–58

in Swat, 119–20, 182–86

Times Square bomber, 240–45

U.S. drone attacks, xvii–xviii, 190, 206–7, 243, 246, 255–65

U.S. war on, 98–99, 107, 113, 190, 238, 251, 261

See also names of specific groups, e.g., Taliban

textile industry, 18–19, 22, 48

Thatta (city), 6

Times Square bomber, xvi, 240–45

Toosi, Nahal, 184

traditional culture. *See* rural culture; tribal society

Transparency International, 37, 279

tribal society

education, 65–66

elopement and kidnapping, 63–66

honor killings, 50–54, 62, 67–72

justice system, 51–52, 67

leadership structures, 10, 50–52, 61, 64, 66–68

Mai rape case, xviii–xix, 53–54

sexual predation, 61–62

women's roles, 60–61

UN Human Rights Council, 260

United Arab Emirates, 176

United family, 35

United States

Afghanistan war, xv, 103, 196, 239, 251, 264–65

covert activity in Pakistan, xvii–xviii, 113, 117, 148, 249–50

drone attacks on Pakistan, xvii–xviii, 190, 206–7, 243, 246, 255–65

Enhanced Partnership with Pakistan Act, 247–48, 260, 268

flood and earthquake relief, 251, 264

Iraq War, xv, 141

Koran burnings, xvii

military aid, 98–99, 238–39, 247–48

Pakistani immigrants, 238, 240, 243

Pakistani's negative views of, 143, 147–48, 152, 237–45, 264–65

September 11, 2001, attacks, xv, 113, 141

trust deficit with Pakistan, 244–55

war against terror, 98–99, 107, 238, 251, 261

UN Security Council, 121

upper classes, 25–44

charities, 29

domestic violence, 57–59

education, 26

feudal families, 8–9, 25–26, 31

governance roles, 28–29

honor killings, 56

marriage customs, 55–56

religious practices, 26–27, 29, 145

servants, 26–27, 29, 30, 57–59

social events, 39

terrorist attacks, 27–28, 30

travel and mobility, 26

urban lifestyles, 25–28

women's education and careers, 54, 59–62

See also poverty; ruling elite

urban culture, 15–21

affluence, 25–28

education, 17

employment, 16–18

inflation, 20–21

Islamization, 21–23

liberal elite, 140

urban culture (*cont'd*):
   population growth, 15–17
   poverty, 9, 19–21
   textile industry, 18–19
Urdu businessmen, 44–45
U.S. Institute for Peace, 95, 141,
   250–51

Violence Against Women Watch Group,
   52

Waali of Swat, 182, 184
waderas (hereditary chiefs), 10
Wahhabi sect, 86, 135
Walmart, 18
wheat, 7–8, 20
Wikileaks, 115, 246, 262
women, 50–72
   adultery laws, 63
   child labor, 57–58
   education, 54, 59–62, 65–66, 180–81,
      194, 292–93
   elopement, 64–66
   fashion, 54–55, 144
   field labor, 11, 60–61
   flogging of Chand Bibi, 201–3
   gold jewelry, 185
   in government, 59–60, 62, 70, 282,
      286
   honor killings, 50–54, 62
   kidnapping and rape, 63, 70
   legislation on, 63, 70–71
   literacy rates, 9–10, 60
   marriage customs, 9, 51–52, 54,
      60–61, 66
   religious practices, 137, 144
   sexual predation, 61–62
   See also honor system
Women's Protection Bill, 63
women's rights groups, 52, 69–70

Xe Services, 249

Yusuf, Fatehuddin, 75–76
Yusuf, Huma, 78–79, 151
Yusuf, Mohammed, 75–76

Zakaria, Rafia, 259
Zamin, Shah, 148
zamindars (landowners), 10
Zardari, Asif Ali, 266–72
   on Afiaa Siddiqui, 255
   blasphemy law policies, 85
   conflict with Chaudhry, 234–36, 275
   corruption charges, 33, 36, 128,
      234–35, 266–68, 270–71, 279
   economic policies, 20
   floods of 2010, 5, 13, 270
   immunity from prosecution, 234–36,
      267
   international policies, 268
   investigation of Bhutto's murder,
      224–26, 268–69
   ISI policies, 109–10
   Long March of 2009, 93, 128, 231–34
   peace deal with Taliban, 120
   police policies, 229–30
   presidency, 34, 63, 203, 224, 231, 246
   religious allies, 84
   revocations of power, 270, 287–88
   security expenditures, 98–99
   Shiism, 86
   unpopularity, 127–28, 247, 268–72
   on U.S. drone attacks, 257
   wealth, 36
Zardari, Bilawal Bhutto, 283
Zia ul-Haq, Mohammed, xv, 32,
      100–101, 116, 140
   Afghan policies, 104–5
   blasphemy law, 79
   death, 86, 104, 223
   Hudood Ordinances, 63
   Islamization program, 86, 94, 103–6,
      135–36, 140, 196
   Sufi allies, 133

ABOUT THE AUTHOR

PAMELA CONSTABLE is a foreign correspondent and former deputy foreign editor at *The Washington Post*. Since 1998, she has reported extensively from Pakistan, Afghanistan, and India as well as Iraq. Before joining the *Post* in 1994, she was a foreign correspondent and foreign policy reporter for *The Boston Globe,* where she covered South and Central America for a decade, focusing on Chile and Haiti, as well as parts of Asia and the former Soviet Union. Constable is author of *Fragments of Grace: My Search for Meaning in the Strife of South Asia* and co-author of *A Nation of Enemies: Chile Under Pinochet.* A graduate of Brown University, she is a member of the Council on Foreign Relations, a winner of the Maria Moors Cabot Prize, and a former fellow at the Alicia Patterson Foundation and the Woodrow Wilson International Center for Scholars. She is the founder of the Afghan Stray Animal League, which operates a shelter and clinic for needy small animals in Kabul.

ABOUT THE TYPE

This book was set in Garamond, a typeface originally designed by the Parisian typecutter Claude Garamond (1480–1561). This version of Garamond was modeled on a 1592 specimen sheet from the Egenolff-Berner foundry, which was produced from types assumed to have been brought to Frankfurt by the punchcutter Jacques Sabon.

Claude Garamond's distinguished romans and italics first appeared in *Opera Ciceronis* in 1543–44. The Garamond types are clear, open, and elegant.